D0728204

NATION'S FORTRESS

Books by Robert Kempinski

Fiction

Balance of Terror

Nonfiction

Introduction to Bonsai

NATION'S FORTRESS

Robert Kempinski

Mahogany Row Studio

Nation's Fortress

© Robert Kempinski 2019

Published 2019

Printed in the United States of America

Library of Congress Cataloguing – Publication Data

ISBN: 9781798771082

Published by Mahogany Row Studio

Melbourne Florida

Acknowledgements

My father-in-law, Julian Maxey, spoke with me on many occasions about his action in the Korean War. When I would relay these stories to my wife, she said he rarely, if ever, told anyone about his experience. Perhaps my time in Korea with the Army, albeit under much different circumstances, formed a kinship. As he aged, he would recount the tales in no order. Unfortunately, in his later years he contracted emphysema and as he succumbed to the disease, he started telling me his memories more frequently, especially the events surrounding the "Direct Order." I decided to write down what he told me after he passed so his children and grandchildren would know what he endured. In doing so, I recalled my father, Robert Kempinski, who passed in 1999, telling me about his service in World War II. Interviews with my brothers along with my memories led to the "Secret Mission."

This process took a couple of years and while spending evenings researching and writing my wife said I should look at the genealogical information my mother-in-law, Janice Maxey, had collected. It provided a solid time line and details of the Maxey family's lineage and their military service going all the way back to the American Revolution and the Battle of Yorktown. It seemed natural to compile these stories into one volume that spans the Maxey and Kempinski families.

Obviously, it would have been impossible to write this book without the support of my loving spouse, Terry Maxey Kempinski. I thank her for sharing her family's history, allowing me the time to write, and helping review the text. I also must give great thanks to my twin brother, Bernard. He and I collaborated on a prior novel. In this book, he provided the art work for "War Colt," portions of the cover design, and contributed most of the Civil War letters in "Seeing the Elephant." My daughter, Jennifer, helped edit the book. She regularly offered advice on diction, grammar, story pacing and structure and earned my appreciation. As did Stephanie Clewer, a co-worker, who was kind enough to edit the draft. She did wonders with her suggestions. Finally, I must thank the Kempinski family and the Maxey family for their service and incredible contributions to our country. May they all rest in peace.

Dedicated to Julian Maxey, hero and inspiration

The Nation's Fortress

"Wars may be fought with weapons, but they are won by men. It is the spirit of the men who follow and of the man who leads that gains the victory."

General George Patton Cavalry Journal (September 1933)

Wearing ivory handled pistols, General George Patton directed convoy traffic at a critical road junction during the Third US Army's thrust into the German flank at the Battle of the Bulge. This flamboyant feat, along with many others by the colorful General, have been recounted in books and even transformed into a movie, "Patton", in 1974. Another General, George Washington, the United States' first President, suffered frigid temperatures and risk of drowning along with his men of the First Continental Army as they crossed the Delaware River. The middle of the night attack on the Hessians at Trenton highlighted his brilliant military career and helped cement him as an American icon.

Yet another George, Colonel George Armstrong Custer, a charismatic US Army Cavalry officer, had his story replete with flowing golden locks and a mortal battle at Little Big Horn carved into the American consciousness. Each of these officers shaped the nation's history. And while history has chosen to scrutinize and record the lives and actions of each of these leaders, they have something more basic in common. Each commanded soldiers, troops willing to follow orders, and each counted on them to enact their strategies.

Since the American Revolution, about 50 million soldiers have served in the US military. Each of these, from the veteran medal winners to those washed out of training camp never to see a battlefield, have stories. These accounts, sometimes written in memoirs, or in private diaries, or boasted with bold bravado in bar rooms, or even kept in private haunted memories, have shaped the world's history as much as the actions of their leaders. Through their courage, their sweat, their blood and many times their lives, American soldiers have built, like brick upon brick, a fortress for their country.

What is it that makes such soldiers willing to follow orders and commands, knowing they could lead to injury and perhaps death? There are as many motives as there are soldiers. They have stood together driven by notions of patriotism, duty to serve and perhaps, even revenge. The draft pulled in many who had no choice. Others did it for opportunity: to escape from economic stagnation or from stifling relationships. The thrill of adventure lured others looking to shoot, to fly, to parachute, to climb mountains, to dive underwater, and to travel to the earth's extremes. A subset viewed it as a personal quest, testing their mettle against the basic challenges of strength, endurance, and flesh against steel, learning to be led and learning to lead. And some did it to kill: to satisfy a primal bloodlust to hunt and to be hunted with a chance to emerge victorious. The military as a vast melting caldron brings together all these soldiers regardless of their motivations, and through tradition-bound processes melds them into a force aimed to do their leader's bidding.

The merging of these units takes arbitrary assignment and through indoctrination creates cohesion. But chance never leaves the equation. George Custer said his main attribute of success was "luck." The soldiers of the 82nd Airborne Division crossing the English Channel on D-Day had no say in their destiny. Randomness determined which plane took a flak burst and blew up in mid-air while it allowed others to jump to test their fate to a sniper's aim while floating suspended below a silk parachute. It allowed others to last until the ballistic dynamics of an artillery shell shrieking through the air settled the odds. In World War II alone, over three million US soldiers tested their luck, and many did not win. The survivors may not have understood this going in, but the crucible of battle reinforced in all the happenstance and their fortune in making it. These soldiers stored that process into their mental fabric.

What if we could peer into the subconscious imprint of all soldiers, not necessarily the leaders, but all the men and women whom have served--to delve into their memories and document the collective experience? What would we learn, and would it be possible to use the knowledge to some greater end? In the accounts that follow, we examine two American families, one in America longer than the country, and the other a relative new-comer of the 19th century. Both families have a direct line of soldiers with stories that while unique, captured the experience of many throughout the history of the United States. Perhaps someday, by taking advantage of their collective experience, we may determine a way to rid ourselves of soldiers and wars.

The following stories are based on true events and, where possible, contain the recollections, correspondence or history of the participants from the direct descendants of the Maxey and Kempinski families. Their paths were not easy, and for some their sacrifice large. Putting these tales to paper honors these soldiers despite the nature of their travails. The more contemporary entries sprung from the actual verbal lore passed from the participants. The earlier stories came after detailed research of the family history and available historical documents, and were developed with painstaking attention to detail. Obviously not all the dialogue was captured in the historical records, so literary license helped craft the tales, however, the basic fact is these are true stories of real soldiers etched into the bricks of the nation's fortress.

THE STOIC CINCINNATUS

ROBERT KEMPINSKI

From the archives of the Daughters of the American Revolution, Richmond Virginia. Scanned from the original, now stored on digital stock.

State of Virginia, Buckingham County

On this 30th day of July 1841, personally appeared before us Justices of the Peace in and for the said County, John Maxey, a resident of said county and state, aged 84 years, who being the first duly sworn according to the law doth on his oath make the following Declaration in order to obtain the benefit of the act of Congress passed June 7, 1832:

That he entered the service of the United States on the first day of March in the year 1778 and served until discharged on the first day of June, making a tour of three months. His officers were Colonel Harvey, Major Name unknown, and Captain William Anderson and Harding Perkins. That his three months tour was served at Albemarle Barracks in guarding the British prisoners at that place. That he was drafted into service; that the county through which he passed was that lying between Buckingham County Courthouse, and the Albemarle Barrack on Albemarle County- these counties being separated by the James River; and that the names of the Continental Regiments and com-panies that he served with were unknown, that he has no docu-mentary evidence having lost his original discharge nor does he know of anyone whose testimony he can procure, who can testify to his services in this tour. That he again entered the services of the United States (living at the same place on the first of September 1781 and was marched to Yorktown in the State of Virginia – par-ticipated in and witnessed the surrender of the British forces at that place was marched thence according to the best of his recollection to Winchester, State of Virginia- and being honorable discharged he returned home on the first day of December, making a second tour of three months; that his officers were Colonel Towles, Major

John Moseby and Captain Nathaniel Cunningham; that having lost his original discharge from this tour also, he has no documentary evidence, nor does he know of any person whose testimony he can procure, who can testify to the length of this later tour, that he hereby relinquishes every claim whatsoever to a pension or annuity except the present; and declares this his name is not on the pension roll or the agency of any State in the Union."

Sworn and subscribed the day & year aforesaid before us

S/ John Ayers, JP

S/ John M Harris, JP

S./ John Maxey Senior

State of Virginia Buckingham County

"On this 4th day of September 1841 personally appeared before me a Justice of the Peace in and for said County, John Maxey, the claimant named within, and being duly sworn according to law doth upon his oath, assign the following reasons for not making earlier application for his pension: That in the year 1834, William N Patterson undertook to procure his pension, obtain the necessary evidence, took my declaration in open Court, and promised me he would attend to it, until it was acted on at Washington; that two or three years afterwards he applied to Mr. Patterson to note something about it when said Patterson informed him that he had lost or mislaid it; that having already been put to [too] much trouble about it, and feeling still able and willing to work for his low living, he took no other steps towards it until he was struck down with the palsy, and rendered unable any longer to support by his labor; that he then proceeded to make the within Declaration.

He further testifies, in addition to what is stated in his Declaration, that he was, after the surrender of Yorktown, marched to Winchester in guarding the prisoners to that place served in that capacity until relieved by a company of militia from Frederick County Virginia; that he then and there procured his discharge, gave it to his Captain to draw his pay upon, and ultimately lost both his discharge and his pay for two months – the pay for one month he received in form of a certificate which he afterwards used in payment of his taxes at home; that he was in active service from the date of his enlistment till he was discharged.

S/ John Ayers, JP S/ John Maxey

[John Ayers, a clergyman, and Isaac Baber gave the standard supporting affidavit.]"

Questions put to John Maxey, the within named claimant, and his answers thereto:

1.   What year were you born?

Answer – In Buckingham County, State of Virginia in the year 1756.

2.   Have you any record of your age and if so where is it?

Answer – Yes in Abram Maxey's possession.

3.   Where were you living when called into service; where have you lived since the revolutionary war and where do you live now?

Answer – In the county of Buckingham; have lived there since the Revolutionary War, and now live there.

4.   How were you called into service; were you drafted; did you volunteer or were you a substitute, and if in substitute, for whom?

Answer – I was drafted as a substitute.

5.   State the names of some of the regular officers who were with the troops when you served, such Continental and militia regiments as you can recollect and the general circumstances of your service.

Answer – The first call I substituted for Benjamin Hart and ordered to report to the Albemarle Barracks in Charlottesville under Sergeant Alexander McClardy. We rode horses to Charlottesville in a day and mustered on the ground of the school. Militia captains gave orders and we rehearsed drill and practiced musket shooting. The third day we broke camp and marched north toward the barracks where Thomas Jefferson had arranged the receipt of several thousand prisoners, British and Hessians, captured from the Battle of Saratoga. We made camp and spent much of March and April felling trees and making huts for us and overseeing the prisoners. Duty was light, and the prisoners were poor having marched in January through March from the north. British officers were allowed to come and go as long as they found housing within a day's horse ride of the camp.

Most of the guard were militia like me but we had a few veterans. They regaled us with the grit of combat and built our resolve. I worried how long we were to watch the prisoners as spring planting weather was arriving soon. Anon, the weather broke and the dogwoods bloomed so Captain William Dugrid secured our release and we rode home with orders to maintain our flintlock and brown hunting shirts and white smocks for the future.

6.   What were the circumstances of your second service?

Answer - September 1, 1781, I substituted for my brother, Shadrach Maxey, he was married. I was back into duty with the Virginia Militia. We had orders to rendezvous in Charlottesville, on the fields north of Mitchie Tavern. A line of Buckingham County men marched north under Major John Overstreet of Prince Edward, through Scottsville, and took a bateau across the James at Carter's Ferry, fare waived for the militia. We picked up two horses and a wagon with three bushels of meal, dried beef, bacon and four flintlocks of good quality. Next day we reached Mitchie Tavern where some British officer prisoners were quartered; they turned out to see us. We secured our junction with the Marquis Lafayette and fell under his command reporting to Colonel Towles. We just missed action where the militia had foiled an expedition by British Colonel Banastre Tarlton who had forced the State Legislature in Charlottesville to disperse. Tarlton must have been taught a lesson by his crushing defeat at Cowpens a few months earlier so he moved southeast to avoid action in Charlottesville.

We were constantly under motion heading south east toward Richmond following the British. We'd make a few miles and camp. Before dawn, we struck the tents, rolled them and moved out continuing southeast. As the sun gained in the sky and we'd find a stream or well, the officers offered halt for a water call. Non-commissioned officers had me and six or so others collect canteens to fetch water. Rarely did we have a chance to fully quench our thirst as the company's throats waited. I recall we were always thirsty, not like when we hunted and we could drink whenever we wanted. The officers forced water discipline and many a man felt the sting of the whip for a dry canteen. Hungry too. We were not allowed to eat prior to noon, and then it was hard tack or jerky. Sergeants ordered stacking of arms and knapsacks unweighed. My water party would scurry for refresh of the canteens then we'd have a spell to chew on the meager rations. The company officers messed together with cooked food carried by their servants but we were not allowed to cook until night.

After we crossed the Rapidan at Raccoon Ford, General Cornwallis attempted to strike our flank. The Marquis foiled this attempt by moving us at night along an old path, since called the "Marquis Road," and took a strong position on high ground behind Mechums River. Cornwallis however withdrew toward the coast.

The next day we joined troops with General Wayne's men from Pennsylvania, but all under command of Lafayette. The northerners looked ready for business with hard faces and blue coats. Their continental uniforms contrasted with our frocks and hunting overalls of linen. After a few days of march, we took a day cleaning and repairing, passing out ammunition, mending flint-locks, and carriages, especially wheels, as the trails were hard on the spokes. I was good with a spokeshave and could whittle a rod quick as any in the company.

We neared Richmond, where the rumors said Lord Cornwallis with the British army now lay. Troops were anxious for a shot as we saw some of the handiwork his lordship left in our countryside in burned out structures and tobacco sheds. Our officers had us march through Richmond rather quickly but urged our resolve by reminding us of the damage done by the enemy.

Within a day, we approached Williamsburg chasing after the enemy, when our spirits buoyed with the joining of troops under the command of the well-known Baron Steuben. With the larger force, mood of our officers turned serious and rightly so for near Bacon's Bridge the British reversed course. It seems our growing force and hasty pace squeezed them. With a flurry of orders, we formed for a fight eager to pay back for some of the damage we saw, yet the redcoats did not come. With dark we set camp.

While we rested, word passed General Wayne was anxious to do something about Colonel Simcoe's British horse and mounted infantry. They were either foraging for food or committing some plunder on our fellow Virginians. We learned they destroyed American magazines at the mouth of the Rivanna. To our front, a rumor reached Wayne's ear the enemy was less than a mile off. Before you could wink, the Pennsylvania brigade left their tents and baggage and marched at dark. Each put a piece of white paper in their hats which our eyes could readily see as they passed through the camp. Under the moonlight, we could also see they had their flints out and faces grim.

While we rested, the northern men fought their need for sleep and marched and counter marched until they reached an area called the Bowling Green, where local folk told them Simcoe had been the evening before but no longer. Well before day-break, our officers woke us and with haste we moved out. We linked up with Wayne's men before noon but Wayne kept us in reserve and ordered a brigade under Colonel Richard Butler to engage Simcoe. At Spencer's Ordinary, we could see Butler's men maneuver and wheel, like well-trained troops and after a few hours a brief but intense skirmish took place. Butler's men did well, handling the British roughly and rescuing stolen cattle. Wayne moved the rest of the Pennsylvania men to support Butler, but Simcoe retreated which was just as well as rumor said Lord Cornwallis was moving to support his subordinate. The marquis marched us through the field of the Battle of Hotwater and here for the first time I saw the remnants of conflict. The sight left me feeling ill at ease, almost sick. I endeavored to overcome this temperament but the friendly and enemy gore sickened me. We didn't have much time to ponder their plight as our light troops under the Marquis moved with Wayne's men. We kept on the move for the rest of the day, then we heard rumor the redcoats have decamped and crossed the James River.

Our brigade marched on, and found the edge of a field where we laid on arms through the darkness in drill order but resting about ten miles from the enemy. We took small sips from the canteen and tried to sleep. With first sun, we marched until the middle of the afternoon when we heard firing in the distance. Our advance encountered the enemy's pickets, protecting their companies now stomping in the open. When perhaps within one hundred and twenty yards of the enemy, the northern men closed column and reformed into line with weapons pointed. They advanced as a battalion then started firing all along the front. We mustered in line to the rear deferring to the more experienced troops. Our regiment of light infantry with a couple of artillery pieces set a line on a hill to the rear. We could see the British light infantry's colorful coats set dress-right-dress and their second line following with shouldered musket. Wayne must have underestimated the enemy for it was not a rear covering force on the north bank, but his whole unit. While we moved back and forth, we saw the British main body split into two thrusts, one to the left and one to the right and put Wayne's men at true risk. Through the smoke of the muskets the northern boys seemed to take a licking from the Redcoats. Orders were given us to retreat. We were inexperienced, exhausted with hunger having eaten nothing all day but a few wild raspberries. Despite dizziness, and with difficulty I stayed in formation during our hasty departure. We managed to keep close to our leaders, and continued running until their fire could not set upon us. For some odd reason, the attackers stopped at the ground we just held. Reflecting, the affair had to take no more than five minutes, but at the front-line, the northerners squared off less than sixty yards from the enemy, plenty close for violence. The Virginians escaped loss, but Wayne's men were hit hard; maybe one hundred killed and wounded with some officers captured. The carnage even took some horses, killing all the steeds pulling the artillery and several cannons lost. The British had men go down but not as many as us. Perhaps Wayne made an impetuous charge into Simcoe's troops for revenge but the Continentals paid the price.

As the Pennsylvania men fell back, we joined them for about two miles where we met the Marquis' main fighting force. There we took our breath and ate some plain ground Indian meal. I assisted with dressing some wounds of Wayne's men.

Next morning, we raised a white flag and an officer led a surgeon, and a burial party to the battle scene to accord last respects to the dead. An equal number of the enemy did the same, rubbing shoulders with men they were firing at the day before. After the action, we visited the field; and could discern the ground occupied by both sides from the pieces of the torn cartridges which were scattered and spent in lines where the troops leveled shot at each other. I could throw a stone from one line to the other as the combatants were that close.

7.   Was this at Jamestown?

Answer - Yes, but by day, we could see the British had left Jamestown so we marched and crossed the James River at Westover Plantation the home of late Colonel Bird, the gambler and once the wealthiest planter in the State, until his debts caused him to commit suicide. There was nothing like his sublime estate in Buckingham.

8.   Why did the British leave despite winning the ground?

Answer - No idea, perhaps they knew the Marquis' larger force lay near and Lord Cornwallis feared an ambush. We were told the British numbered about eight thousand men but they probably heard of our swelling numbers. Or a report of a French fleet on the river below made them wary of being surrounded. I will say the news of the fleet confirmed great joy and our sour mood from Jamestown improved with the army back on the alert and ready for the enemy. Yet, we didn't engage, instead kept southwest of Lord's men to shut any escape option to North Carolina.

Within two days we encamped on the south bank of James River, and could see the part of French fleet indeed. We were massing a large force. We then recrossed the James River on barges and encamped at Williamsburg. The great number of soldiers inflated my confidence, for as militia we had never seen such a formidable force including impressive ships of the line.

Then on September 14th General Washington arrived. Our militia was paraded to receive him and I caught a glimpse as he rode a splendid white steed along the lines quartered in Williamsburg. He was as tall as his reputation and his presence alone seemed to account for another thousand men and further encouraged us, especially as he was a fellow Virginian.

9.   You met the future president?

Answer – Yes indeed, as soldiers, of course we didn't know he'd be president then.

10.   Was the Battle at York next?

Answer - Not for a few days. We had a comfortable bivouac, about two hundred yards from William and Mary College, now used as a hospital. My eyes confirmed what I had heard about Williamsburg, as the most populous, and most influential of the American colonies. The neat streets laid out in regular array gave the impression of wealth and elegance. No wonder so many good ideas originated there.

Around Williamsburg the Continental army had swelled to nine-thousand men, and the French under Marquis Rochambeau with the Virginia militia raised the total to 15,000 all under General Washington. So many general officers, and the arrival of many new soldiers seem to energize everyone. Discipline became the order of the day, quite a change for a militia, but it generated pride in our formidable fighting force. We got caught up in the sensation and joined in daily practice. The regulars gave us good example, as their five years of fighting seemed to prove. These men led the exercise and put us through various evolutions. Soon we behaved like seasoned troops, albeit without the bite of real fire.

Then officers ordered a parade so off to our posts we wheeled by platoons marching smartly in step to the accompaniment of fine music, much pageantry and in front of many spectators. The whole unit marched off, saluting the Marquis and field officer of the day.

11.   When did you set upon Yorktown?

Answer - On the 28th we moved as an Army toward the enemy, strongly dug in at Little Yorks, as it was called then. Upon our approach their pickets fell back, seeming to not deign a fight. We changed ground once or twice then and finally sited close to their enemy's main lines. In front of us was Pigeon Hill, rising ground topped with stately Loblolly pine blocked our view and British soldiers our advance. Their officers, like ours, I suppose, recognized the mound as a gateway to York. Below, the city lay on a flat, sandy plain. Aside the structures ran a pilotable river which, as you know, served as a strong port of commerce, but now was full of French ships of the line.

We set positions. Americans on the right side of the hill and the commanders placed the French on the left, with our lines touching both sides of the river encircling York for a siege. In the bay, the French naval fleet bottled up the few British ships.

Each day, we had troops on fatigue staying busy making obstacles such as gabions and fascines. I preferred this woodwork over moving the heavy iron artillery closer and closer to the lines. At first dark, whole regiments, again wearing white cards in their caps so we could see them, passed through the lines and laid ready with arms providing cover while the rest built the trenches, and high parapets for the siege. When we went out for cover duty, we would use the trees for protection but occasionally a heavy shot would fling through and cause damage.

When Colonel Schamel, adjutant-general to the whole Continental army died after an encounter with clever cavalry troops, it seemed the General had enough and we charged Pigeon Hill in the morning, and took it. We then stretched temporary works among the pines now facing directly into York. It seemed we spent more time digging and filling casks with dirt than anything, but our leaders occasionally sent a Militia patrol into the dark. If we'd ran into a British unit, a few shots might be exchanged, but both sides would generally slip away, as the darkness really won.

On the night 6th of October, we moved en-masse and opened a new parallel the closest ever from the enemy works. As we worked the dirt, the British made every exertion to harass us unprotected diggers, and no wonder as the royals must have felt the slow crush of our army as we moved ever closer. Nonetheless, we dug and built, until October 9th our artillery began to fire. The scene viewed from the camp caused wonder and some fear, particularly after dark. The shells from the both sides, especially the mortars, trailed vivid red traces as they passed high in the air, arcing toward their targets and bursting in a blinding detonation. General Washington rode through one evening and espied a young lady helping with camp mess chores and asked her, "Are you not afraid of the cannonballs." She replied, "No, the bullets would not cheat the gallows, that it would not do for the men to fight and starve too." Her spunk caused quite a sensation in the ranks.

On October 11, we made a second line within three hundred yards of the enemy's front. Motivated men erected new batteries in almost point-blank range of the British shot. An additional number of cannon were brought forward, some twenty-four pounders and 12 inch howitzers. Tumultuous shelling from French and American heavy cannon fired in platoons, four at a time, and the mortars three at a time, kept up a constant fire silencing the British front pieces. Shells from behind their works still coursed overhead doing damage. We stood watches in-between the opposing artillery and repelled attacks, especially towards the end as the enemy sensing desperation sent two charges to advance from their lines, and within rifle shot of our second parallel.

Shortly after dark on the night of the 14th, the well-prepared British redoubts were taken by charge. We were on the right of the Pennsylvania men. Further left of them were the French. Wayne's batteries had kept a constant fire upon the positions through the day. At night the Marquis moved us out, supported by Wayne's northerners moving in favorable dark for the assault. Upon our movement, our batteries had ceased firing and there appeared a dead calm. We, light infantry, following Colonel Hamilton blazed the way. When the business was over in our sector, not a gun was fired by us; the bayonet only used. Ten or twelve of our Virginia infantry were killed. Further down the line, the French encountered the center of the British line and suffered greater losses.

A regiment of reserves behind us immediately started connecting the freshly taken redoubts by digging a ditch parallel to our earlier work. The British took alarm regarding our propinquity and made their escape into their main trenches. As they moved out there came tremendous fire from their rear breaking the quiet in our sector. It seemed firing was going on in all directions, but particularly toward our unit, where our reserves were digging new positions. Fortunately, due to the terrain, the shot passed over-head. In less than an hour we displaced the light sand and had ourselves under cover.

The next day, there was heavy fire from our batteries hours on end. We placed shot upon shot into the town from every direction devastating the structures. Only those dug in bomb-proofs could have survived, yet it must have been living Hades for them as the bombardment seemed endless. Around noon, a French mortar shell found a target in British frigate with ensuing conflagration burning it to the water's edge, whereupon it blew up making the ground around our position shake.

Sometime on the 16th, the enemy retired from their positions without hardly a sound. As soon we as realized it, our division manned their vacated lines and we moved closer to York. Firing from our batteries continued without intermission. Enemy fire also continued and the din dulled the senses. The next day, though, before our relief came in the morning, the British firing stopped. A drummer mounted the enemy's parapet, and beat an excessive cadence, and immediately a red-coated officer, holding up a white handkerchief, appeared in front of their works and moved toward us waving the truce cloth. The drummer accompanied him, beating a soulful march. Our batteries ceased and a loud hurrah emanated from behind our position. One of the officers ran from our lines and pulled a handkerchief from his blue blazer. He placed it over the other's eyes. The drummer returned whence he came, and the emissary whisked somewhere behind us.

We were all enough to know the enemy had surrendered, so we stood the ready but hopefully expectant until the 18th. Then a bevy of British officers rode past from the devastated town and surrendered their swords to our leaders. I heard later the swords were returned.

11. The surrender came on the 19th.

Answer - Indeed. Our division manned the lines again. Everything was quiet as we restocked our equipment and supplies. When the swords were turned, they had already signed the Articles of Capitulation. The British army paraded and marched out with their colors furled. Drums draped in black fabric and black ribbons dangling from their fifes mimicked the poor tone reflected in their defeat. General O'Hara, a stocky man with florid face flushed with tears, led the formation, as it seemed Lord Cornwallis excused himself from marching out with the troops. They stacked their arms and returned to town.

12.   The enemy returned to town?

Answer – It had to do with the articles of capitulation. Surrender brought mayhem, the British caused much confusion and riot among the remains of the town. Many of their soldiers seemed inebriated; strange behavior for those surrendered but maybe the lifting of the siege relieved them of more than one could imagine. We went on heightened alert when an American sentinel guarding a stock was killed by a redcoat with a blade. Our officers sent us on patrol with strict orders to administer capital punishment for justice. After a few days, I gladly turned over this distasteful assignment.

York lay tremendously shattered, destroyed by continuous shelling from our side. Houses burned, several dead lay by the market house and others sick with the scourge of small pox, and dead animals nearly everywhere. Despair overtook me to have to have witnessed such a waste of humanity. Yet, within a few hours some civilians appeared having found their way back from wherever they were holed out.

The Army availed themselves of the enemy's fine supply of stores and clothing. The Continental Army saw to it each officer received sixty dollars and enlisted men, thirty dollars.

13.   When did you depart?

Answer - We marched under Captain Cunningham escorting prisoners to Winchester. There I was discharged to my relief, glad to be finished with the conflict.

14.   Did you ever receive a discharge from the service, and if so, by whom was it given and what has become of it?

Answer. Yes; Captain Cunningham but alas I don't know what became of it.

15.   State the names of persons to whom you are known in your present neighborhood and who can testify as to your character for veracity and their belief in your services as a soldier in the

revolution.

Answer. George Chambers, Ed Maxey, Isaac Baber, George Baber, John Agee, Wm Maxey, Reverend John Ayres, Clopton Chambers

The affidavit of Mr. Charles Howell of Buckingham County Virginia (aged 82 years) to establish the pension claim of John Maxey of said County and State who states that he recollects that said Maxey was drafted and marched to the Albemarle Barracks under a draft of three months; he was also drafted and marched to the Eastern part of Virginia on a three months tour both of which times he marched from the County of Buckingham and in the last mentioned tour he was at the Battle of Little York in 1781 – and this affiant was there with him.

Chas. Howell S/ Chas. Howell

This is to certify that I have known John Maxey, now claiming a Pension and whose declaration is now with the Commissioner of Pensions for the period of fifty-one years; that I saw him while he was on duty at Yorktown, but never knew the length of his tour; that I have always understood he went from that place to Winchester on duty; that he has always been regarded as a soldier of the Revolution, and is now so regarded by his neighbors, some of whom have known him and lived by him for the term of fifty years, that I have read his Declaration, and believe every word he there states concerning his Revolutionary Services; & that he now is, and has been for the past forty-odd years, and exemplary member of the Baptist Church sustaining in all the relations of a man and Christian, and unimpeachable character.

S/ Reverend John Ayres

Revy. Pensioner

Veteran was pensioned at the rate of $20 per annum commencing March 4th, 1831, for service as a private for 6 months in the Virginia militia.

Washington Is Burning

Washington Is Burning

1685

A King in the Garden of Fontainebleau
Crimson roses portend blood that flew.
Huguenots march with the setting sun
leaving estates, culture, but not the one.

England received a hesitant generation
Yet the new world beckons without cessation.
Ever the burning memories, home lost
More depart for America, ocean tossed.

Settled in Virginia the tribe adopts.
They work the land for bountiful crops.
And join the militia to protect their till
Switching from farm to military drill.

1812

Britain impresses, and blockades trade.

Declaring war, on paper, America dismayed.

The news travels on ship and horse

But slowly does it make its course.

Sailed from Plymounth, Lieutenant Maxey

Captains the Whitig, a horrid taxi.

A Jonah, soon to be lost to the depth

For what the sea wants, the sea has kept.

Into the Chesapeake carrying dispatches

For the US government, secured in hatches.

The recipient obliges and captures the schooner

Lt Maxey, the first unwitting prisoner.

Near Portsmouth, chivalry loomed

And the vessel returned again to spume.

Make haste to London, with frantic news

The cousin departs, n'ere America to cruise.

1814

Time moves slowly, busy with the Emperor

Britain ignores their younger pesterer.

Yet Maxey's news sends redcoats,

To the Chesapeake in gunboats.

Cockburn raids the islands and generates fear

Militia responds to protect their sphere.

March to here, trod through the dirt

Abraham Maxey dons his field shirt.

A private in Boaz Ford's Company

7th Virginia Militia moving free.

Soldiers deploy, not knowing the next attack

Stand to the ready, can they take the wrack?

To Canada, and to then USA quick

Ross, free of Waterloo, lands in Benedict.

To teach the upstart a lesson

He aims for the congressional session.

Birds aflight, news jars the commonwealth

Officers scramble, and the troops tighten belts.

Abraham breathes in the hot August air

Marches with haste into the glare.

Men join at each city they pass

The group growing strong, one mass.

Some carry muskets, but most

Just bring vim, vigor, and boasts.

With feints and jousts, seasoned English troops

March across pastoral Tidewater in groups.

While angry trainbands filled with patriotism

Merge on Washington for a Redcoat exorcism.

Winder and Armstrong lack what it takes

They dither and dally their soldiers forsake.

At Blandensburg a defense they muster,

Green militia will lose in the bluster.

"Weapons, cartridges and ball," they declare

"We'll teach the British to take care."

Yet the supply man decides receipts do need

And the Virginia militia to the battle cedes.

To the Capitol the invaders head like banshee.

With no experience, the greens panicked and flee.

They run through the city, and head to hills

While hardened soldiers give their fill.

Citizens frantic, fill wagons with goods

And head west toward the backwoods.

Madisons scamper with White House possessions.

They cross the Potomac, a meal in mid-session.

The Generals enter and enjoy their repast

Courtesy of what the fourth US president amassed.

After a victory toast they torch the city

Brazenly burning the young government's dignity.

The militia watch helpless from across the river

As the flames send the evening aquiver.

Yet Abram's prayers answered, a large storm arrives

And douses the fire with fury surprised.

The citizens ashamed, the Capitol in embers

Alexandria without a shot surrendered.

Yet in a fortnight the tides turned

General Smith at Baltimore has learned.

He organizes a grand defense.

With the courage of McHenry, the battle quenched.

Scott Key observed old Glory endured

And soon the tone of war had cured.

Abraham returns to the farm in Buckingham.

His time served converted to an engram.

He fathers a family and has three sons

Grateful the conflict has had its run.

SEEING THE ELEPHANT

With Bernard Kempinski

1971

Abandoned by her siblings and cousins, Terry Maxey, the youngest girl of the childhood brood, decided not to be afraid of the dim attic, but rather to explore. She climbed over the stacks of boxes in the top floor of the old farm house using the filtered light creeping past the lone window. A pile of many years of yellow National Geographic magazines, leather bound books, and cases of old farm receipts collected dust, but her eyes skipped over them and alighted on a small but old leather chest secured with a tarnished clasp. She picked up the sooty container with thoughts of a secret treasure. Using her hand to brush aside the years of settled dirt, she saw it was not a case, but rather a thick leather-bound scrap book with unsecured hasp. Under the cover lay a set of modern papers, old newspaper clips and letters amassed by someone, but now forgotten in the pile of family detritus. As she turned the first page a type written note fell out. Her lips moved as the fifth grader read the words.

"In April 1862, near the town of Shiloh, Yankee and Confederate forces faced off in the first major battle of the Tennessee campaign and killed in two days almost as many men that died in the revolution 90 years earlier. In addition to the dead, nearly 20,000 more were wounded. Carnage of this scale had not been seen by the Army of Tennessee and it overloaded the capabilities of the Confederate medical system. Uncle Abraham spent the night in the field, when they found him and brought him to the only hospital in town, the largest home in Corinth."

The remainder of the page although dry now, had been water damaged and unreadable so she flipped it over and found a set of yellowed handwritten letters.

Letter from Columbus, KY December 1, 1861

Dear Mother and Father,

We are now camped at Fort DeRussey near Columbus, KY overlooking the mighty Mississippi River. We arrived by the cars and moved to a camp north of the town on the bluff.

Columbus is a nice enough place. The town has several substantial buildings made of brick and lumber. There is a steamship wharf and railroad depot here. They conduct a brisk trade as ships come up from the south to exchange cargo at the wharf and depot. Trains also come and go with regular frequency.

We see very few ships from the north, just an occasional small raft or skiff every now and then. The Army has erected a redoubt at the top of the bluff with several heavy cannons looking down on the river. Nearly every day they practice firing the guns. The dull roar echoes across the river and we can spot the splash of the balls in the river. I can't imagine any Yankee ship captain foolish enough to sail beneath the bluff.

Sometimes we see staff officers take a steamer north, presumably to reconnoiter, but they usually return before night fall none the worse for the wear.

Sampson is doing well now that the men have elected him captain. He stands tall and is the model of martial demeanor. His braids arrived a few days ago and he found a local seamstress to sew them on. I am proud of my older brother, but insist he show me no favoritism.

Our camp is situated on high ground. The ground is wet from the snow and rain, but not as muddy as other camps I have visited. We have erected nice little cabins with many of the comforts of home. We built a mud and straw hearth with a chimney made from a barrel for our cabin. We take turns gathering firewood. After we scoured the local forests, we turned to the nearby fences and an abandoned barn. I suspect they will be stripped clean too in a few days, though the some of the officers fuss about our taking fences, etc.

Tom Potter from Shelby County has a way with the pans and we have made him our cook. Our rations have been meager, much of the bacon has maggots and the hardtack impossible to chew. Nonetheless, Potter manages to make a good coosh from it all using onions, potatoes or other items we can purchase or find around town. It's not like Mother's fritters and bacon, but it ain't bad either.

I fashioned a bed from small logs, vines, and straw I gathered nearby. With a fire in the hearth and my wool blanket I can sleep quite comfortably. If it weren't for the incessant martial activities, this would make a nice homestead.

We have been issued smoothbore muskets by the Army, those weapons are well made but appear ancient. It is near impossible to hit what we aim at. Oh, how I wish I had my squirrel gun with me instead.

We are learning to load and fire quite rapidly. When the whole company line fires in a volley, the fire and smoke billows and the sound crackles across the fields. After a few volleys the front is filled with an impenetrable layer of smoke. Aiming is impossible, so we just add to the smoke as we continue to fire our muskets as fast as possible, with no idea of any execution we may be performing.

They have given us impressive 18 inch bayonets which we have learned to append to our muskets with amazing alacrity when given the command, "Fix bayonets." When the regiment moves forward in line with fixed bayonets, it makes for a bristling steel tipped wall that can only but sweep all before it. When not used on the musket, the bayonet makes a handy tool for digging and chopping. Many of the men brought Bowie or other large knives with them. They brag about how they will use them in close combat, but I am not sanguine about those prospects. I'll be happy to stick with the bayonet for such close work should the need arise.

We usually drill three times a day, except Sundays. A first I enjoyed it. The manual of arms having many movements, formation changes, bugle calls and drum rolls to learn. With all the practice, we have learned our evolutions by heart. But the routine has become dull after week upon week of the same drills. So, I jumped at a chance to volunteer for a patrol across the river. We were going to intercept a Federal cavalry scouting party local farmers reported.

About 100 of us under Captain Sommerville from A Company took a steam boat across the river an hour before dawn. Everyone was silent as we slipped across the river. Our nerves were drawn tight expecting to see Yankees under every bush. I felt as if my heart was in my throat when we stepped on the far shore.

We marched a few miles inland and saw nothing but quiet farms, low swamps, and empty woods. When we reached a hard-packed dirt road, we deployed into skirmish order across it. Every eye strained to the north expecting at any second to see the enemy across the misty fields. But all we saw were shifting shadows and an occasional dove. After a few hours, the drummer sounded recall. We formed up and marched back to the landing. We took the steamer back across just as the sun set. So much for my first action.

With love your devoted son,

Abraham

March 3, 1862

Letter from Fort Pillow,

Dear Mother and Father,

 We have departed Columbus in haste without ever firing a shot or so much as seeing a Yankee. I left behind my nice bed and cabin. Oh, how I miss it now. The past few nights we have slept under the stars. The men are huddled against each other to try to stay warm.

 Whatever possessed our officers to retreat from Columbus without a shot is beyond me. I hope they know what they are doing.

 We arrived at Fort Pillow and it is an utterly unremarkable place. Other than the redoubts against the shore and the trenches dug in an arc around it, there is not much else here. Hopefully we can build cabins soon to get away from the winter snow and rain.

 Our rations have been very sparse as we moved south. Our wagons have not been able to rendezvous with the railroads or supply boats. There is not much to forage this late in the winter, so the men and the animals are hungry.

 They say a steamer will arrive tomorrow with rations, so maybe Potter can work his magic once again.

 Rumors of a Yankee invasion are rife. The fall of Fort Donelson and Henry was especially worrisome news. But we are confident we can drive the Yankees back, if only our thunder head-ed officers can just arrange the meeting.

 Sampson is doing well. The men look up to him. He manages to keep a cheerful outlook, even when all around him are complaining. I think he is taking well to Army life. I have been well even though we have been subject to some cold, raw weather. The same can't be said for many of the others in our company. About one third of them have been sick with the various ailments, mostly ague and the trots. The doctors don't have much medicine to offer, so they must suffer through it. We did leave several men behind at

Columbus as they were too sick to march. Often a hot meal and a warm night is all it takes to cure them. Still, several men have died from disease. We usually bury them outside the camps.

After the glorious news from Manassas, I thought I would be home soon. But the recent news has been bleak. The loss of the forts has been a blow to the cause. The whole of Tennessee is open to invasion.

Your loving son,

Abraham

Tennessee open to invasion, seems so strange, so she paused to try to understand. Then she lifted Abraham's letter to find a smaller note written by a different hand.

April 9, 1862

Dear Parents of Abraham Maxey,

I am writing on behalf of your son, Abraham. He was under my care in the makeshift hospital at Corinth. He came to the station a few days after the battle and at first, although his wound was great, he seemed to recover, he even had a good appetite and graciously took some bread and tea. Then his pallor turned and he lapsed. We offered what comfort we could, but alas he did not have the Angel's Glow, and passed to the lord two weeks after being wounded. He had this letter on his person, so I am sending it, and apologize for the delay as we have had many to care for.

With the lord's grace,

Abigale Martin

She wondered if these letters could really be over a hundred years old. She held the paper up to the light and thought about Abraham. She had not heard about him and wondered how or if he was related to her, seeing as how they shared the same last name. She gingerly put the letter aside, and picked up the next sheet. This one was on thicker and coarser paper, and not nearly as yellowed as the previous sheet.

April 5, 1862

Dear Mother and Father,

It appears we will be going into battle tomorrow, and I thought I would take a chance to write a few words. We are in good health and spirits, though the past three nights have been cold and wet. The rain has turned the roads to soup. We have marched barely 5 miles a day in the slop. Our clothes are caked with mud. I hope I get a chance to wash them soon. I managed to keep an extra pair of socks dry and I am wearing them now.

This evening the weather is dry, but they are not permitting any camp fires. We have not had rations issued in a few days. I saved a piece of bacon and a cracker, so I am not too hungry. But the other men in the company ate all their rations on the first day and now they are foraging for food. I am glad I can rest instead. My blanket and oil skin make for a pretty warm and snug cocoon.

Many of local citizens have been generous in giving us what food they can spare. I got a nice fresh biscuit from a young girl two days ago as we left Corinth. We smiled and waved as we marched by. But there are few farms in this area. The land is rather flat with many woods and scant roads and trails. The underbrush is not too bad and we can move across the country without too much difficulty.

Most of the boys have adopted to army life. I tolerate it well enough, but brother Sampson seems to have an affinity. The other men in the company look up to him and he acts like a natural leader. I suspect he will do well if our luck holds out.

We are now in Taylor's brigade. He is truly a martial leader. We will follow him anywhere.

Captain Somerville is sick now, Bill Grimes from Shelby county is taking over the company. He has a quiet demeanor, but he takes the leadership responsibility to heart.

None of us have been in battle before. Some of the boys from Forrest's cavalry that escaped from Fort Donelson have been teasing us, saying, "we're in for it now." But, I suspect they are do-ing it to bolster their own courage. None of us have seen a Yankee yet, but I suspect we will do our duty when the time comes.

With trust in God, I am sincerely your son,

Abraham Maxey.

PS. Sampson just stopped by and asked me to pass his greetings too. He is too busy to write now as they have him orga-nizing picket duty. If I am lucky, he will let me sleep.

The young girl frowned as remorse creased her brow. It sounds so sad, imagine her great-, great-, great, or how many greats, grandmother receiving such a note from a son who had died. It still seems hard. She reread the words, shook her head, then moved the notes aside and found another on the next page of the scrap book.

4th TN. Volunteers Murfreesboro

November 30th, 1862

Dear Father, Mother,

It has been some time since I wrote to you all. I have heard from you two or three times. I have been in Kentucky since I wrote to you and have been in two very hard battles there and in Tennessee since Corinth where Abraham succumbed to his leg wound. Not a day passes I don't rue his demise but since I have seen a great deal and could tell you more than I could write. The grand cause of our nation will require a sacrifice be paid in full.

In our last engagement at Perryville, our regiment lost nearly half our men killed or taken prisoners. William Johnson and John Finn we suppose are taken. We have not heard from them since the fight. It happens often good men just disappear. Would news of them appear back home, please let me know. Our regiment now barely could make a company. They have combined us with the 5th Tennessee as they too have been greatly reduced. I know a few of the boys in that unit, but many are strangers to me.

Our regiment used everything we had. I have no blanket nor any clothes but what I have had shared with those less fortunate than I. I have got the suit on you sent me. I like it very well. I lack for shoes as do many in the regiment. Father, could you have me a pair of boots made? The siege and movement have used our supplies. The local folk would provide for us, but they too are lacking due to the deprivations of the campaign. The Yankees fleeced the area as they moved through. I found a warmer coat as I suspect the chill is coming.

Yours in faith, Sampson Maxey

Sampson Maxey, another relative she guessed. Battles in Kentucky and Tennessee. Poor lad, no shoes, but as long as it wasn't too cold, he might have been alright. She ran around all summer with no shoes. What he must of have seen she really had no idea, so she reached for another sheet and read.

January 10, 1864 Dalton, GA

Dear Father, Mother

With the winter arrived, we are probably camped until the weather breaks. We have had occasional snow and hard frost every morning. After the siege, and our retreat from Chattanooga, we camp in the northern portion of Georgia. The troops scour the country for provisions, but find little in the spent land; the devastation wrought by battle scars the soil and leaves many a fine home naught but a chimney and pile of ashes. Yet we manage to find stores for meals and forage for the animals. From my view, the war looks to linger and only the Father knows the result. My faith has been taxed, yet remains strong with the realization we must go forward with our duty. While encamped, I long for the farm; however, it is impossible for me to make the ride to visit. If only I could take a bateau along the river sitting just below the bluffs, I might see home, yet I daydream as there is no time for such a luxury.

The enemy is using the rivers. Rumor has it river action led to our recent retreat from Lookout Mountain. The Bluecoats now move relatively free across Tennessee and we pray our officers make moves to stop this, if not I fear for the safety of our neighbors. The longer we struggle, the greater the cost. While I don't know the Lord's ways, we need all your prayers for on them depends the safety of our people. If we don't win, then I fear for the manner in which we will live under the hands of the Red Republicans.

John was well when I received the last letter. I can't vouch for the movements of the Army, but it's possible we will be fighting together. Write to me, Care 4 Regt. Tenn.

Yours in faith, Sampson."

Terry squinted at the 4 Regt. Tenn. and thought it must be some sort of code. Why all this talk of Tennessee? Maybe these letters were not her relatives at all, but why would they be in the attic.

Her curiosity built so she reached for the next sheet, a crumpled and badly aged sheet of yellowed parchment. She barely made out the date, Jan 12, 1865. Almost a whole year after the earlier letter.

Jan 12, 1865

Tupelo, Mississippi

We find ourselves a battered army seeking solace in the confines of Tupelo. We marched here in haste after the battle at Nashville. You may have heard it was a horrid engagement and now the Army of Tennessee is in tatters. It may be irony we tend to our wounds here, not far from our first engagement near Corinth that took brother Abraham. Yet now, nearly all the Buckingham men, save myself, are gone, either lost to the heaven, or disappeared with no notice.

I went sick the past few weeks and dropped weight but now the Yankee pursuit has stopped I seem to have managed to recover and put back some pounds. I managed to find winter clothes to fend off the elements as the loss of so many soldiers has freed their belongings.

The regiment is to be reconstituted and we will be sent to some other division, but the men don't have the same zeal. Watching corn fields razed by cannon and shot as if it were clearly cut to the roots by a knife with the same havoc wrecked upon flesh tests our mettle. Seeing most of the houses throughout the country are deserted or abandoned makes us wonder what do we have to return to. Rank weeds now grow all over once proud land. Probably there is not now one acre cultivated, where before the war, there were hun-dreds. This area is now the most desolate country, and no human being can realize or comprehend the dreadful devastation and horrors created by war, until they have been in its track.

I have not received word nor letter in several months and do hope this manages to find home. I pray the depredation of this conflict has not found the farm and you can manage the livestock and crops with your sons gone. I also pray I may have the fortune to return and this infernal battle ceases.

43

In God's will, Sampson

There was a pounding at the door, and her sisters called her name. "Come on out, Terry," they yelled and cracked open the attic door. Happy to be found, she replaced the letters in the scrap book and bounced over the boxes to the portal, joining the gang in their children's game. As she did so, a single sheet fell from the scrap book back into the box.

Greensboro, North Carolina

April 27, 1865

Dear Parents,

We have been running picket duty near the front but there has been no fight. The pickets don't fire at each other now. We go down to the edge of the creek on our side and the Yankees come down on their side and talk to each other. The men on picket opposite are from New York, and seem very tired of the war. Yet no more tired than me.

We learned yesterday we are to stack arms and head home; we have been mustered out. The war is over. Could I have indeed lasted, while so many did not? Regardless, I plan to make way to Buckingham and to take up the good vocation of farming. I plan to adhere to orders and take what may come, as it has to be better than these past years of conflict.

It may be I will reach home before this letter, but I look forward to seeing you and the family soon.

With grateful prayers, S.

An engraving of the Battle of Shiloh, April 1862

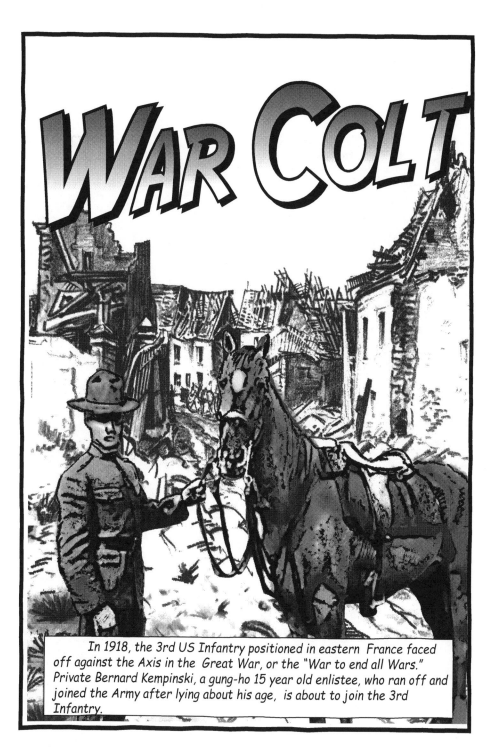

In 1918, the 3rd US Infantry positioned in eastern France faced off against the Axis in the Great War, or the "War to end all Wars." Private Bernard Kempinski, a gung-ho 15 year old enlistee, who ran off and joined the Army after lying about his age, is about to join the 3rd Infantry.

Although only involved in fighting for about one year, the US Army suffered 116,800 killed and 204,000 wounded. The total number of deaths for the rest of the belligerents is unknown, but was probably more than 100 times American losses. People were not the only ones that suffered. Eight million horses perished in the war.
The Great War, the war to end all wars, did not quite accomplish that. The ensuing armistice set the stage for the next World War in 20 years.
Private Kempinski survived to return home, marry, and raise a family.
He died on Thanksgiving Day, November, 1955.

THE SECRET MISSION

Chapter 1

The hallway of the tenement felt only a bit warmer than the outside December air, yet the chill on his back was not from the cold but the anticipation of the President's speech, coming over the radio in just a few minutes.

"Hurry, Mom, it's starting," Robert Kempinski yelled from across the hallway, his teenage voice cracking with the anticipation of the President's speech, sounding like it did several years ago before it changed to its manly version. "Mr. Truba has the radio on and the President is getting ready to speak."

The teenager darted back into the living room of his neighbor's apartment and seized a spot near the large wood-framed RCA Victor radio. Despite the hour, noon on a Monday, nearly all the residents of his building had gathered around the radio, the most modern in the five-story tenement on the southeast side of Manhattan.

Within the stuffy room, clouded by the adults' cigars and cigarettes, someone coughed.

"Quiet everyone," Mr. Truba hollered.

Kempinski scanned the glum faces huddled on the sparse furniture. His best friend, Frank Gustav, absently stared at the cloth radio grill as did his older brother, Teddy, eyes set thin in defiance.

The static crackled and Speaker of the House, Sam Rayburn announced, "Senators and Representatives of the Seventy-seventh Congress, I have the distinguished honor of presenting the President of the United States."

Applause could be heard as the music *Hail to the Chief* played in the background.

Kempinski hunched low and adjusted his itchy and now sweaty woolen underwear.

"Yesterday, December 7, 1941," Franklin Roosevelt spoke in a voice familiar from the weekly fireside chats, slowly, with presidential intent, "—a date which will live in infamy—the United States of America was suddenly and deliberately attacked by naval and air forces of the Empire of Japan....."

Kempinski wondered what infamy meant as his mom, Sophie Kempinski, entered the room.

"Here, Mom, next to me," Kempinski beckoned to his mother.

"Shhh," Mr. Truba hushed.

"Japan has, therefore, undertaken a surprise offensive extending throughout the Pacific area. The facts of yesterday and today speak for themselves. The people of the United States have already formed their opinions and well understand the implications to the very life and safety of our nation.

As Commander-in-Chief of the Army and Navy, I have directed that all measures be taken for our defense. But always will our whole nation remember the character of the onslaught against us."

The rest of the speech was a blur, and over soon. Kempinski, Teddy, and Frank Gustav listened raptly as the adults in the room discussed what war would mean for their part of New York City.

Mr. Truba, a union negotiator, remarked, "We have no choice, we have to go to war, as FDR said, it was an unprovoked attack on Pearl Harbor."

Kempinski's father, Bernard, a gaunt man in a dark wool

suit, who made his living as a window washer, shook his head. "We may have no choice, but it is going to be difficult." His face, a grim mask like a funeral shroud, recalled the horrific memories as a soldier in Pershing's Army in the Great War. "It will not just be Japan, but Germany, too. We'll be fighting them in Europe. Two days ago, they say a U-boat sunk a ship off Perth Amboy. Some window washers from Jersey said they could see the flames from Asbury Park. My son is in the Merchant Marine; will he be on the next ship to go down?"

Teddy stuck out his chin. His muscles, broad from body-building routines, flexed underneath his navy-blue pullover sweater. "Don't worry about me, Dad, I can keep those Jerry U-boats off my back."

Kempinski regarded his older brother with awe. Although Teddy had only joined the Merchant Marine six months ago, he had already made several cruises to Europe, mostly England, delivering all manner of supplies in support of the Lend Lease program. He was on his Christmas shore leave and had regaled his young brother and other kids in the neighborhood with stories of submarines, airplanes and encounters with icebergs.

Sophie and Mary Truba left and re-entered the room with cups and a spun aluminum pot of steaming roasted java. "Have some coffee, everyone. Except for you, Bobby and Franky, it's milk for you."

"Ah, come on, Mom, I can have coffee," complained Kempinski. "I'm almost sixteen. I'm going to be a soldier."

Sophie patted his head facetiously, prideful yet concerned. "Some soldier you'd be." Her accent combined eastern European pitch with south side Manhattan pace.

The boys grudgingly took the milk, even though it was a treat to have it in a grim economy. They retreated from the somber discussion to the back of the hallway. Kempinski opened the double sash window and he and Gustav stepped onto the grating of the black and rusty metal fire-escape landing.

Splayed before them was the dressed-right-dress façade of lower east side Manhattan tenements; brown stone apartments six or seven stories tall that housed New York's working class; truck drivers, bakers, nurses, carpenters, bricklayers, and garbage men. Along Avenue B, running north-south in the Alphabet City area of the East Village, the first floor of the corner buildings had retail shops, anchoring the city layout providing identification for the city residents negotiating the maze.

The rectangular grid of the island borough defined distances in blocks, and whole neighborhoods could exist between one avenue and the next. Crowded and dense, each section had a neighborly feel, but with residents living in such proximity meals, arguments, celebrations, and other private moments were shared.

The taller of the two, Kempinski scanned the neighborhood vista, surprised by the lack of activity; someone was always doing something along the block. A darkness seemed to have draped the neighborhood. He shuddered and pulled his wool overcoat tighter around his spare shoulders, turned lean like all residents of the tenement by the tough years of The Depression. "I don't know about you, Franky, but I'm going to join the Army."

"How are you going to join, Bobby? You're only fifteen!"

Kempinski adjusted his plaid hat over his slicked back dark hair, hiding a partially receding hairline that made him appear older than he was. "I'll be sixteen next week. If my parents agree, I can enlist."

"No way, you must be 18, and maybe if you're 17 with parent's permission, but your mom and dad aren't going to sign. They are scared enough over Teddy joining the Merchant Marine."

"He's eighteen, and besides, he joined the Merchant Marine to make money."

"What's wrong with the Merchant Marine?" said Gustav defensively and pulled his newsboy cap tight over his dark eyebrows making his eyes peek out menacingly. "I want to go to sea, but the navy is not my cup of tea. Too many regulations."

"Yeah, but you can't fly in the Merchant Marine. I'm going to be in the Army Air Corps and fly planes. I'm going to be a pilot."

Six months later

"What do you say, Mom? I can't stay home while everyone is doing his or her part," said Kempinski in the apartment kitchen. "If you are sixteen, you can join with your parent's approval."

His mother reached across the simple painted wooden table and held his hands with gentle love. "Bobby, you are just a boy. The war effort is important, but you're too young. Stay in school, read your books, and learn. That's how you can do your part."

"But Louie, Dopey Joe and Lefty have all enlisted."

"They are all older than you. Our family has done its part. Your dad fought in the Great War not long ago, and now Teddy is away at sea all the time. I'm already a nervous wreck wondering if his ship will make it. I don't need to worry about my little boy, too."

"I'm not a little boy. I'm sixteen and I can kill Krauts."

Sophie retracted her hands and crossed her arms over her hand knitted sweater. "That's enough, young man. While your dad is away in Chicago, you can prove what kind of man you are by helping me around the house."

"But Mom!"

"No 'but Moms.' Now do your chores."

Kempinski dejectedly pulled on his grey overcoat and in one smooth motion, grabbed the kitchen trash can and headed down two flights of dimly lit stairs to the bins outside the tenement stoop. The empty cans lined the steps like a metallic platoon silently guarding the east entrance to the canyon of brick tenements. As he transferred the household waste to the bin, Gustav appeared next to the landing.

"Why so blue, Bobby?" Gustav asked.

"My mom won't sign the Army papers."

"I knew she wouldn't."

"Everyone else is going off to battle to win the war."

"I have a feeling we'll get our chance. My Dad says it's going to be a long and big war. Do you hear what Japan is doing in China and the Philippines? My mom is so scared. She lived in Europe during the Great War and remembers how all the boys in her town never came back. 'All dead,' she said." Gustav's mood sagged, overcoming its usually goofy but happy-go-lucky quality.

"They aren't going to get us. We're too tough."

"You think so?" Gustav shrugged, his face returning to its normal carefree state. After a few seconds, he said, "I have something to make you feel better. Look what I snitched from my uncle's gun cabinet." Gustav reached into his overcoat pocket and removed two .270 Winchester rifle rounds, their brass casings glinting in the city light.

"Wow, neat!"

"You want to shoot them?"

Kempinski moved toward Gustav, his eyes glistening in wild excitement. "Yeah, target practice shooting Jerrys. You have a gun?"

"No, I don't have his rifle, but if you just punch this little round part here," Gustav pointed to the primer at the end of the cartridge. "The bullet will shoot."

"Really? How are we going to do that?"

"I don't know. Let's snoop around the super's tool box, maybe we can find something."

Gustav put the rounds back in his pocket and the two boys bounded around and under the red brick stoop toward the building superintendent's basement workshop. The door was unlocked, and they found the well-used grey steel toolbox on a shelf next to the steaming boiler. Gustav rummaged in the beat-up box.

"There's a hammer and pliers. Think that will work?"

"If you hold it, I'll hit a nail against the little round part."

"All right come on."

"How about on the roof?" Kempinski pointed up. "We can make some targets like Jerry soldiers."

The boys rounded up some chalk and raced up the fire escape to the roof. Designed for emergency egress from the tenement, the boys used the external stairway as a private route up and down from the tarred rooftop– one of their favorite spots to pass time. With the chalk, Kempinski sketched some crude human silhouettes on the side wall of the roof. Gustav took pliers and held one of the rifle rounds between its jaws.

"I get to aim the first one." Gustav eyeballed the ene-my, about ten feet away. He steadied the pliers against a roof waste vent while Kempinski took a nail and held it up to the primer.

"Hold it still. Here goes!" He smacked the hammer onto the nail and struck the primer. The ensuing explosion knocked them both off their feet.

The young lads did not know the pressure of gases driving a rifle bullet could reach about fifty thousand pounds per square inch and temperature of 3,500 degrees Fahrenheit. Unsupported by the steel chamber of the rifle, the brass cartridge shredded in the air, sending flame and splintered shards of jagged metal in all directions.

Kempinski stood, his eyes seeing spots and ears ringing, shaking his head.

"My hand, my hand!" Gustav moaned.

Blood oozed from Gustav's hand, covered in black burns.

"Franky, your hand is bleeding."

Gustav groaned.

Kempinski reached into his coat pocket and pulled out a handkerchief. "Here, wrap it in this. We have to find Mr. Goldberg."

He helped Gustav to his feet and guided him as they climbed down the fire escape; a task made difficult by Gustav's damaged hand.

Holding Gustav by his arm, he ushered him to the corner drug store. They burst into the glass fronted shop. Mr. Goldberg, the pharmacist in a white smock covering a fat double-Windsor knotted tie, was a kindly old man who served as the city block's resident medical expert dispensing pills, advice and the occasional bloodletting.

"Mr. Goldberg, you have to help Franky. He hurt his hand," Kempinski exclaimed.

Mr. Goldberg looked up from the white marble counter where he was sorting pills. He frowned when he saw the bloody handkerchief on Gustav's hand. He moved quickly around the counter and reached for the injury. "What happened?"

Kempinski glanced toward Gustav, who's his eyes flickered nervously. "He fell off the fire escape."

"Oh, no. Let me see."

Goldberg gently unwrapped the handkerchief and examined the hand. A quizzical expression crossed his face. "But your hand is burned and lacerated. How did the fire escape do that?"

Kempinski backed away a step. "I don't know," his expression guilty.

"Boys," he elongated the word. "What were you doing?"

"Oh heck, Mr. Goldberg, we were doing target practice shooting Jerrys and the bullet blew up." Kempinski dropped his gaze.

"A bullet blew up? I don't understand."

Kempinski related the story while Gustav shook his head in agreement, in too much pain to talk.

"Don't tell our moms, please," begged Kempinski through a black powder-stained face. "She'll never let us be soldiers."

"You have to tell your parents, boys. But first let me see the damage." Goldberg moved Gustav to a deep white enameled sink near the mixing table and tended to the wound.

Goldberg sprinkled sulfa powder over the cuts and wrapped the hand in a bandage. "It's not too bad. I don't think you need stitches. Just keep it clean and wrapped tight for a few days."

"Thanks, Mr. Goldberg," replied Gustav.

"Now I will leave it to you to tell your parents the truth. If your mom has any questions, she can see me." Goldberg patted the lads on their backs. "And for God's sake, boys, no more bullets, there is enough shooting in the world."

Later in the evening, after Mrs. Gustav and Sophie's anger wore away, they agreed the boys could go to the movies to forget about the accident.

The boys walked the five city blocks to the theater, the Roxy's large art deco neon sign serving as a navigation beacon. They paid ten cents each for admission and settled into their cushy velvet seats just as the first newsreel started.

The screen depicted bleak accounts of German attacks in Europe and crushing Japanese advances across the Pacific. The report of the fall of Corregidor to the Japanese cast a pall over the theater, everyone privately wondering if the war could be won against the ferocious might of the Japanese and German alliance. Up-beat US government-provided vignettes followed with reports about American military hardware production and the will of the people to contribute to the effort.

Following the news, the boys watched the cartoons and the feature western movie. As the theater lights came on, Kempinski and Gustav headed home.

"Franky, what did you think about the news? I can't believe the Japanese beat the Army."

"I hear they fight like savages. They don't surrender, and they kill their prisoners," Franky said as he held up his bandaged hand.

"If only there were something we could do. We're only sixteen, but we can fight. We can show the Jerrys and the Japs how to take a New York licking."

"Yeah Bobby, just wait 'till some New Yorkers show them a thing or two."

They walked a block in silence until they passed an Army recruiting office on the way home. Although evening, it was still open, and several people were talking with the recruiting sergeant.

"Hey, let's go in and see how to sign up," Kempinski said, feeling like an adult.

"Not me, I'm going into the Merchant Marine."

"Yeah, well you watch from here."

Kempinski punched open the door and walked over to a sergeant writing at a desk. The soldier smiled broadly and gestured for him to take a seat. Gustav stomped his feet in impatience in the cool spring air as the non-commissioned officer talked with Kem--inski, and then took some papers from his desk.

Fifteen minutes later, Kempinski burst out the door holding some government forms in his hand.

"Franky, listen to this. If I get my mom to sign, they will consider me for enlistment."

"Get outta here, there's no way they will take a sixteen-year-old."

Kempinski titled his head. "Umm, I know. I told them I was seventeen."

"What? You mother is going to be mad."

"All I have to do is show her the papers, and if she signs, I'm in."

"Phew, I don't want to be around when she learns." Gustav shook his head and gave a dismissive wave with his good hand.

When they reached the tenement, Kempinski bid good-night to Gustav and hid the Army forms under his coat. He said hello to his mother then went to the bedroom he used to share with his brother. On the way home from the recruitment office, he had pondered how to approach his mom to get her to change her mind. He concluded it would be best to do it in the morning after she had a night to sleep.

The next morning, Kempinski got up before his mother and lit the stove. He fixed her eggs and kielbasa, a luxury in wartime rationing. Sophie entered the kitchen.

"What's that smell? Kielbasa?"

"Morning Mom," Kempinski replied as cheerfully and brightly as he could. "I made you breakfast."

His mom wiped the sleep from her eyes, eyeing her son with an askew glance. "Feeling guilty about Franky's hand, are you son?"

"No, not at all. Umm, well, yeah, a little bit." The contrite approach might help him achieve his aim, getting his mom to sign the underage waiver. "I made you breakfast to show you I can be a man of the house."

"Very nice. Your father will be impressed."

Kempinski pulled a chair out for Sophie and served her the eggs and sausage. She sat down and Kempinski joined her, his hands shaking almost as much as the butterflies fluttering in his stomach. After she finished her portion, she picked up the plate and turned to the sink, where she spied the enlistment papers on the counter next to the drainage rack. "What's this?" she asked.

"Oh, Mom, you won't believe it," Kempinski beamed. "I stopped at the Army recruitment center last night and the sergeant there told me how to be a pilot in the Army Air Corps. He wrote out some papers and said all you need to do is sign them, and I can be an Army pilot."

Sophie dropped the dish into the sink. "Sign your papers?" she exclaimed. "You are only sixteen years old!"

"Well, you see Mom, I told them I was seventeen, but if you sign, they will never know."

Sophie's face turned bright red. "I am not going to sign them, no matter what the army promised you. You are too young." She reached for the papers and tossed them in the trashcan. "No more talk about the army until you grow up. Now get ready for school."

Kempinski sulked to his room, gathered his schoolbooks and wrapped a thick red rubber strap with a metal clip around them. As he reentered the kitchen with his books bundled under his arm, he noticed his mom had left. He passed the trashcan, considering longingly the enlistment papers. If Sophie happened to change her mind, he couldn't leave them there. He plucked them out of the trash. Smoothing the sheets on the counter, he saw they were still in good shape save for one small oil stain from the sausage. He carefully stashed them in his fabric-covered loose-leaf binder and rewrapped the stack of books with the rubber strap.

After lunch in the Peter Stuyvesant High School cafeteria with Gustav and a few other friends, the school bell announced it was time to go back to class. The boys gathered their belongings and headed out of the cafeteria.

Kempinski tugged on Gustav's sweater. "Psst, Franky, I need you to do me a favor."

"Huh? Why are you whispering, Bobby?"

With a puckered chin, he said in a forlorn way. "I need you to sign for my mom on this note, like we used to do when we played hooky."

"Right now? We'll be late for Mr. Finbar's Latin class. And this bandage makes my penmanship terrible."

Sticking out of Kempinski's loose-leaf binder were a few sheets of paper; he pulled out one page and pointed to a blank line near the bottom following lots of fine print. "It will only take a second. Sign 'Sophie Kempinski' right here."

After glancing at the paper, Gustav's face froze in fear. "Bobby, this isn't an absence note; it's some sort of Army form."

"That's right. It's an Army pilot application. They don't know what my mom's signature looks like."

"I don't know, Bobby. We could get in a lot of trouble."

"No, we won't. The Army needs as many pilots as it can get. Lots of guys are doing it."

"OK, but don't tell anyone it was me."

"Of course not, you flat tire. I can't tell anyone. They have to think my mom signed it."

Kempinski handed the form to Gustav and then turned his back and hunched over slightly. "Here, sign it on my back."

Gustav quickly scribbled 'Mrs. Sofia Kempinski,' in what he hoped resembled adult penmanship.

"Good luck, Bobby. You are going to need it."

"Oh, boy Franky, this is so keen. I can't wait." He placed the paper carefully back in his loose-leaf binder and raced down the hall to Mr. Finbar's classroom.

Gustav accompanied Kempinski as they took the long way home from school past the Army recruitment office. There was a line outside the door of twenty or so men waiting like restless tigers to learn how they could do their part. Kempinski gulped. Waiting would make him late for dinner, but it didn't matter. He would be a soldier. He thrust back his shoulders as stiff as he could and walked past the row of rough men to the end of the line.

The eager volunteers glanced at Kempinski, and quickly returned to their jack jawing about their upcoming career choice and how they were going to win the war single handedly. After a half hour, the two boys reached a sergeant, a tall thin man with slightly grey temples, lots of overseas stripes along his arm, and fruit salad of service ribbons nearly up to his chin. It wasn't the same non-commissioned officer whom had previously given Kempinski the papers.

"Hello, I'm Robert Kempinski, and here are my enlistment papers. My mom signed them." Kempinski handed the papers across the desk. "I'm going to be a pilot."

The sergeant reached for them but kept his eyes on Kempinski. For a quick second, he glanced at Gustav and then back to Kempinski. "Is that so?" he asked, scanning the forms. "So, Sergeant Wilson drew these up for you? Hmm, a waiver for underage. How old are you, son?"

Kempinski froze, the sergeant's glance piercing him. It took all the courage he could muster. He said, "I'm seventeen." His voice cracked. He swallowed and continued with as much bravado left in his mind, "Born on December 13, 1924."

The senior sergeant studied Kempinski for a long moment and then Gustav. "Well, you sure don't look seventeen. Neither does your buddy. He looks like he's twelve."

Gustav jerked back his head in indignation. "I'm not twelve. I'm sixteen."

"Where are your papers then?"

Gustav stepped back, semi-stunned. "Umm, I'm not joining today. Only Bobby is."

"I see. Well, since Sergeant Wilson started your paperwork, he must finish it. He will be here tomorrow. Come back then. Meanwhile, I will put these in Sergeant Wilson's in-box. "

Kempinski didn't know what to do, so he stood there by the desk.

"Soldier," the grisly sergeant bellowed, "don't just stand there taking up space. Make a smart about-face and get moving. I've other men to process."

"Yes sir." Kempinski jerked to attention.

"Don't call me sir, you 'cruit. I work for a living. Now, move out on the double."

The next morning, Kempinski left for school with nervous excitement. He had had a vivid dream of strapping himself into a tight cockpit of an Army Air Corps fighter plane and performing all kinds of maneuvers in a cloudless sky.

His exhilaration compromised his concentration on his classes. He was still feeling ten feet tall when he arrived at the tenement.

"Hey Mom, I'm home!" He opened the door to the kitchen of the apartment.

He stopped short upon seeing his mom sitting at the kitchen table. She had some documents in front of her, her eyes red and handkerchief in hand.

"Robert, get in here right now," she spoke in a stern voice. Kempinski always knew he was in trouble when his mom called him by his proper given name. "Do you know a Sergeant Wilson?"

"Uh, uh…" he stammered.

"Well, Sergeant Wilson stopped by today to see me about your enlistment. It seems there were some problems with my signature. I needed to sign several forms." She stared into Kempinski's eyes. "Sergeant Wilson knew you weren't old enough, and he was kind enough to explain the situation to me."

Kempinski's heart leapt to his throat.

"How could you do this, son? You are too young."

His eyes dropped to the floor, "Mom, I'm sorry. I just really, really, want to fly. The Army needs pilots and I want to do my part."

Sophie's eyes moved over his face. "You are just like your father." She paused. "I know you want to do your part, everyone does, but still, you are too young to join the Army."

She stared wistfully out the kitchen window into the other tenement kitchen next door. She seemed to carefully consider the next sentence. "I managed to call Chicago today with the telephone at the union hall to talk to your father." Kempinski felt his face flush and his pulse quicken knowing his father was involved. "He and I agree we will let you join the Army Air Corps when you turn seventeen, provided you do well in school before then, and you act on your best behavior, but your Dad says you can't join the infantry or the cavalry like he did when he was your age. The Air Corps only."

"Seventeen? Really Mom?"

"Six months from now."

"I know, I know. Thanks, Mom." Kempinski dropped his books and ran to hug his mother. She returned his embrace and patted him on the shoulder, fighting back more tears.

Chapter 2

The winds of war changed in the spring of 1943. News reels reported the massive Russian victory at Stalingrad, when the second brutal winter in a row had taken its toll on the German army. Combined with the progress made by the Allies in Northern Africa and Italy, hopes kindled the war might end someday. With soaring spirits, the Saturday Evening Post published a patriotic illustration of Rosie The Riveter, encouraging American women to replace men in factories, supporting the war effort.

Kempinski and Gustav, wearing only shirts and pants, taking advantage of the warm spring air, sat on the porch of their tenement admiring the cover of the weekly magazine when a friend from around the block approached them.

"Hey, Bobby, hey Franky, whatcha doing?" Dominick Varchek was a burly, older classmate, thanks to being left behind in the third and fifth grades.

"Not much Dom, just scoping this dame on the cover of the Post," replied Kempinski, "You think she's real?"

"Yeah, she's real alright, in fact, she's making my tank," Varchek replied.

"Your tank? Whadaya mean?" Gustav blurted.

"The Army finally realized what they need to win this war, and they called me in. I report to Fort Dix this weekend. I'm going to drive a tank." Varchek hooked his thumbs around his red suspenders and thrust out his chest, straining his one-size-too-small plaid shirt.

"A tank?"

"Yeah, how hep is that? The Army recognized my mechanical abilities and assigned me to the armor. I'm going to drive a tank all the way to Berlin and back."

"I wonder what it's like to drive a tank," mused Gustav, removing his newsboy cap and rubbing his hair.

"It might be swell, but it doesn't compare to flying." Kempinski rose, thrusting his arms out like airplane wings. "Have you heard about the new Mustang? The P-51? That's what I'm going to do. Fly right over your tanks and shoot 'em up."

The boys laughed. Then Varchek said, "Hey, how'd you'ze like to help me out? I'm going to sell my car to settle some bills."

"You have a car?"

"Yeah, I have a '27 Model A Sports Coupe," Varchek answered, pride obvious in his voice. "I keep it by my Aunt's place in Staten Island. They used it for a delivery service and it was all beat up, but in the last few months, I've fixed it up pretty good. I was thinking I'd drive it to Fort Dix, but then I found out the Army won't let you have a car during basic training. My Aunt says she can't watch it while I'm gone, so I need to sell it."

Kempinski and Gustav turned their faces towards each other, amazed one of their friends owned a car. "I've never driven a car," said Gustav.

"Me neither. But, er, I drove a tractor a couple of times the summer Teddy and I spent upstate when my Mom was sick," replied Kempinski.

"It's easy to drive, and the Sports Coupe is a piece of cake to maintain."

"Yeah, maybe for you. You're a mechanic."

"Oh, come on Franky, we can fix things too," chided Kempinski. "My dad always gave me repair chores to do at the Union Hall."

"Right, so where are we going to get money for a car?"

"I have six dollars saved up for when I join the Air Corps."

"I got less, maybe four dollars."

"Lookit guys, I was going to ask twenty bucks for it. Like I said, it's not in the best shape. But ten bucks for now helps me settle my bills and you guys can give me the rest when I come home on leave."

"What are we going to do with a car?" questioned Gustav.

"Are you for real? First, the shebas love it. Second, you'll get practice driving and it will give you a head start on the other guys when you are in the service."

"Yeah, makes sense," said Kempinski, rubbing his chin, thinking over Varchek's logic.

"I'll tell you what. I'll take you to Staten Island and teach you how to drive it. Then it's all yours."

"Go to Staten Island, now?" questioned Gustav his lips puckered like he just tasted a lemon.

"Sure, Franky, we can take the ferry and be back with the car before dinner."

"Now you're talking," Varchek beamed and placed his

hands under his suspenders and pushed them out like a country farmer.

"Let me go upstairs to get my money."

"Me too," added Gustav.

Kempinski grabbed Gustav by his shoulder. "Better not say anything to your mom."

"Yeah, let's keep it quiet." Gustav nodded.

The ferry ride from the Battery Terminal took thirty minutes, but the salty air combined with the excitement of picking up the car made the trip seem like it took forever. When they arrived at the Staten Island ferry dock, they took a bus to Varchek's aunt's house. Twenty minutes later, they arrived at their destination: a two-story duplex with a dirt driveway and small garage in the back. Next to the garage was a well-worn and faded yellow and partially-rusty Ford Model-A Sports Coupe.

"You really have a car," said Kempinski.

"What's da matter? You'ze didn't believe me?"

"It seems kind of beat up," commented Gustav. "It's a jalopy; this fender, it's lopsided."

"Whad'ya expect for twenty bucks? It's not new, but it's easy to fix. As for the fender, you just use this wrench I keep here in the rumble seat to tighten up this nut. Let me show you."

Varchek realigned the fender, tightening the nut and then sat in the frayed driver's seat. Kempinski sat on the passenger side. "Here's how to start the car. Pay attention to the steps."

"First, make sure the gas valve is inline." Varchek reached under the dash on the passenger side and turned a well-worn brass valve. Then he pushed a chrome lever on the left side of the steering column. "This here is the timing – it controls the engine spark.

You retard it."

"Retard it?"

"Yeah, Bobby, just push it all the way up. Then pull out this here lever – the throttle, it controls the gas. This works best if almost all the way out."

Varchek reached over to the passenger side and turned a silver knob clockwise. "This knob is the choke and fuel mixture."

"Oh, I know about the choke from the tractor on the farm. All the way out when it's cold, right?"

"That's it. Wow, maybe you will be able to fly a plane."

Kempinski turned to Gustav and smiled, arching his shoulders in teenage bravado.

Holding his nose like he had smelled something foul, Gustav turned away.

The mechanic continued, "When the engine is warm, you don't need the choke."

Placing his left foot on the clutch pedal, Varchek said, "You push this pedal to disengage the clutch and then with your other foot, push the starter button. As soon as it starts, you push in the choke. Got it?"

A twist of his head belied how he really felt but Kempinski replied, "I think so." He pointed toward the floor board. "What about the gas pedal, like on the tractor?"

"When starting you don't use the gas pedal, that's what the throttle is for, 'cause your foot is on the starter button," Varchek answered.

"Ah, I see."

"Okay, let's do it." Varchek pushed the starter button and the engine sputtered but didn't start. "It's cold, let's try again."

Again, the engine turned but didn't crank.

"What's wrong, Dom?"

"Hmm, hold on a second, maybe the gas has some water in it. Let me show you a trick." He went into the garage and returned with a small metal bottle. He removed the air cleaner top and poured some liquid into the carburetor.

"Now, quick, hit the starter button."

The starter fluid did the trick; the engine turned over, sputtered, and then settled into a steady, reliable hum.

"Runs like a kitten." Varchek beamed.

As the car continued to idle, the beat-up door at the back of the house opened. A matronly lady with her hair wrapped in a dark blue kerchief and wearing a gingham print house coat and matching apron appeared. "Oh, Dommy, it's you. I didn't know you were here."

"Hi, Aunt Zelda. I have great news. I'm going to Fort Dix Saturday to join the Army. I'm in the armor. My friends here have bought the car. They are going to drive it home."

"The Army," she paused, "and so soon. Oh, my." She motioned to the others. "Well, then, you and your friends have to stay for dinner."

Kempinski and Gustav grimaced. "Oh, thank you ma'am," said Kempinski, "but Franky and I need to get back to Manhattan before six o'clock."

"Is that so? Then Dom, you must stay, with you going away into the army and all. It's the least I can do."

"Okay, Aunt Zelda. Let me help these guys get on their way and then we can have some chow."

Quickly illustrating the shift pattern, Varchek worked the clutch pedal and stick shift showing his friends how to engage the clutch and use the three gears. With Kempinski in the driver's seat, Varchek in the passenger seat, and Gustav in the rumble seat, they headed out for a practice run.

"Oh, boy, this is great," said Kempinski as he appeared to master the process of shifting.

"You're a natural, Bobby. The tank has plenty of gas, so just follow the road until you come to the tracks and then make a left across the tracks and head to the ferry. They'll let you drive right onto the ferry. It's only a nickel for a car."

Kempinski nodded. He had watched cars board on the trip to Staten Island.

"Okay, stop here and I'll head back to my aunt's house. See you tomorrow in Manhattan."

While Varchek waved goodbye, Kempinski drove off with Gustav staying in the rumble seat – he liked the air blowing in his face. Next, they took turns driving the car around the streets of Staten Island. Not as adept as Kempinski, Gustav had trouble slipping the clutch, nearly stalling the car several times. After some time driving around the area, they lost track of where they were. Kempinski took over driving. "Hey, it must be getting late; we better head toward the ferry. Which way did Dommy say it was?"

"He said something like 'left across the railroad tracks.'"

"Where are the tracks?"

"I think a few blocks behind us," said Gustav, rubbing his chin.

Turning around, they drove a few long blocks until they spied some railroad tracks. The sun was getting low in the sky.

"Didn't Dommy say the tracks led to the ferry?"

"I think so." Gustav nodded. "I'm not sure."

"Well, the sun is in front of us, so that's west. If we turn right on the tracks, we should head north to the ferry terminal. Hey, let's just drive down the tracks. It's a bit bumpy, but it will be the quickest."

"I guess so."

Kempinski turned the car onto the tracks and straddled one of the rails as the wheelbase wasn't wide enough to cover both rails. The ride was terrible. Every time they hit a railroad tie, the car bounced up and down.

After several minutes Kempinski said, "I don't think this was a good idea. We have to get off the tracks."

As he scanned ahead for a road crossing, the car approached a turnout in the tracks. The iron rails made a 'V' and the front right tire wedged into it and stuck, as if a brake had been applied. The two boys were thrown forward as the car jerked to a halt, stalling the engine in third gear.

"What the heck?" hollered Kempinski.

"That hurt, I banged my head on the roof bar," Gustav exclaimed, replacing his newsboy cap on his head. "What happened?"

"I don't know. The car stalled. We have to restart it. Let's see, what to do?"

Adjusting the knobs and levers like Varchek had showed him, Kempinski pushed the starter button with his foot, but the engine just turned over and didn't catch. After several more tries, it sounded like the battery was getting weak.

In exasperation, Gustav said, "Oh, boy, it won't start. Maybe we need the starter fluid Dom used."

"Not with a dead battery. We have to try to push start it. Get out and push."

The two lads got behind the car and pushed but they couldn't overcome the wedged wheel.

"Drat, it's stuck against the rail." Kempinski grunted. "Let's push it the other way."

As hard as they tried, they couldn't budge the car. As they toiled, the sun lowered in the sky and darkness approached.

"Bobby, what are we going to do?"

"Hmm, this is bad, Franky. It's almost dark. We have to get out of here."

"What about the car?"

"Forget about it."

"You mean leave it here?" Gustav sounded desperate.

"What else can we do? We can't get help here in the boondocks of Staten Island. Plus, where were we going to keep a car in Manhattan anyway?"

"But what about our ten dollars?"

"Gone. Geez, pissed away. Let's get out of here. We'll have plenty of explaining to do as it is."

The next day, having concocted a story about visiting Varchek's aunt for dinner, the duo escaped without getting into trouble. They never mentioned the Model A or their lost ten dollars. After breakfast, they donned some old baseball uniform shirts over their wool pants, and with felt newsboy caps and low-cut leather shoes, they walked to the East River Baseball Field for some practice to reduce their chances of seeing Varchek.

"My mom says my dad is coming home in a week or so," Kempinski said. "His union business in Chicago is finished."

"That's great."

"Yeah, I miss him. Plus, I can talk to him about exactly when I can enlist in the Army Air Corps."

"Speaking of the Air Corps." Gustav gave Kempinski a

blank stare. "Did you hear about Skinny Joe?"

"No, what about him?"

"His mother got a telegram two days ago from the Army. He's missing in action. His plane didn't return from a mission over France."

"Oh, no. I wonder if he parachuted out."

"According to my mom, the telegram had no details. His mom locked herself up in the apartment and won't talk to anyone."

"I'm sure he's hiding in the woods trying to link up with the French resistance. They rescue a lot of downed flyers."

Gustav shrugged and the rest of the walk to the field was in silence.

The pair joined up with other kids for a game of sandlot baseball at the sparse but adequate empty field. Kempinski took out his old baseball and some electrical tape he got from the super's tool box and rewrapped the beat-up ball with the sticky, black, cloth tape. He took the pitcher's mound, which was a flat spot about sixty feet from the trash can lid used as home plate and started to warm up with the neighborhood kid playing catcher. Tommy Leonid, a strapping youth, stepped into the batter's box, comprised of two lines scratched into the dirt by the end of an old broom stick instead of chalk lines like a regulation diamond.

"I'm going to be number three, Babe Ruth, today," yelled Kempinski to Leonid.

Leonid said, "Yeah, well I'm number five, Joe DiMaggio. Just try to get one by me."

And Kempinski did, throwing fastballs, curves, and the occasional screwball. After the game, he collected his ball, with the tape now thoroughly frayed, and headed home with Gustav.

"Did you see the ball I hit today, Franky?" Kempinski smiled. "That would have been a home run in Yankee Stadium."

"Yeah, right, and my shot would have ended up in Brooklyn if Tommy didn't catch it. You only got a home run because you run fast."

"Yeah, well I am the fastest guy on the east side."

"Psh." Gustav blew between his lips. "How is your speed going to get our ten dollars back?"

"Hmm, maybe we should ask Varchek for refund. I mean his car stopped running on the tracks."

"Right! And who is going to tell him his car is crushed underneath a train?"

"True, probably better if we avoid him for a while. In a few days he'll be driving tanks, and I sure wouldn't want him to think of me as a Kraut facing his Sherman."

Both lads smiled.

"You know with my dad coming back, maybe he can get me some work at the Union Hall. The window washers always have little jobs to do."

"You mean you want to get a union card?" said Gustav.

"Nah, not a card, just some odd jobs to make some money before joining the Army Air Corps. After all, my dad used to be the president of the union. He still has some clout."

"With you joining the Air Corps this summer, I was thinking." Gustav hesitated. "I'd go ahead and join the Mariners Union. Last time he was in town, Teddy gave me the name of the guy who signs up apprentices."

"An apprentice seaman?"

Gustav shook his head. "Not a seaman, but an engineer, an oiler actually." Gustav turned his lower lip. "One thing worries me, the guy at the Union Hall told me I might as well be joining the navy. According to some new law, something like, uhhh, the

Merchant Marine Act, in times of war, merchant mariners are considered part of the navy and part of the uniformed service. But still, being on a merchant ship can be a great job."

"Tell me about it. Every time Teddy comes home, he has more adventures to tell. Of course, with Teddy, you're never sure what to believe."

Gustav hitched his pants as if he was uncertain. "Do you think the Merchant Marine is right for me? The guy at the Union Hall asked me if I was sure. He said more men were lost in the Merchant Marine than any other service. The German U-boats have sunk so many ships."

"I think it's for you. I can't picture you as a soldier, and certainly not a marine."

"Well, if any U-boat torpedoes my ship, I'll swim over to them and punch a hole in their side."

Kempinski chuckled. "Don't worry, Franky. You'll be fine; it's the other guys that get hit. They won't mess with New Yorkers."

The third Saturday in June of the year 1943 started as a special day. Sophie Kempinski, her young daughter, Sandy, and son, Robert, dressed in their Sunday-best clothes and took the city bus to Grand Central Station. The station hummed as the axle in the city's transportation hub with soldiers, sailors, businessmen, students, families, and children scurrying under the domed promenade with purpose in their steps due to the war. War bond banners hung from the mezzanine and United Service Organization (or USO booths had lines of servicemen waiting for a care package of cigarettes and chocolate.

Kempinski, wearing a brand-new black Tyrolean felt hat with a yellow feather, led his mom and sister through the crowd and found the track number. They nibbled on waxed paper-wrapped Kruschiki cookies leftover from Easter dinner while they waited for the train from Chicago to arrive. As the steam engine chugged into the station, Kempinski jostled in front of the dozen or so people waiting. The conductor jumped out the open passenger doors followed by a steady stream of travelers, mostly soldiers and business men. After several had passed, Kempinski spotted his father.

"Hey, Dad, over here," he shouted and then turned to his mother. "He's coming, Mom."

Bernard Kempinski, wearing a dark double-breasted suit with shiny shoes and a natty fedora, spotted his son waving and ran to him, dropped his bag and gave him a hug. "How's my favorite son doing?"

"Ah, Dad, come on. I've been good."

"That's what I hear."

He found his wife and toddler and they embraced.

"It's great to be back. There's nowhere like New York. Let's head home."

As they boarded the city bus, Kempinski sidled up to his dad. "Hey, Dad, when we get a chance, can we talk about the Air Corps? I've been doing a lot of reading at the library."

"Oh, the Air Corps. The flyboys. A little later son, we'll have plenty of time to talk." He reached over and rubbed his son's head even though now they were the same height.

"Okay, Dad."

Several days later, Bernard Kempinski accompanied his son to the recruitment station and together they discussed enlisting in the army. It turned out Sergeant Wilson, the non-commissioned officer, or NCO, they spoke to and Bernard Kempinski had been in the same division, the Third Infantry, at the Marne in France during the Great War. As a favor to a fellow veteran, Sergeant Wilson said he would put in a good word for Kempinski's selection into the Aviation Cadet program and went to talk to the officer in charge. The NCO came back with a serious expression and stood in front of Kempinski. "What was it you wanted, soldier?"

"The Air Corps, Sergeant Wilson."

"Well, then," Wilson paused with a deadly serious expression, "welcome to the Air Corps." Wilson changed his face to a broad grin and turned to Bernard Kempinski. "The Lieutenant sends his compliments." Then, addressing the younger Kempinski, "The Lieutenant also said to tell you the Aviation Cadet Corps is extremely competitive and you will have to pass special physical and aptitude tests. If you don't pass, it will be the infantry for you."

Father and son viewed each other. Kempinski gulped slightly. "I'll pass, don't worry Dad."

"You are to report on July 1 to the New York Recruiting Office at 39 Whitehall Street for your aptitude test. If you pass, you'll get a flight physical and a report date, probably near your eighteenth birthday. Do what you can to prepare. The wash out rate has been pretty high. Flying is in big demand."

They shook hands and left, with father placing his arm proudly around his son.

For the next month, Kempinski visited the New York Public library on Fifth Avenue between 40th and 42nd street every night. He roamed the vast rooms reading all the articles and books he could find about flying. One evening, the librarian told him she noticed him each night and his choice of books and asked if he was going to be a pilot. Kempinski said yes, he was, as long as he passed the test. She told him her brother was an Air Corps pilot and home on leave. Maybe he could give him some tips. Kempinski nodded vigorously and the next night the pilot was at the library.

He said he only had a few minutes, but they were golden for Kempinski. The pilot explained the written exams were like high school history and math, so not hard, but the psychomotor tests, designed to measure coordination needed for flying, were difficult. In one test, lights flashed, and buzzers announced every mistake while the candidate had to operate make-believe aircraft controls. The pilot advised focusing on the dials and not the lights. Kempinski practiced what the pilot told him and on July 1, passed the aptitude test with flying colors.

Passing the test placed Kempinski in the Aviation Cadet program and qualified him for training as a pilot, bombardier, and navigator, even though he didn't have a college degree, nor had he finished high school. Two days later, he had his first ever medical exam. A bit embarrassed to have to take off his clothes in front of the nurses, he nonetheless qualified "One A," fully fit for duty. After a week, a letter arrived from the Army assigning him a report date of December 11, 1943, two days before his eighteenth birthday.

The summer passed quickly with news of the war showing progress in some areas but defeat in others. The list of casualties continued to grow and many families in the neighborhood received unwelcome telegrams or visits from Army officers with bad news. Nonetheless, as December neared, Kempinski could barely contain his desire to join the fighting to help win the war.

On December 4, 1943, Bernard Kempinski said over dinner, "Well, Son, you have one week before you leave for active duty."

Peeping over his borscht soup, Kempinski's favorite, he beamed with enthusiasm. "I'd go today, Dad, if I could."

"Well, try to wait, because tomorrow, I'm taking you and Franky to the Giants game. I got three tickets hoping Teddy would be back, but he's still at sea, so Franky agreed to go."

"It's the Giants and Redskins, Dad! How'd you get tickets?"

"The guys at the Union Hall appreciated how much you helped out this summer, so they took up a collection and bought us the tickets."

"Gee, that was swell of them."

Sophie Kempinski smiled, but her restless eyes revealed a touch of sadness. "You have fun boys; it may be a while before you can again."

Bernard Kempinski was an avid Giants football fan and in the past years, he and his sons would go to at least one game a season. The son rooted for the Redskins to be contrary to his father and liven up their discussions.

The Giants and Redskins had a running rivalry with the Redskins' winning the 1937 and 1942 Championships. The 1943 season so far had confounded the New York team. The teams were scheduled to play back-to-back games on two consecutive Sundays, December 5 and December 12. The Giants trailed the Redskins by two games, so the December 5 game would help determine the division champion, a process the NFL stuck to despite the war-depleted rosters.

Sunday afternoon at Giants Stadium, Bernard Kempinski, along with his son and Frank Gustav, settled into their seats. As the players warmed up on the field, Kempinski pointed to them with a gloved finger.

"Hey, Franky, look at those Giants, all wearing leather helmets, what a bunch of sissies."

Several of the spectators sitting around them chuckled. 1943 was the first year the league mandated players wear leather helmets and they were not popular with the fans. It made recognizing the players difficult.

Gustav said, "You root for the Redskins and these fans will make you wish you had one," The lad sided with the older Kempinski in his fan allegiance.

"Easy, boys, the game hasn't even started," coached Bernard Kempinski. As he spoke, a beer hawker holding a wooden tray loaded with paper cups filled with sloshing beer climbed the steep aisle steps past their row yelling.

"Beeeeer heeeerah!"

"Since you boys will be men next week, how about your first beer?" offered Bernard Kempinski.

"Sure!" Kempinski and Gustav replied in unison.

Bernard Kempinski motioned to the vendor. "Three beers this way. These men are joining up next week and they're thirsty."

"You got it, Mista."

The nearby spectators, hearing about the future, turned to the soon-to-be men and shook their hands, offering congratulations, making Kempinski tingle with excitement.

The game started, and the teams played in a well-fought contest, the Giant's defense shutting down the star Redskin quarter-back, Sam Baugh. Kempinski, surrounded by Giants fans, toned down his cheering. As the final second ticked, the fans near the fence erupted onto the field. Several rows up, Bernard Kempinski smiled at his son. "Well, chalk one up for the Giants."

"Oh, they were lucky, Dad, Sammy had a bad game."

"Maybe so, but it's better for you to save your luck; you'll need it in the Air Corps."

"I don't need luck, Dad."

"Oh, yes you do, Son. We'll pray for you, and with the Good Lord willing, luck will bring you home in one piece."

Chapter 3

After morning Catholic Mass, then a full breakfast, Kempinski hugged his mother and father goodbye and left for the induction station, taking the subway to the Fort Totten Recruit Reception Center. He wore a simple suit under his dark overcoat with a change of underwear in a small satchel. Sophie Kempinski had cried while his father stood proudly stoic. Sandy, his younger sister, had asked when he would return. Kempinski had rubbed her head and said, "Soon."

The reception center was a blur. Sergeants met the recruits at the train station, shouting all manner of commands. Kempinski was instructed to board a bus to Fort Dix. Once there, he got in a long line where he checked in for duty and was issued an Aviation Cadet uniform with overcoat. The uniform was the same as for officers, except for the cap, which had a blue band and the Air Corps winged-propeller instead of the eagle. He went through orientation and would ship out tomorrow for Biloxi, Mississippi for Air Cadet training, a combination of enlisted Basic Training and Officer Candidate School. As an Aviation Cadet, he would draw pay of seventy-five dollars a month, the rate of a private on flight status.

His first dinner in the Army was derisively called "shit on a shingle," corned beef in gravy on toast and, although it tasted like its nickname, he wolfed it down, not having had lunch. He spent the evening on a wood-and-canvas cot in a field house-turned dormitory. The constant noise of hundreds of men snoring and whispering, with doors opening and closing, made it hard for him to sleep and he lay still, thinking about what it was going to be like flying with the birds in the clouds. He finally drifted off while his imaginary plane made loops.

At dawn the next day, olive-drab buses took the sleepy cadets to the train station. Even at the early hour, the place vibrated with activity – daily scores of passenger trains and even more freight trains passed through the main line, cramming the transport of war into the nation's business. Railroads made a mini-renaissance during the first few years of the war, with gasoline and tire rationing putting a halt on the growing pre-war automobile market. Trains handled the movement of millions of soldiers across the nation as well as the deployment of military supplies and equipment.

Kempinski crammed onto a passenger train heading south with a party atmosphere. Even though the compartments were crowded, morale was high as the soldiers made new friends, some passing around a flask of giggle water. A large hulking man wearing a hat two sizes too small for his enormous head deep-set with prize fighter eyes, squinting as if ready for a punch, asked Kempinski if the seat next to him was occupied.

"Nah, have a seat," Kempinski said, sticking out his hand. "Bob Kempinski."

"Kempinski, eh." The big man's hand swallowed Kempinski's. "Polacken! Ja też. I'm Louie Kowalski," he said in Polish.

"Yeah, my grandfather was born in Poland, but I don't speak Polish." Kempinski smiled.

"Oh, okay. Where are you from?"

"Manhattan, East Side."

"Heh, I'm from Brooklyn. Nice to meetcha."

"Same here."

"You ever been to Mississippi?"

"Nope, never past Jersey."

"Me, neither." The big man crumbled into the seat, an awkward assemblage of elbows, knees and ankles.

"Hey, how are you going to fit in a cockpit?"

"Don't worry, I'll fit alright even if I have to stretch the metal."

"Well, you look strong enough."

Both men smiled.

The troop train arrived in Biloxi at 6:00AM after three days of travel. Kempinski departed through the passenger door with his small bag and rumpled uniform followed by his new friend, Kowalski. They boarded a bulbous green Army bus for the ride to Keesler Air Field, one of the largest Army Air Corp basic training bases established at the beginning of the war. In three years, the base saw ten million dollars spent on construction with over 12,000 carpenters, plumbers, roofers, painters, and laborers erecting the base. Even with all the construction, there weren't enough barracks to house all the troops passing through, and many inductees and cadets had to live in a tent city comprised of square six-man tents, affectionately called "tentments" by the soldiers.

The bus disgorged the cadets to a cacophony of sergeants yelling orders, herding them into a long line outside a mess hall tent. As they queued for morning chow, a dull rumbling sound amassed in the distance. Within seconds, the sound grew and resonated throughout the area. Kempinski scanned the sky, trying to determine the direction from which it was coming, when one of the new cadets pointed over the mess hall crying, "Look!"

A shadow passed over them, cast by the distinctive outline of a Liberator, the B-24 bomber. Four radial engines with eight cylinders each – the twenty-four cylinders and pistons totaling thousands of horsepower - rattled the area. A second plane thundered overhead, followed by another, and then another. Kempinski craned his neck as he watched the dark green planes with bright orange tail markings gain altitude and then trace gentle arcs in the sky as the student pilots practiced getting into formation. The ear-throbbing vibration of the squadron filled him with awe and pride as his skin tensed with goose bumps.

"Holy Moly, would you look at them?" said Kowalski, his jaw dropped making his face even larger.

"That's why we're here, bud, to fly them and kill Nazis," offered Kempinski as they watched the planes fly off into the horizon.

"Alright, you sorry sacks," yelled the sergeant. "The welcome show is over. Get in the mess hall. You have five army minutes to grab some chow and re-form out here. Now move out."

After wolfing down a breakfast of powdered eggs and ham, the men marched in a ragtag manner to a medical tent where they received shots for tropical diseases possible to contract in the Deep South.

Kempinski rubbed his arm where he had just received three shots. "So, this is the south. I thought it was supposed to be warm."

"If this is warm, then I don't want to see cold," replied Kowalski, hugging his chest.

"The Sarge says we are going to be assigned a tent. I wonder what it's like to sleep under canvas?"

"I'm so tired, I could sleep in a barn right now."

A muscular NCO built like Jim Thorpe wearing combat boots ordered, "Cadets, fall in on this cable. Move it! Move it! You are on army time now."

The soldiers moved in mass to create a straight row, placing their toes against a steel cable stretched and staked along the ground.

"Alright, listen up: I will call out tent assignments. When we are done, you'll fall out, find your tent, and unpack your gear. You have ten minutes to fall back on this cable." The NCO unfolded a sheet of paper and started calling names. "Adams, Ambromowitz, Anderson, Andrews, Autehcon, and Archer, Tent 48. Ardwell, Ax-emore,…" and so on. Kempinski heard his tent assignment. Since Kowalski's name was alphabetically near Kempinski's, their tents ended up near each other.

"Hey, Louis, you're only two tents away."

"Yeah, good, Bobby, I'll see you in a few minutes."

Kempinski found his tent, dropped his bag on an open bunk and was nodding to his future tent mates when the sergeant called fall in again. The troops ran out to the area between the rows of tents.

"Attent-Shun!" commanded the sergeant. The men stiffened their backs, standing rigid.

"Alright, you pisswad air kay-dets," bellowed the sergeant, facing the men. They had formed in rows on the packed-clay field. "Welcome to Keesler Army Airfield. I'm Sergeant Nash. Before any of you think you are going to fly the US Government's airplanes, you are going to have to prove to me your worth. You will move when I say so, you will run when I say so, you will eat when I say so, you will sleep when I say so, and you will shit when I say so. Do you understand?"

A few men murmured and nodded.

"What? I can't hear you! Do you understand?" demanded the sergeant, even louder than before.

This time the men yelled in unison, "Yes, sergeant!"

The sergeant did an about-face. An officer, a captain, marched to the front of the sergeant and they exchanged salutes. "Good morning, Aviation Cadets." The captain paused, glancing at the unresponsive assembled company. "Good morning, cadets," the captain repeated, this time louder.

The men got the message. "Good morning, Sir!" they replied with extra volume.

"I'm Captain Smithson, your company commander while you are here at Kessler."

Smithson had a purple scar running from the side of his neck to his left ear, and several rows of campaign ribbons over the left pocket of his tunic. "Party time is over, men. We are at war. We are here to learn to kill the Jerrys and the Japs. It's up to Sergeant Nash to whip you poor excuses for humanity into shape.

If any of you fail to live up to our standards, we will wash you out and send you to the infantry. Do you understand?"

This time the men exclaimed vigorously in unison, "Yes, Sir!"

For the next four weeks, the captain and the sergeant became the cadets' interface with the rest of the world, leading and directing their every move. Early in the war, air cadet training had resembled West Point training, complete with hazing, but as the war progressed, the need for air crews meant the phasing out of the senior hazing and incorporating an extreme focus on generating the most proficient air crew members possible in a short amount of time. The company commander and platoon sergeant trained the cadets in close-order drill, marching everywhere, squaring off corners as they executed a column left or column right marching turn. The cadre also led them in physical fitness and escorted them to classes in basic academic subjects, such as refresher courses in physics and math, with more detailed training in map reading, aircraft recognition using silhouettes and photos, and the military code and decoding. Gaps in the schedule were filled with Morse code classes.

While Kempinski found the regimentation of camp rigorous, he enjoyed it. The marching, saluting, pulling guard duty, attention to uniform dress, and other aspects of military life thrust upon them were tedious, but gave purpose to what they were doing. Anytime a plane flew overhead, Kempinski would watch it and yearn for his chance to be behind the controls.

The third week of training, the company boarded a transport cattle-car for a drive to the edge of the base. When they arrived, the men piled out onto a grassy field.

Sergeant Nash bellowed out, "Alright, men, today we are taking chemical weapon defense familiarization training."

The cadets collectively shrugged their shoulders, horrified; they had heard rumors about how the training entailed smelling real mustard agent. Kempinski whispered to Kowalski. "This is nuts."

He recalled the stories his dad told about the ghastly mustard gas in the trenches of WWI and how a person's skin when exposed to it would burn, blister, and die. Or, if breathed in, would cause a slow, painful death.

Nash explained. "Form a line in the grass. When we ignite the gas grenade, check which way is upwind. As soon as you smell newly mown hay, run in the downwind direction as fast as you can until you reach the wood line."

"Sarge, don't we get gas masks or anything?" asked one of the troops.

"Your dumbass, Uncle Sam isn't trying to kill you yet. This is familiarization training. This is a training agent. You'll get gas mask training later today. For now, you only need to find out which way is downwind. Can you blockheads figure that out?"

"Yes, Sergeant!" the group hollered.

"Alright, then move out."

The company formed the line and several guys moistened their fingers and stuck them in the air. "It's coming from that way."

Kempinski watched the tree tops and he and Kowalski agreed which direction to run. Then Nash's voice came over a megaphone. "Fire in the hole. The grenade is pulled."

The men tensed up and sniffed. Kempinski surveyed the other guys, then pulled on Kowalski's shirt. "Let's go."

"Why, I ain't smelled no hay yet."

"You flat tire, we're from the city; we don't know what fresh mown hay smells like! And I, for one, don't intend to find out."

Kempinski turned and started running. With his natural speed, he quickly out-distanced the other troops and was first to reach the defined assembly point.

In between huffs, and a few seconds later, Kowalski caught up. "Did you smell the hay?"

"No, I wasn't taking any chances."

"Well, I guess you're right, but this here is some serious stuff."

"Tell me about it."

One morning as they fell in for physical fitness training, or PT as the cadets called it, Kempinski whispered over to Kowalski, "Hey Louie, I hear we are getting this weekend off."

"Yeah, I heard it too," replied the big man in his best stage whisper. "If we pass the test, we get a Saturday night pass."

"Want to head to town for some fun?"

"Soitently, I could use a beer."

"You drink beer?"

"All the time, before Uncle Sam got my ass."

"Yeah me too," added Kempinski, remembering the beer he had with his father at the Giants-Redskin game.

As promised, the cadre gave the men overnight passes for Saturday night and Sunday morning. They men cleaned up and put on their brown cadet Class A uniforms with leather flight jackets. The January air on the Gulf Coast had a hard chill. This would be their first chance to visit the southern coastal town of Biloxi.

"So, Bobby, where are we headed?"

"Listen," said Kempinski. "Two of the guys in my tent want to take a cab to Biloxi; there's supposed to be a hoofer for the cadets, a chance to meet some of the local broads."

"Sounds good to me."

"Sure does. Meet us at 1830 by the Post Exchange. We can catch a cab there."

The cadets met as planned and piled into a Checker Cab for the short trip to Biloxi. They didn't have to go far. Along the Irish Hill Road from the base into Biloxi several bars, pawn shops, and assorted buildings catering to the military had appeared with the construction boom.

As they piled out of the cab, Kowalski paid the driver, stood up, and said, "Hey, before heading to the dance, let's get us a few brews." He pointed to a wood-framed building with a sign, "Bubba's Place." A small sheet tacked to the door frame read "Military Welcome!" "Here we go boys," he continued. "What about that joint?"

"Hey, aren't the gin mills on this road off limits?" asked one of the guys.

"Don't worry; lots of other GIs heading in. They don't enforce that rule."

Kempinski and his tent mates followed Kowalski across the street. There was only one window covered with butcher paper and the only door was the one they entered. The bar was dimly lit and as Kempinski's eyes adjusted to the light, he could see it was nearly full of air cadets, enlisted soldiers, and civilians. The group sidled up to an old paneled bar, a survivor of the past century. Kowalski ordered a round. The men took their beers, but couldn't find an open spot, so they stood near a roof support beam.

Kempinski raised his mug. "To the Air Corps."

"Hear, hear!" the others said and sipped their drinks. A few nearby cadets and airmen joined in on the toast. Then, one after another, the men offered salutations and gulped their beer. In no time, Kowalski had ordered another round and the men moved to a recently vacated table. As they got situated, four civilians dressed in a motley assortment of coarse jackets over plaid shirts and dark pants approached the group. The civilian in front, a pasty-faced, rotund Mississippian with dark hair mostly slicked down except for a twisted cowlick that stood like a peacock feather said, "Hey, y'all fly boys, this is our regular table. Go find ya'll someplace else."

"Oh yeah, says who?" replied Kowalski. "Dis here table don't belong to nobody."

Another one of the locals, a lanky one with a gaunt face and buckteeth said, "Golly, did y'all hear how he talks? What are you, some kind of Yankee?"

"Yeah, I am as a matter of fact. You got a problem with that?"

The rotund one said to the others, "Lookee here, this Yan-kee fly boy thinks he can rule our roost."

Kempinski stood and pointed, "He's not the only one; we are all from the north. You can tell because our legs are both the same length."

"Ya'll better watch yo mouth boy."

"That's soldier to you, cracker," replied Kowalski, embold-ened by the beer and several weeks of army training.

As the words heated, the other Air Cadets and a few Marines in the bar turned their attention to the confrontation, watching expectantly to see what might happen.

"Ya'll ain't no soldier boys, ya'll's kaydettes. Ooh, big time fly boys. We'ze sick of ya'll coming into our town and acting like ya'll own the place," the rotund one pushed his face into Kempin-ski's, "I could whip ya'll's ass in a Biloxi minute."

"Yeah, we'll see," Kempinski assumed a boxing pose taught by the New York YMCA Golden Gloves program.

The pasty-faced local took a swing and Kempinski ducked under it, the one beer having no ill effect on his reflexes. He quick-ly countered with a right-hand jab to the fat man's midsection. The local exhaled loudly and doubled over, his face lowering into a quickly-delivered left arm uppercut. The punch, solidly landed on the chin, knocked him sideways and into a table with three US Marines. The Marines stood issuing epithets as the collision of the fat man spilled their beer. They pushed him off the table. Meanwhile, the other locals swarmed and locked into close order with the soldiers.

In the melee, the lanky local lunged for Kempinski and grabbed him with one arm around the neck. Then Kempinski felt a sharp pain in his back.

"You sum-a-bitch," yelled Kowalski, as he saw the lanky local pull a pocket knife from Kempinski's back. "You stabbed my friend!"

Kowalski used his long arms to grab the lanky guy's arms and pulled him off Kempinski and pummeled the attacker in fast succession with his fists. Lanky staggered and dropped his knife. Kowalski, in a display of amazing strength, grabbed the now-dazed southerner and lifted him and swung the man like a Saturday night wrestler 180 degrees in the air, then let go of him. The stunned local flew into a nearby table and crashed to the floor.

Meanwhile, the marines had turned the fat Mississippian face up across their table and were taking turns punching him. The rest of the patrons surged back and forth as each tried to size up another and make their next move.

Kempinski was ready for action except for a funny sensation in his back. He reached around his torso, trying to assess the damage from the knife.

"That bastard stabbed me."

"I saw it. Forget him, he's out for the night. We got to get you out of here."

Kowalski collared Kempinski and, with the two other cab mates, pushed their way to the door, knocking over two locals who tried to stop them. Outside, Kowalski pulled Kempinski to the alley next to the bar. "Let me see your back."

"It doesn't hurt too bad."

"Come on, that's borrowed brass. Let me see your back." This time it was a command.

Kempinski bent over and pulled up his jacket and shirt.

"Shit, his knife got through your jacket and shirt. There's some blood but not too bad. The leather jacket saved you. Good thing it was only a pocket knife." Kowalski paused. "I think you'll need stitches, though."

"Damn, first let me back in there and kick his ass."

"Ah, forget about it. Save it for the Nazis. He isn't going anywhere with the marines using him as a punching bag," Kowalski smiled and good-naturedly slapped his friend.

"Youch, that smarts," shrieked Kempinski, "You don't know your own strength."

"Oh, sorry. Well, we need to get you to the base aid station."

The group hailed a waiting Checker Cab and headed back to the base. The MPs stopped the cab at the entrance gate and made the cabbie open the trunk. The cadets stared straight ahead.

Kempinski whispered to Kowalski, "What are they doing? Do they know about the fight?"

"Nah, I doubt it. They're checking for contraband. They search all vehicles entering the base. Stay tight."

The MPs waved the cab through and the cadets directed the cabbie to the aid station for their battalion. The doctor's aide on duty at the medical station was dubious, but nonetheless accepted the excuse he fell onto a doorknob and sewed two stitches into Kempinski's back. Sprinkling sulfa powder and applying a big bandage, he released the cadets back to their unit, but not before revoking their Saturday night passes.

Kempinski and Kowalski walked back to their tent, recalling their night and laughing. "How do you like our first night out and we restart the Civil War," Kempinski said smiling "And the north won again!"

"True, but now we're stuck on the base," moaned Kowalski.

"Maybe so, but it might be a good thing. I need to clean the blood from my shirt and sew up the hole."

"You go clean up; meanwhile, I think the guys in my tent may have figured out how to sneak some giggle juice onto the base."

"Really?" Kempinski's face stretched in astonishment. "How they'd do that?"

"One of the guys is from Long Beach and he said he might get some moonshine by hiding it inside the spare tire of one of the taxi cabs."

"That's hep. Sounds like trouble, though."

"Exactly what I thought." Kowalski made a mock serious expression, then broke into a grin. "Let's go find out."

"You first."

The rest of the weekend passed without incident, mostly because the moonshine never showed up, but the lack of activity helped alleviate the soreness in Kempinski's back. Monday morning when they fell in for physical training, Kowalski brushed by Kempinski and asked, "Your back okay for PT?"

"I'll be alright; the Randolf Shuffle isn't going to hurt."

Kowalski nodded.

After the troops lined up for PT, instead of breaking into the double-spaced order to start their stretching and calisthenics, Captain Smithson approached the front of the company and announced, "The boys in Alpha Company have challenged us to a football game. We have two weeks, right before you graduate to next phase, to organize. Any of you blockheads know how to play football? Raise your hands."

Kempinski raised his arm, despite the twinge from his wounded back. Several others did likewise. He motioned over to Kowalski and mouthed, "Raise your hand." Kowalski did so but hesitantly.

The captain surveyed the hands, "Good, that's enough for a team. You men fall out behind Sergeant Nash."

Kempinski and Kowalski dropped behind their squads and double-timed to the rear of Sergeant Nash who was standing behind the platoon. They formed a squad line behind the sergeant.

Captain Smithson commanded, "The rest of you, atten-HUT! Sergeant Nash, take these men on a five-mile run. Football players stand fast."

Groans and snide comments from the formation were drowned out by Nash's command. "Company, right face. Forward, march!"

Nash's voice had extra edge. He relished taking what he viewed as slackers on the extra-long run. After a few steps, Nash bellowed, "Double-time, march!"

Captain Smithson watched the company jog away then he motioned to the newly-formed football team. "Alright, men, Bravo Company has never lost a challenge game to Alpha Company. This is serious business; there is pride and possibly some dough riding on the outcome. Do you understand?"

"Yes, sir!" replied the group.

"We start practice today. As football players, you'll be

exempt from KP and guard duty." A small cheer arose from the players.

The Bravo Company football squad practiced each evening after regular training. Unlike the NFL, the company team played with rudimentary equipment, including second-hand football pants and high-topped leather cleats, but no helmets. Some of the guys cut up old sheets and tied them to their elbows, but for the most part, the players were unprotected. The linemen practiced blocking drills by pushing the company jeep padded with an old mattress.

With his good speed, Kempinski snagged the wing back position. Playing was a good break from the demands of military training and served as a reminder his civilian life had only been interrupted a few weeks ago, though it seemed liked ages had passed.

On one practice play where Kempinski was to run interference for the half back, he took a hard shot to the abdomen by a charging Kowalski busting through to break up the play. The blow knocked him to the ground where he couldn't breathe. Gasping for air, he heaved his chest with seemingly no effect. Captain Smithson jogged over. "You alright?" he asked.

Kempinski couldn't find the air to reply.

"Oh, Kowalski just knocked the wind out of you. Here, let me see your belt." Smithson reached down and jerked Kempinski off the ground by his football belt. The sudden arching of his back stretched his diaphragm and sucked air into his lungs.

"You two guys carry him over to the bench. Watson, you give Kempinski a blow for a few series."

Still gasping, on the sidelines Kempinski watched the team play a few series of downs, where he marveled at Kowalski's progress. The big man's size and animalistic strength made him a natural middle linebacker. Although he had never played football before, he quickly picked up on the key aspect of the game, to hit people, and he found it easy to bowl over the other players in practice.

Hit after hit, soon his own offensive line didn't to want to face him. When another player went down after a Kowalski hit, Captain Smithson called him to the sidelines.

"Alright, bruiser," the captain-turned-coach said to Kowalski, "You are beating up our team. From now on, I want you to run the practice plays at half-speed. Save the full-speed for the actual game."

Then Captain Smithson blew a whistle and huddled the team around him. "Take a knee, men. We're shaping up well, but the key to winning this game will be to keep things simple – we'll have only a few plays, but we'll rely on execution. We practice them over and over and we will win the game."

"Shoot, sir, all we have to do is let Kowalski loose on them," suggested one of the bruised linemen. The team laughed and Kowalski shrugged his head in mock humility.

With only a few days of practice in between basic training classes, the team got somewhat better before the big game arrived. It turned out Alpha Company had two former college football players on their squad, but even they had trouble handling the one-man wrecking crew of Kowalski. He bowled over the Alpha Company players and caused havoc like what he did during Bravo Company's practices. The two veteran college players tried to neutralize Kowalski on one play by setting up a crack-back block, but the big man managed to fend it off by literally throwing the first blocker off him, even though he hit Kowalski low on the legs. When the final whistle blew, Kempinski had scored a touchdown and Kowalski had knocked out three of the opposing players. Bravo Company won 14-0.

Captain Smithson, after collecting his winnings from the other company commander, gave the cadets the rest of the weekend off. The game had been planned to coincide with the culmination of the first phase of cadet Basic Training. Next, the cadets whom passed the army's grueling air crew selection process advanced to ground school. The cadets were to use the weekend to get ready for the serious business of actual flying.

The week after the football game, the cadets finalized their basic training and waited for their reassignment to a primary flight school. In 1943, nearly all primary flight school was taught by civilian instructors at contract flight schools. The army had nearly perfected the system to identify trainees for pilot, navigator, and bombardier positions and sent cadets all over the country based on a series of physical, psychological, and motor skills tests. By mid-week, after enduring three days of testing and probing, Kempinski and Kowalski went over to the base PX for one of their two week-ly-allotted beers. Sitting in the sun with their beer, the men reflected on their training and their passing to the next stage.

"Well, we made it so far Kowals, but I can't believe so many guys washed out of basic," commented Kempinski.

"Yeah, and most are headed to infantry. What a drag."

"But the rumor is they are washing out pilots like crazy in primary. Too many pilots in the queue. Supposedly, they need gunners and radio operators."

"What would you do?"

"Whadya mean?"

"If you washed out."

Kempinski paused, his face twitching as he pondered the question, then he tugged on his beer, a new-found appreciation, gained courtesy of the Army. "Listen, you know what, we just need to pay more attention. We did good in basic. We'll do fine in primary."

Kowalski raised his beer bottle and the men clinked them together, "Yeah, you're right. To the Air Corps."

"Watch out, Adolf, the New Yorkers are coming," replied Kempinski.

Chapter 4

Both Kempinski and Kowalski were transferred to Gulfport Army Airfield base for basic flight school. While only a short bus ride from Keesler, the transfer from basic engendered a mental shift in the cadets. One reason was the contracted civilian team conducting the primary training offered no military supervision, so the cadets set up their own internal chain of command. Civilian instructors allowed the army to make pilots in the most efficient and minimal amount of time, especially since diverting actual pilots from combat to primary training was not possible. Weeks of regular army Basic Training would now be replaced by the partially relaxed, by army standards, actual learning to fly.

The newly arrived cadets massed in a large, but sparse, wooden framed building. Each took a seat on a backless bench where the paint on the cross members was worn to bare wood by the thousand cadet boots that had preceded this class. Kempinski listened as the flight school commander, standing behind a simple wooden podium, briefed the cadet pilots in their orientation: the training process would require sixty flying hours of primary training in five weeks, weather permitting. Primary flying training would be in four standard phases. In the pre-solo phase, he would learn the general operation of a light aircraft and achieve proficiency in forced landing techniques and in recovering from stalls and spins. In the second, or intermediate phase, he'd review the pre-solo work, and then learn precision of control by flying standard courses or patterns, known as elementary 8s, lazy 8s, pylon 8s, and chandelles. The idea of doing those maneuvers in an aircraft gave him a thrill but also brought some concern as the ideas seemed so unlike anything he had ever done. By the time the captain briefed the third, or accuracy, phase, which demanded high proficiency in various types of landing approaches and landings, Kempinski's mixed emotions were partially overwhelmed, and his mind raced to imagine all he would do. Then in a moment, he told himself to calm down, take it step by step. But when the captain described the fourth, or acrobatic, phase where he would perform loops, Immelmann turns, slow rolls, half-rolls, and snap rolls, Kempinski's mind turn to glee and he reverted to the boy who would dream in his bed of flying over and through the clouds chasing down German fighters. He barely heard the captain describe the rest of the training: how the ratio of dual to solo hours was flexible within the limitation a minimum of forty percent and a maximum of fifty percent of the total time was to be dual-- each student in primary was required to make at least 175 landings. The captain's advice about paying attention and studying hard broke through Kempinski's imaginary haze and he took heed. He knew wash out was always one mistake away.

Taking the captain's advice, Kempinski bore down in pre-solo, paying strict attention to all lessons, especially those related to the actual aircraft operation. Barely knowing how to drive a car, the shift to flying a plane seemed like a huge mountain and despite the detailed training and his desire, Kempinski lacked confidence in his ability to pilot a plane. Complicating matters was the apparent change in Army Air Corps needs. Rumor had turned to fact and the army announced it had plenty of pilots but lacking were air crews - gunners and radiomen. Hence, the wash out rate for cadet pilots had increased significantly. At the start of the war, Kempinski heard cadets could afford to make a minor mistake or two. Now, one mistake, especially while operating the plane, and he would automatically washout.

"Good morning Cadets, I'm Charlie Johnson, your flight instructor," said a tall gawky pilot in army khakis with civilian insignia as he sauntered in front of his five assigned cadets. Johnson had a definite non-military bearing personified by his forward hunching shoulders and a strange backwards tilt of his flight cap, but his face conveyed a seriousness amplified by an absurdly asymmetrical nose Kempinski found intimidating. "In the next few weeks, we are going to try to make you boys into army aviators. If you do what I say, you will be fine. You don't do as I say, and you will wash out." Johnson paused for effect. "Understood?"

"Yes sir," replied Kempinski with his flight mates.

The ground school portion was unlike anything Kempinski had ever tried. The classes were non-stop covering the basics of aerodynamics, the mechanics of the plane, navigation, weather, radio operation, along with more physics, mathematics and a host of other topics. The army required the cadets to memorize the flight manuals and the layout of all the instruments and controls of their first airplane, a Boeing Stearman PT-17 Kaydet biplane, a plane with two wings. Kempinski studied hard and had no trouble learn-ing the technology, but he struggled with the spatial orientation portion of the training. Yet despite the rigor, Kempinski passed the ground school exam and was ready for the actual flight instruction.

On a Monday morning, Johnson escorted four cadets, including Kempinski, to the flight line and next to a slightly used PT-17 with bright blue fuselage and glaring yellow wings. Each cadet wore a utility jumpsuit with leather pull over cap and goggles, and a parachute they had checked out of the Parachute Room. The PT-17 had an open cockpit for low altitude flight, so there was no need for cold weather clothing for high altitude flight. The Kaydet, although obsolete for WW2, gained favor by the Air Corps for its durability and effectiveness as a basic trainer. It was simple to fly and could take the abuse meted out by the raw trainees. Johnson, also wearing a leather jacket but over khakis with a tie tucked in under his second button, walked around the aircraft, quizzing the cadets about the purpose, function and movement of each major portion of the flying machine. Satisfied the ground training had been retained, he said "Men, this is your first day of actual flying. I will take each of you up to get you used to the bird and its controls. You'll take the stick for a few minutes then I will return the aircraft to ground where we'll change out to the next guy. As we taxi in, I'll give you a debrief on how you did."

Kempinski was second in line, so he waited on the grass field with the two other cadets with a combination of unbridled enthusiasm and trepidation. He watched his flight mate board the lithe plane with its throaty radial engine. The trainee taxied down the runway and lifted off in a line with several other trainers. The planes darted like yellow birds gracefully across the Mississippi sky. Each instructor had a certain assigned airspace, and soon the planes disappeared in the distance. While they waited, Kempinski fidgeted with his parachute. Getting all the straps adjusted properly took some time and, even so, it was uncomfortable, so he undid the leg straps, reminding himself to redo them prior to boarding the aircraft. Then to fight nerves, he rubbed the rosary beads he always kept in his pocket, saying a few Hail Mary's for inspiration. About twenty minutes or so later, the yellow trainers started lining up for landing. Kempinski's mouth dried like a raisin in the sun and his palms oozed sweat as his turn to fly for the first time approached.

After five planes had landed, Johnson's Kaydet touched down, taxied next to the team, and the engine sputtered to a stop. The first student, beaming broadly, climbed out of the back cockpit. Johnson waved to Kempinski, who, with butterflies as active as the training fleet floated in his stomach, approached the aircraft.

"How many hours of flying have you had cadet?"

Taken aback by the question, Kempinski stuttered, "Ah, none, sir."

"Then we will start from the beginning. Go to the front of the plane and when you see me give a thumbs up, using both hands give the propeller a good turn clockwise, then get out of the way and quickly strap yourself into the rear seat. And, by the way, don't call me sir. I'm a civilian trying to teach you how to fly, that's all."

"Yes sir, I mean yes," Kempinski said as he moved to the propeller. Then watching Johnson like a hawk, he saw the thumbs up, and gave a mighty yank to the propeller. It turned easier than he expected, and the hefty radial engine coughed to life. He then eagerly put his foot on the wing step and threw his other leg over the side opening, once painted bright yellow but now showing aluminum polished by the other students that had gone before. Kempinski first redid his parachute harness, then tightened the seat belt as he had done many times in the ground trainer, then placed the earmuffs and goggles over this hat. His eyes bounced off each instrument in the cockpit and confirmed that he knew all the functions.

Johnson talked over the Gosport Tube, a simple one-way tube connected to the trainee's ear muffs. As a communication system, it enabled the instructor to communicate with the trainee, but not vice versa. The trainees had to nod or give hand signals which the instructor could see in a rear-view mirror. "Now, Kempinski, put your feet on the rudder pedals, and your right hand softly on the stick. All set?"

"Roger," said Kempinski while nodding his head.

"Just feel what I do." The instructor gunned the throt-tle while pushing the rudder; the plane moved left and then to the right, in a series of small S-shaped turns, necessary as one could not see directly to the front of the plane until they reached the end of the runway. Kempinski craned his neck over the dashboard to watch the instructor. 'Pay attention to what he does,' Kempinski said to himself. 'Learn his every move.'

As they reached the end of the taxiway, the instructor called out, "Check the manifold," as he gunned the engine. Kempinski glanced at the gauge on the lower right of the instrument panel, like he learned in ground school, and verified the pressure in the manifolds was sufficient to create the power needed for takeoff.

He gave the instructor a thumbs-up so Johnson could see it in his rear-view mirror.

They both looked to the right, left and then toward the control tower. A light turned green – cleared to go. Johnson gave another dart left and right, then Kempinski could feel Johnson move the pedals as the plane turned onto the runway and started to accelerate. Whipping wind made Kempinski adjust his goggles as his pulse quickened; the windshield didn't offer much protection from the air stream. He could hardly believe he was about to be airborne.

As the plane moved down the runway it bounced gently on the grass and when the bouncing stopped, Kempinski's stomach made a somersault. He glanced at the grass runway and saw the shadow of the plane quickly separate from the aircraft and fall away as they climbed. He was in the air! For a few moments, the exhilaration tingled through his being and seemed to burst from his fingers as they quivered around the control stick until Johnson called out some instruction.

"You watch your climb rate, too steep and you'll stall. Keep the manifold pressure constant until you reach your cruising speed." Johnson then banked the plane in a lazy curve to the left as they climbed to three thousand feet. "Our assigned training area is just south of Biloxi over the gulf. We'll keep the coast in sight at all times on this flight."

Once the plane leveled off, the engine droned its distinctive rumble. Johnson said firmly, but calmly, "We are high enough for you to get used to the controls. Take the stick and rudders and make a gentle turn to the right. Try to keep the flight coordinator in the middle."

Kempinski gulped once and pushed the stick to the right while pushing the right pedal. The needle gyrated wildly to the right so Kempinski tried to correct and the gauge rolled harshly to the left.

"Woah," Johnson said, "gentle, this here is like a baby; you coax it into moves." Johnson took control and leveled out the plane. "Try again."

Kempinski flashed back to his time driving the Model T when he tried to feather the clutch to start the car stalled on the train tracks. He used the same feeling on the stick and rudder pedal. This time the needle moved slowly, and the plane banked to the right.

"That was better, now take it the other way."

Kempinski did and this time it was easier. 'This isn't too hard,' he thought, then the plane bucked like a bronco and he inadvertently pushed the stick forward. The plane nosed down quickly.

"We're diving, pull back gently on the stick," Johnson commanded firmly, but sounding not the least bit concerned. "You hit an air pocket. You will run into those once in a while."

Kempinski, now sweating despite the cool air, pulled back on the stick, but he went too far and the plane pulled up, with a high angle of attack.

"Again, down with the nose or we'll stall, easy though, like holding a baby."

Kempinski tried, but again the plane nosed down and up like a roller coaster.

"Let me have it," intoned Johnson. He quickly quieted the plane. "It's time to head back."

Johnson navigated the plane back to the traffic pattern next to the airfield and joined the other trainers lining up to land. "You watch the windsock and line up on that," Johnson said into the tube. "The Kaydet is pretty lousy in a cross wind, but the grass field is wide enough to land into the wind." As he spoke he floated the bird down onto the runway with hardly any bump and steered the plane to the other waiting cadets.

While taxing back in, Johnson debriefed Kempinski. "Not too bad for your first try. You got the hang of turning, but that up and down motion is called pilot-induced oscillation. You'll have to learn to control that or it's an automatic wash out. Oscillate near the ground and you'll auger in and prang the plane or worse."

Kempinski slumped back in his seat. He really wanted to ask how to control it, but instead pipped, "Yes, sir."

While his remaining flight mates flew with Johnson, Kempinski reflected on his first flight. 'Darn it, the front and back motion of the control stick was tricky'. He needed to find a way to practice. He spent the rest of the time rerunning the flight over in his mind.

Back at the barracks, Kempinski searched for Kowalski. "How'd it go Kowals?"

Kowalski turned and Kempinski could immediately see the answer, his eyes and jaw seemed slack, making him the most downcast he had seen. "Geeze Bobby, I really screwed up."

"What?"

"Well to start with, I barely fit inside the cockpit. Then when we got airborne, I got seasick, well, I guess they call it airsick. Lost all my cookies and couldn't see straight enough to even fly the plane."

"Oh no, what did you instructor say?"

"I got one more chance to do it again. If I can't get my stomach under control, they will board me. It could be mechanics school, unless I go for the infantry."

"Well, go see the doc, maybe they have something you can take."

"No, I can't have that on my record. I still really want to fly. I think tomorrow I won't eat any food; nothing to upchuck."

Kempinski gave his friend a pat on the shoulder, "Yeah, maybe that will work," he said, but inside he wasn't so sure. Kowalski had become a good friend and his concern took his mind off his own problems.

The next day had the cadets on the flight line again. Kempinski's flight with the instructor went fairly well, although he did have a small problem with vertical oscillation and a bumpy landing. The instructor downgraded him on his flight sheet, but not low enough to wash him out. After evening chow, Kempinski found Kowalski sitting on his bunk in the barracks even more forlorn than yesterday.

"Hey buddy, you missed dinner," Kempinski said more like a question.

Kowalski hung his head between his massive shoulders, "You won't believe it, Bobby, even with no food in my gut, I felt worse than yesterday. My instructor has recommended a review board. I go tomorrow morning, I may get washed out."

"Damn Kowals, that's a raw deal."

"Something about my inner ear they think. I won't be able to fly."

"What are you going to do?"

"I don't know, they say the Air Corps needs mechanics. Maybe I'll do that."

"Tough luck, but you know aircraft mechanics do important work. They could use a smart guy like you to keep the planes flying."

"I know Bobby, what can I do? I mean when the Japs bombed Pearl Harbor, I was so mad." Kempinski could see the veins in his friend's neck stand out. Kempinski too felt his muscles tighten.

"Me too, Kowals, I wanted to kill those bastards. " He stood and adjusted his flight jacket.

Kowalski raised his chin. "I thought flying would be great, a chance to get some revenge, but now…" his voice trailed with disappointment.

"You can still fight, heck every job someone does is important."

"True, but I want to kill those Nazis, kill those Japs, make them pay."

Kempinski beheld his friend, then nodded his head in understanding. He sat on the bunk next to Kowalski's massive body. He, too, had that feeling and he knew piloting a plane was much harder than he thought. What would he do if he washed out?

The cadets were still for a few minutes then Kowalski broke the silence. "I think I'm going to sign up for the infantry."

"The walking army?" Kempinski was taken aback as transfer to the infantry was used as a threat for the air cadets. Nobody volunteers for that.

"Yeah, those guys see all the action."

"True, but at ground level,"

"What's the difference, I can still take on the Jerrys."

After a pause where he visualized a newsreel showing Kowalski on the front lines taking on the Werhmacht, Kempinski said, "You may be right. I mean you are the strongest and toughest in the squadron. Remember how you handled those shit kickers in the bar in Biloxi."

The big man cracked a smile "And you with a stab wound wanting to go back and finish them off."

Kempinski too smiled, "Well if you go infantry, I'm sure you'll do well."

"Thanks, Bobby."

After sharing a beer, probably their last one together, the men returned to their bunks. Kempinski lay on his mattress and studied the white painted ceiling pondering what he would do if he washed out. His confidence had eroded a bit, but in his heart, he still wanted to fly. He remembered his father's ad-monishment, "no infantry." He reviewed his flight once more in his mind and as he balanced his performance with his friend's decision, he too decided that, come what may, he would try his best.

Next up on the flight schedule was a near solo event. This meant the training missions would be flying dual, but the cadet would do nearly all the flying, including the landing. As the cadets walked to the flight line, Kempinski kept quiet, and so did the others, as the palatable tension reflected this key point in the primary training. After the unaided dual flight, cadets would take their first solo. The two flights would determine washouts. Looming above the threat of washout, though, was the unspoken. Flying accidents in the cadet corps during solos were extremely high, but with the accelerated training schedule there was no other way to generate the air crews needed.

Kempinski managed to execute his dual-flight with a marginal passing score. Some minor pilot induced oscillation almost failed his mission. Compounding the problem, for some reason, Kempinski had difficulty lining up the plane in steady approach. As they walked back to the ready room from the flight line, Instructor Johnson waved to Kempinski. "Hey Kempinski, come here."

Kempinski moved quickly to Johnson, who paused a moment to allow the other cadets in the flight to get out of earshot. "Your flight technique is good except for the oscillation. You know sometimes that can be due to the structural response of the control stick. I'm going to recommend you try a different plane tomorrow for your first solo."

"Do you really think it could make a difference?"

"You never know, not all these birds fly the same. Just make sure you try a different tail number tomorrow."

"Roger, Mr. Johnson."

Johnson made a faint smirk, but when placed under his unusual nose, it came across like a grimace. Kempinski backed away quickly and considered this latest development. He didn't have enough mechanical experience to fully understand what Johnson meant, but he was willing to give it a try. The stress of learning to fly had been taking his toll, and while each successive mission seemed to be giving the other cadets more confidence, Kempinski thought he was getting worse. That Kowalski was heading to the elimination boards today lodged in the back of his mind and didn't help his own confidence.

Morning formation the next day felt strange to Kempinski as Kowalski was missing. His airsickness caused the flight review board to eliminate the big man from further training. His bunk was empty and no one was certain where he was headed, but the thoughts didn't linger as Kempinski, like all the other cadets, had more to worry about. Today was the first solo day for the cadet host.

The morning flight schedule, however, was delayed due to a rain shower that soaked the field. After waiting what seemed like forever for the weather to clear and for the other cadets ahead of him to fly, Kempinski took his turn in the cockpit, a different Kaydette than he had flown before. The controls all felt the same so he focused on his instruction and checklist. The take off and prescribed maneuvers went according to the plan, even the level flight was fairly smooth, no oscillation, although now he was alone without the weight of the instructor, the plane flew much livelier. Next, he had to do a fly by and then line up for landing. Kempinski did fine managing to keep his P-17 level as he passed the control tower and set up his gradual turn to land. Then out of the corner of his eye, he saw one of the yellow winged P-17s landing several spots in front of him hit the runway hard, bounce once and cart-wheel over onto its left wing. The fuselage appeared to bend in half and the top wing broke. Immediately, the control tower flashed the red light and the planes, according to standard operating procedure, were to continue to circle the field. Kempinski kept glancing back at the crashed aircraft wondering who it was and it caused him to get a bit jittery. The Kaydet responded by starting to gently oscil-late like a porpoise skimming the surface for school fish. Quickly, Kempinski threw the plane into a gradual turn that seemed to quell the oscillations, but the damage had been done and his confidence seemed to ebb like air passing the cockpit. As he finished the turn for the downwind leg of the airport lap, the plane started to oscillate again. Kempinski tried to tweak the control stick but each push seemed to magnify the plane's reaction. This time the oscillations were more pronounced and certainly visible to the ground observers. It took four laps of the airfield to clear the accident, and by the time Kempinski made his final approach for landing he had managed to quell the unwanted vertical movements although he was still quite nervous.

The landing was going to be made into a slight, but steady, cross wind. To compensate, Kempinski's training told him to maintain wings level and the aircraft position near the runway centerline during approach. As trained, he pointed the nose into the wind so the aircraft approached the runway slightly skewed with respect to the runway centerline, or as Johnson called it 'crabbing', as the movement resembled a Blue Claw crab moving along the ground. This gave the impression of approaching the runway flying sideways, which Kempinski found a bit disorienting but nonetheless, he tried to maintain his position on the runway by balancing the crosswind component with engine thrust. He kept the stick steady to keep the wings level throughout the approach and just before the flare, he applied the rudder on the downwind side to eliminate the crab, with a simultaneous application of opposite aileron to maintain a wings-level attitude. In theory, at touch down this would keep the aircraft velocity vector and bank angle aligned with the runway, and the aircraft positioned near the center.

What Kempinski didn't factor into his flare was the muddy runway caused by the morning rain. The left main wheel hit first and dug in deeply to the mud acting much like a strong brake. The aircraft started to head in a slightly skewed direction from the aircraft's intended direction exerting a side force on the wheels. On a P-17, this force is in front of the aircraft's center of gravity, and the resulting movement rotated the Stearman's heading even further from its direction of motion. This increased the force and the process reinforced itself leading to the beginning of ground loop or a fishtailing of the airplane. To avoid a ground loop, Kempinski needed to respond to the unplanned turning quickly, while sufficient control authority was available to counteract it. Unfortunately, this was not covered in detail in his training; Kempinski hesitated and once the Kaydet rotated beyond a certain point, there was nothing he could do to stop it from rotating further. The ground loop caused a violent jerk and the plane bounced hard twice but fortunately did not flip like the bird that crashed earlier.

Once the plane settled on the landing strip, Kempinski applied the brakes and taxied the plane to the allotted parking area on the grass. Cursing silently to himself he climbed out of the cockpit. A crew chief and Charlie Johnson came over to the plane and started to inspect the undercarriage for potential damage.

"How did it feel taxiing over?" asked the crew chief. "Any strange vibration?"

"No. None I could feel," Kempinski nearly whispered, somewhat embarrassed and disappointed to have spun the plane on the ground.

Having completed scanning the aircraft, Johnson watched Kempinski climbing out of the cockpit. The clenched jaw and pursed lips told Kempinski he was headed to the board for possible elimination.

The other cadets in his flight dropped their gaze and avoided eye contact with Kempinski. He peeled off his leather helmet and ran his hand through his slicked back hair; shoulders slumped as the stress of the flight faded, yet he had a strange mindset: a combination of disappointment and relief. He took a seat on the grass and gazed at his boots while the next cadet boarded the trainer. He thought about what lay next. He had heard the disposition of eliminees at the classification centers followed a constant pattern. A board of officers would inform them of the alternative types of training available. Usually washouts were sent to a basic training center for reassignment to gunnery or to technical training in preparation for combat-crew or ground-crew assignment as an enlisted man. It was important for morale, for student and for the men who had been classified for aircrew training, to recycle the ones as quickly as possible. What seemed to surprise him the most was he was not disappointed--flying was hard and he did his best. If he had better luck, maybe he would be given a second chance, but even if he wasn't, he decided he, unlike his friend, Kowalski, was still going to fly; he would ask to be a radioman or gunner on an air crew.

In the evening, Kempinski walked over to the company orderly room, a plain white chamber next to the commander's area, with various bulletin boards and posters nailed to crude lumber walls. He quickly checked the after-flight rating sheets and as expected, he failed his flight. Next to his name was an "X" meaning he had to report to the company commander first thing in the morning. He took small consolation there were eight others with an "X" by their name.

In the morning, after a surprisingly fitful sleep, Kempinski put on a fresh uniform, shined his shoes so they reflected the sky and double checked his gig line between his belt and shirt. He checked his tie in a mirror in the restroom, making sure it was properly tucked into his shirt and his hat sat at just the right angle. He thought he'd looked his military best to impress his commander and be assigned to a crew and not mechanics school, or even the infantry. The other cadets in the barracks ignored the group heading to the orderly room and Kempinski didn't begrudge them for it. He had acted the same way the last few days.

Kempinski stood fourth in line for processing by the elimination board. He reported to the company commander whom he hadn't seen since the first day orientation. A burly man with a butch style crew cut, whose graying hair stood straight up in front as if it had some sort of electrical charge, nonetheless commanded the room with his presence and the parallel bars on his shoulder.

The commander reviewed some papers from a stack in front of him.

Studying the papers, he said in a fairly heavy southern drawl, "Ahright let's see her-ah, Kemmmmpens," he paused. "Golly, how do you pronounce that son?"

"It's Kem-pin-ski sir."

"Kem-pin-ski, ahright seems easy enough. From New York, eh."

"Yes sir."

"Well, I'm from Texas son, and you know, this man's army is glad to have patriotic Americans wherever they are from." The commander glanced down at the paper. "I see you had good scores in all your quals but you can't seem to fly. Ground looped one of the birds." He pursed his lips. "I'm sorry to tell you son, but that is grounds for elimination from the cadet corps. He made eye contact with Kempinski. After a moment, he added. "But you know, with the change in the strategic situation, the Air Corps needs crew members. Infantry would be a waste for you, son. What do you want to do?"

Kempinski answered back without a moment's hesitation. "Kill Nazis from the air, Sir."

"That's the spirit son. We are going to reassign you to radio school. I'd be proud to have you on my crew."

"Yes sir."

The commander signed a form and passed it to the first sergeant.

"Dismissed."

After the group was boarded, the orderly room corporal gave the eliminees one hour to report back to the company headquarters with their duffle bags packed. Kempinski noticed the downcast mood in the rest of the men, but he didn't feel bad. All the men with him were reassigned to radio school and Kempinski already started to contemplate how he would learn the radio operations. He recalled fooling around with his uncle's radio one time as they peeked inside the case in their apartment, but the tubes and wires seemed like magic to him. He figured they all had a purpose and he decided we would work hard and learn all he could about radio operation.

Kempinski collected his few belongings in a duffle bag and headed back to the assembly point. The group gathered and, while they waited for the Army to make its next move, they speculated on their future; radio school followed by gunner school then perhaps a crew assignment. One of the guys said the Air Corps radio schools were Scott-Field in St. Louis, Sioux Falls, South Dakota, or Homestead, Florida.

"Wow, talk about the boondocks," offered Kempinski, "They got indoor plumbing in those places?"

The quip managed to bring a smile to the other men. The corporal ordered the men to fall in and then marched the men to a holding barracks where they waited for a bus. Along the way, they could see the training aircraft forming up for a takeoff, destination unknown.

The bus took them back to Keesler Air Force Base where the soldiers queued up at a classification center. They waited for two days, pulling KP and sweeping up the winter grass and gravel paths while the barracks filled up with other eliminees. On the third day, Kempinski's name was called in formation and he was given orders to radio school in St Louis. He and a host of others were transferred to a train station. After a twenty-hour train ride and bus trip, he arrived at Scott Air Field, home of the US Army Air Corp radio school.

Chapter 5

March 2, 1944

-.. . .- .-. -- --- -- .- -. -.. -.. .- -.. --..—

That's Morse code for Dear Mom and Dad.

Here we are in the sixth week of COMM School and it's Morse code day and night. I am even starting to think in it. Dots and dashes in my dreams. We should be here five months learning all there is to know about radios. It's not too bad, the weather seems to be warming up and I finally got over my cold I caught on the train ride up here. It might even be nice here when spring finally arrives.

St. Louis is decent, different than New York, but we can go anywhere by streetcar or bus. The University streetcar line runs along the north side of Scott Field. We can ride it all the way downtown. There are some old buildings along the river, factories and warehouses I guess. Some of the guys have taken river boat cruises on the Mississippi, but I think it's been too cold for me. Maybe when it warms up. Last weekend we went to Forest Park Kiel Auditorium, for a big USO show. There were soldiers everywhere but the show was fun, the Kilter Sisters, great song and dance.

We have a little shopping center with a dry cleaner, drugstore, and grocery store on the northwest corner of campus. We can get basic stuff we need at good prices. Radio school is like a large high school or college, in fact, some call it the 'Communications University of the Army Air Forces.' Either way, we sure will know about radios and electronics when we are done. The Army drums it into our heads with tests every couple of days. I finally am learning what all those tubes in Uncle Sam's RCA did.

One thing we learned this week is radio position location. To shoot a radio fix we tune in three stations and draw lines to those stations along a compass direction. Where the lines meet, is where you are. It's usually a small triangle. My first 'fix' covered much of Kansas and Okalhom. Ha, I eventually figured it out though, even though I'm a New Yorker!

Speaking of New York, my roommate is a New Yorker, Tom Kelly. He's an Irish lad and we get along real well. We help each other out with the studies and homework.

I am not sure what happens after radio school, maybe gunner school, but that is at least three and half months away. The newsreels report good news, but I hope there is some action left after we finish all this school; it seems we are kicking the Japs and Krauts back where they belong.

Wishing everything is swell back in NYC.

Love,

Your son, PVT Bob

Chapter 6

"Oh, my Lord, it tastes like a bale of cotton was stuffed down my throat. Now I know what low humidity feels like," coughed Kempinski as he disembarked the green army bus that had transferred the cadre of trainees to Yuma Army Air Field, Arizona for Flexible Gunnery Training.

"You ain't kidding," replied Tom Kelly, a slight man a few inches shorter than Kempinski with a handsome, fair face, dark hair parted to the left like a Hollywood movie star. "It's July, and we are here. I am so hot and thirsty in this desert; I wouldn't be interested if Rita Haywood lay in front of me."

"Darn straight," Kempinski reached for his khaki shirt pocket, sweaty and soiled from their travel, and patted it. "Oh, drat, I'm out of cigarettes. Hey Tom, got any left?"

"Are you kidding, mine ran out somewhere crossing those endless wheat fields."

"Wasn't that something? Miles of grain. I never knew the country was so big."

"For sure, but this place…" Kelly paused, as if searching for the right words. He motioned his arms like a hiker spinning round for bearings. "This place doesn't even look like Earth. Dirt and dust everywhere. How could the Army find something to do here?"

"What do you think? We're going to be flying and shooting stuff all over the place. We sure can't be near a big city. Someone could get killed."

The two men laughed and followed their classmates to the new barracks, a typical two-story type of whitewashed-wooden building the Army built like a bad rash across the country, housing soldiers in the process of training. Yuma Army Airfield was part of the West Coast Training Center--a network of several small civilian airports the US Army took over as the war progressed.

After settling in with bunk assignments and orientation to the company area, their new platoon sergeant, Sergeant First Class Levette, called them out for formation. He was a bald skeleton of a human with a strange accent Kelly guessed was French, but was actually Cajun.

"Today, boys, you learn how to shoot, and after I am finished with you knuckle draggers, you will be able to pick out a Jerry Messerschmitt, and put a belt-load of lead into his most prized possession."

The troops let out a roar; after months of books and classrooms studying radio operation, they craved some physical action.

Levette continued. "We will start with skeet training," pronouncing skeet like it had six E's. "Y'awl be firing a shotgun on a machine gun mount. This will get you used to leading targets and working with a mounted weapon."

Kempinski turned his head to Kelly and in a stage whisper said, "Hey Tom, this might be fun."

"Yeah right, you know the army, they'll figure out a way to

make it miserable."

"True," Kempinski nodded, "the army could queer a funeral."

"Load'em up men, on the double."

The platoon quickly clambered onto two Dodge deuce-and-a-half trucks, having been in the Army long enough to learn that basic skill. The trucks lumbered over dusty, arid roads, past broad expanses of sand and scrub, unremarkable vistas delineated only by a series of freshly-painted signs, large black numbers on white backgrounds; each marked a firing range. At sign five, the truck stopped and the men scrambled from the truck onto a flat area hastily smoothed as an administrative cordon for the training. Kempinski squinted and placed his hands over his eyes to shield them from the rising sun. Temperature was climbing, yet it was only eight AM.

After introductory training on loading and shooting the shotgun, followed by a safety briefing, Levette ordered Kempinski and Kelly onto a five-ton truck with a ring mount. For the next few hours, they shot skeet in the desert, learning about target lead and movement. Despite the scorching heat, Kempinski found it fun, but knew this was only the beginning, more challenging tasks awaited.

Kempinski lined up a target while the truck was moving and pulled the trigger. Kelly laughed as the pellets missed wide. "You ain't gonna get any Krauts that way."

"Yeah, wait until it's your turn," responded Kempinski. "Leading the target with the gun mounted on a ring rack isn't easy."

Kempinski was right, all the cadets failed miserably at hitting skeet with the ring mount shotgun. So Levette coached them, and with several days of practice, the platoon got the hang of it.

After the third day on the truck back to the cantonment area, Kempinski hunched up next to Kelly on the bench seat of the deuce-and-a-half. "Geez, my ears are ringing, even with the cotton ball plugs."

"Mine too, and we haven't even shot the heavy stuff yet."

"Tomorrow, rumor is, we get to train in the pressure chamber."

"I heard," Kelly replied with his voice belying a tinge concern. "A guy in KP told me, 'make sure you don't volunteer to take your mask off to show the effects of high altitude.'"

"Oh, come on, it can't be that bad."

"You just do it and you'll see."

"Hey, gotta learn what it's like, right? We may have to take our masks off in a mission."

"Bobby, you may be gung ho, but I can wait."

"At least our ears will get a break, and it's probably cool in the chamber."

The next day brought altitude familiarization training inside a welded-steel tube. The tube connected to a vacuum pump that sucked the air from the chamber, simulating low oxygen levels at high altitude. On missions, the bombers flew fifteen thousand to thirty thousand feet in the air to use less fuel, but the crew had to breathe through a mask connected to an oxygen bottle.

Kempinski filed into the chamber behind Kelly and they sat facing each other. The sergeant inside the compartment had a sickly pallor, unlike the trainees with bronzed faces after two weeks shooting in the desert sun.

"You put the mask on like this, check for a good fit. Adjust the top and bottom strap by pulling here. Then put on your goggles. Make sure you turn the oxygen valve clockwise before putting it on, otherwise you will be sucking on nothing, and that ain't good."

Kempinski put on his mask as directed and regarded th other trainers as no longer human, but some sort of viral insects with beady eyes and long proboscises. The instructor motioned to put on the headsets.

"Now you can hear me. Without the headset, you will need to use hand signals. The mask will muffle your voices, and combined with the sound of the engines, you won't be able to hear each other."

Kempinski found himself nodding along with the others.

"If your seal is good, raise your thumbs."

Kempinski checked his seal. Each trainee gave the thumbs-up sign.

"Okay, I am opening the valve. The pressure will drop as if we are at an altitude of 25,000 feet. Stay calm and breathe normally."

There was a hissing sound. Kempinski felt nothing. He nervously took in a deep breath. The oxygen seemed a bit stale, but there were no ill effects. After a few minutes, the instructor stood and walked down the center of the chamber, waiting for a nod from each man.

"With the mask, you can function normally at this altitude. Without the mask, you wouldn't stay conscious for long." He paused for dramatic effect. The men knew what was coming next. "To demonstrate this important point, we will need a volunteer to take off his mask."

No one moved.

"Alright, you fighting men, we are not leaving this chamber until someone volunteers, and these bottles will only last an hour."

Avoiding the instructor's gaze, Kelly seemed like was not about to volunteer.

'What the heck,' Kempinski said to himself, raising his

hand.

"That's the spirit. Pull the mask off your face."

Doing as instructed, he took a big empty gulp. He gulped again. It seemed like he was breathing, and turned his head around. "This isn't bad."

The instructor droned over the headsets. "At this altitude, you last one or so minutes. Okay troop, sing a tune."

"Well, I can't carry a tune in a bucket, so how about..." he paused and thought back to tenth grade civics class. "Four score and 20 years ago, our fore...fathers...brought..." The words grew fuzzy as he went along.

"Put your mask back on," the instructor said.

Kelly later told him it happened quickly. Just as President Lincoln would have been getting warmed up, Kempinski went down. The instructor expected it and caught him with what must have been a well-practiced move and slid the mask over Kempinski's face.

"Geez, what a headache," Kempinski said as he rubbed his temples.

Kelly patted him on the back. "Well, if it ain't the desert air, it's the pressure chamber" Then let out a big laugh and said, "And you volunteered. I told you so."

Kempinski smirked. "I guess that's why Dad said never to stick my hand up."

"Well, I'd say you earned a beer. Let's go to the PX."

"Sure thing. I haven't felt this bad since I had pneumonia at Kessler."

The next week introduced the platoon to the Browning 50 caliber machine guns, the same kind mounted in the bombers. They learned how to disassemble and clean the weapon. Reassembly was tricky; the process required the use of a go-no-go gauge to set the timing of the mechanism to eject the spent round and charge the new one. Kempinski's natural mechanical inclination showed the others how to do it. Each time they would master a task, Sergeant Levette would up the challenge.

"Alright, you yard apes, break time is over. Think the last drill was easy?" said Levette, strutting around the classroom like a skinny chicken in a bayou backyard. "Now you must take this gun apart and reassemble, with gloves on your meat hooks."

"What the hell?" Kelly moaned.

"Hey Tom, think about it, we are going to be wearing gloves at altitude, so it's a good idea," he replied, a cigarette dangling from his lip. A non-smoker before joining the Army, the easy access to tobacco and peer pressure made it easy for anyone to pick up the habit. Like most soldiers, he used the rote process of lighting a cigarette to pass time, to break up the hurry-up-and wait mentality of the Army.

The gloved hands complicated the task, but the Ma-deuce machine gun was not a delicate weapon. It was one of the largest machine guns in the Army's arsenal. Against enemy aircraft, it was an effective weapon to wreak havoc on the airplane's structure. Such a heavy weapon had large parts that could be assembled after some practice with the gloves.

Kempinski developed a system and made small piles of machine gun parts. "Kelly, put the receiver parts here and the bolt parts here. It will keep things organized."

Kelly assessed the pile and agreed. "Good idea. Why didn't I think of that?"

When the trainees mastered the gloved reassembly, Levette reached into a box on the instructor's podium and pulled out some black blindfolds, rounded swatches with rubberized strings. "Now it gets interesting. We'll learn which of you sad sacks really knows your weapon. Put on these and when I say go, disassemble your weapon."

The class collectively groaned.

"Well, we knew it was coming. I've been practicing by shutting my eyes," Kempinski mouthed coolly.

"Hmm," Kelly droned as he placed the black blinders on his eyes. "Heck I can't even find the table."

"You flat tire, move forward a step."

"Cut the chatter and get ready," commanded Levette.

All the men donned the coverings and their nervousness seemed palatable. The sergeant grabbed a stopwatch. "Go, start disassembling."

To Kempinski's surprise, he could disassemble the weapon, albeit much slower than if he could see.

After several weeks interspersed with aircraft recognition training, the men were finally back on the range. The trainees took turns firing heavy machine guns from a ring mount – each shot rocked the truck and the eighty-four-pound weapon took some strength and sweat to control. The trainees learned how to aim and fire the weapon, progressing from ground-to-ground targets to ground-to-air. Next came flight training, where the gunners would learn air-to-ground and finally, air-to-air shooting.

After a morning briefing on how to lead the target in air-to-air combat, the men were assigned aircraft for their first airborne combat attempt. Despite weeks of shooting, Kempinski's skin tingled with excitement.

"Kelly, flying above this desert, it might actually be cool in the plane, we can get away from this heat."

Kelly shrugged and mopped his brow with a rag.

The men marched on the flight line to three B-17 bombers lined up to accept the trainees. Each B-17 had six gunners; two waist gunners, a tail gunner, top and bottom ball turrets, and a front gunner. The waist gunners manually aimed and fired one 50 caliber machine gun each. The other gunners had a mechanized hook up; they aimed the gun sight and a motor moved two 50 caliber barrels at the aim point. Army designers loaded the aircraft with machine guns, creating a 'flying fortress' that spewed a wall of lead at incoming enemy attackers.

Weapon assignments were made based on the height of the gunner. The ball turrets could only accept someone five foot eight inches tall or shorter. Once inside the turret, a motor would lower it outside the skin of the aircraft, ensconcing the gunner in a metal and glass cocoon with two deadly stingers. Kempinski got the starboard waist gun while Kelly was a half-inch too tall for the lower ball turret and ended up on the port side opposite his friend.

Levette gathered the men in a semi-circle behind the first bomber. "Listen up, men. This is how your first aerial training mission will work. An AT-23 will be towing a bright orange target drone. You need to know your planes so you don't shoot the wrong one. The Air Corps started using the AT-23 only a few weeks ago. It seems the boys doing the real work in theater complained our gunnery graduates could not hit targets at high altitude. Can you imagine that?"

He walked around the group and sneered as if their marksmanship was in question, "Well, our officers concluded this was due to a lack of adequate training in high-altitude gunnery. It turns out the only target tugs that could operate at altitudes above 10,000 feet were the B-26 Marauder bombers. In a way only the army can, they renamed B-26 the AT-23, and made it a tow tug."

Levette returned to the front of the group and eyed each man carefully. "So, when ya'll are ready, we will take you to altitude, but don't get any ideas, ya'll are to shoot at the sock dragging behind the AT-23. To make a tow aircraft of the poor old B-26, we had to take out all its armor and armament, and covered the turret openings with aluminum. The mechanics added a C-5 tow target windlass pulling a large orange sock. Some duty for a solid old combat plane."

Levette pulled out a large piece of orange fabric. "It's a new target, or sock, as we call it. For now, you will be level flight, so lead it like in training. Now, let's board."

Kempinski bounced with energy at the chance to get back in a plane, and he quickly made his way to the crew hatch, an open portal on the belly of the bird and climbed up the spindly ladder though the rounded-square opening, where his eagerness quickly turned to disdain. The inside of the plane seemed even hotter than outside and worse, the remains of airsickness permeated the cabin.

"Geez, it smells horrible in here," said Kempinski.

Levette heard the comment and yelled from outside the thin aluminum skin of the aircraft. "Get used to it private, you have a mission to do. This bird survived Pearl Harbor and missions in southeast Asia. You'd smell bad too after all she's been through."

Kempinski shook his head in mock disbelief and settled into the olive-drab chromium oxide-coated metal frame and canvas seat, pinching his nose. With his other hand, he felt the heft of the 50-caliber machine gun. Its stiffness surprised him, and the belt feed tray made it even more awkward to move.

Kelly squeezed in next to him, also holding his nose.

"Holy moly, our first ride in a Fortress and it smells worse than a latrine." Kelly's voice was nasally and Kempinski glanced over and laughed.

"Look at us, going to kill Krauts holding our noses."

The pilot started the right inboard engine and the throaty radial engine coughed to a start. Inside the fuselage, the sound reverberated, and both sets of eyes widened. Neither had been inside of a large bomber and the aluminum frame and skin did nothing to attenuate the sound, in fact, the harmonic vibrations might have made it seem even louder.

"My God, listen." Kempinski craned his neck to get a better view outside the gunner's window. The three other engines came to life and the roar filled the crew compartment. While the engines warmed up, Levette crabbed into the rear waist section and over the engine sound hollered they were going to train on medium level gunnery so no oxygen would be needed.

Kempinski nodded and gulped. As the big aircraft taxied down the runway, butterflies attacked his stomach, a different feeling than trying to pilot the Keydet in Mississippi. "Christ, Kelly, I'm not sure I like this."

Kelly shrugged his shoulders. "Huh?" pointing to his ear signifying he couldn't hear.

"Never mind." Kempinski waved off his friend, hoping the strange sensation would fade. You ain't chicken, he thought, but being a passenger in the plane was totally different than piloting.

Levette motioned for them to put on headsets, which they did. As the B-17 took off, the ride was initially smooth, and Kempinski's anxiety quelled. But desert air pockets buffeted the plane with altitude. Kelly and Kempinski bounced in the back and Kempinski's unease returned. As the plane climbed, Levette showed them how to use the 50-caliber handles and bent knees to counter the rough ride, and the two gunners bobbed up and down, like a chorus line in a strange olive drab production number.

Kelly said, "Hey, I'm riding the subway to Canal Street."

Kempinski smiled, beads of sweat rolling down his forehead while his gut roiled.

Soon the pilot announced, "Target one o'clock." A warning the sock would pass on Kempinski's side. The chance for action broke Kempinski's funk and he pulled the charging handle of the ma-chine gun and scanned to the front. Sure enough, there was a bright orange sock trailing the AT-23. Levette announced over the intercom, "Fire when the target is in your designated field!"

Kempinski took aim as the ball turret on top, about fifteen feet in front and above the waist station, opened fire. The twin barrels added to the cacophony onboard. The New Yorker lined up the sights and pulled the trigger, the automatic crack of the large weapon pounded his ears, and the spent cartridges flew from the ejector into the crew compartment. The recoil moved the barrel erratically, and the tracers revealed a wild tongue of flame pulsing in the general vicinity of the target sock.

"Damn," said Kempinski as he let up on the trigger.

Levette corrected him. "Short, well-aimed bursts."

Kempinski readjusted his stance, aimed once again, and let off a ten-round burst. Again, the recoil made the tracers spin wildly. "Applesauce, this ain't easy."

He focused and reacquired the target one more time. The machine gun punched to life as the ammo ran through it. Cordite vapor and the heat from the barrel added to the sensory overload. Completing three passes on the starboard, the pilot reoriented the aircraft and put the target on the port side. While Kelly took his shots, Kempinski pondered the spent cartridges bouncing on the plywood floor of the waist section. At a few cents a round and eight-hundred and fifty rounds per minute, this training must cost Uncle Sam a pretty penny, then he remembered his queasy stomach and the lack of control he sensed being outside the cockpit.

After thirty minutes sending lead airborne, the mission ended and the plane returned to the field. Kempinski and Kelly disembarked through the entry hatch. Levette left the aircraft and took a waiting jeep to meet the tow aircraft.

"That was hep, but hard. I don't think I hit the target," Kempinski moaned. "And it was flying level. What are we gonna do when it's a Kraut pilot flying crazy loops?"

"Are you kidding? I peppered that sock – it'll be Swiss cheese when it comes back," bragged Kelly.

"You are a real Audie Murphy," Kempinski said as he

rubbed his eyes. His stomach calmed now he was on terra firma. "I'm going to need a lot more practice." He pondered telling Kelly about his unease, but figured it was normal for a first flight in a fortress, especially one stinking like the latrine after weekend leave.

The men walked to an assembly area under a fly tent to get out of the Yuma sun and waited for their sergeant. Kelly lit a fag, took a draw, and passed it to Kempinski. He sucked a drag, then coughed. Smoking was still new to him. Within ten minutes, Levette returned with a definite scowl traipsing his emaciated face. Before the jeep fully stopped, he hopped out and roared.

"You sorry sacks!" He paused to rub his head and slouch, "What a piss poor excuse for gunners! Can you believe there was just one hole in the sock, and that was the one the manufacturer put in it to let the air flow? Not one of you sharpshooters hit the target!"

Kempinski raised his eyebrows in a mixture of disbelief and embarrassment, then glanced over to Kelly. His friend avoided eye contact.

The next day, the crew returned to the classroom, and the instructor pulled out a series of white boards with the aerial gunnery geometry charts. The physics of aiming and shooting while airborne were much different than the crew members realized. First, there was the speed of the aircraft to consider, next the effect of relative airspeed on the flight of the bullet mixed with gravity's pull, and finally, the leading of the target's trajectory.

"Geez, Kelly, it's like we are back in high school physics."

"Yeah, maybe for you, I never even took that class. I was sure I was putting my rounds into the target yesterday. How the heck are we going to hit anything?"

"I think that is why they put so many guns on the B-17. Enough bullets in the air are bound to hit something."

The Army recognized the difficulty and gave the crew more

flight time at different altitudes. They learned to control the weapon, to compensate for the recoil, to lead behind and above oncoming targets, and how to use the newly-installed lead computing sights. These devices used a gyroscope to measure turn rates, and moved the gun barrels to take this into account, with the aim point presented through a reflective sight. The only manual input to the sight was the target distance, which was typically handled by dialing in the size of the target's wing span at some known range. For safety and to save ammunition, they sometimes used gun cameras to simulate shooting– the photographs would show probable hits.

As training progressed, barracks' talk turned to their next assignments. After flexible gunnery training, crew members were usually assigned to a stateside crew for assimilation training, and then a combat mission.

On the night before their last high-altitude training flight, Kempinski, Kelly, and a couple of other classmates walked from their quarters. As they crossed the scrub and sandy desert to the simple one story PX, they were silent until the one of the crew asked, "Where are you going to request? Pacific or European theater?"

"Tough choice," replied Kempinski. "European theater. Eighth Air Force. You get to have a swell time in England, beer and shebas, but you have a fifty-fifty chance of getting killed."

"Okay, sure, in the Pacific you have a better chance of living." Kelly turned to face the other men. "But you sleep in a tent in the middle of the jungle, with leeches and snakes and all kinds of creepy crawlers." He moved his hands like he was swatting mosquitos and flies. "And no booze."

The men collectively groaned.

"And how about sharks, with all the time flying over the ocean," said the crewmember who asked the original question. "I don't swim that good."

The men laughed, but the chuckles were tinged with an

edge of anxiety.

"Well, in the Pacific you can get a B-29. They say it's pressurized and a smooth flier, plus the chances of getting some action is better," offered Kempinski. "The air war over Germany is winding down."

"Yeah, and the Japs are down to flying kids as pilots."

"Crazy kids, though. They can't shoot worth a darn, but they ram their plane into whatever they can find," Callaway said.

"Ah, it doesn't matter," groaned Kelly. "You know this Army Air Corps is going to send us wherever they need us."

"That's for sure" They all agreed.

Arriving at the PX, they each purchased one of their weekly allotted beers. They sat on the simple wooden stairs of the building, peering out over the desert, the hell hole the Army hastily built in the hot and dry Arizona desert. Kempinski took off his utility cap and fanned his face, trying to break the blast-furnace heat. "It's crazy business all this flying, bombing and shooting."

"It's a big waste, Bobby," belched Kelly. "But what can we do? Those SOBs attacked us."

"We just keep fighting until we win, then we figure out what to do next."

The men nodded and returned to their beers in silence, pondering their choice between Scylla or Charybdis.

At morning formation, Levette ordered the men to load a full combat outfit: helmets, oxygen masks with bottle, leather flight jacket, pants and boots lined with sheepskin. It seemed ridiculous to have such uniform in the scorching 100 degree Fahrenheit of the desert floor, but at 20,000 feet, the temperature would drop to twenty below zero. They climbed into the training B-17, taking their positions with an assurance developed by rigorous repetition. They bundled their jackets and other gear at their feet. This would be their toughest test to date as the AT-23 and target would be leading their Fortress to an altitude they had not yet flown. Despite the three weeks of nearly daily flight, Kempinski's stomach was still jittery; the thought of high altitude didn't encourage him.

The takeoff and climb was routine. As the pilot lit the oxygen light, the crew donned their cold weather gear and oxygen masks as they had practiced many times. They scanned the sky within their designated area of fire, searching for the target. As Kempinski peered out the starboard window, he could make out an AT-23 about a quarter of a mile off with another B-17 flying alongside. He watched as the tracers arched across the sky, then to his amazement, the tracers started to impact the AT-23. He did a double take and blinked. It must be the angle he had on the other two planes. The two parallel tracer streams continued, and then the port engine of the AT-23 started to smoke. Kempinski called across his intercom, "Do you guys see that? They shot up the tow plane."

Kelly turned to Kempinski's window and said, "Holy cow," just as the other B-17 peeled hard to the left and down in a maneuver Kempinski had only seen a fighter do. From the AT-23, smoke built from the flames spewing out the engine. Soon the propeller feathered, and the sock line was cut with the cloth target fluttering in the wind. The plane banked to port, as the pilot struggled to handle flying with only one engine. The tow plane started to lose altitude and the other B-17 was no longer in Kempinski's field of view.

"Mission abort, safe weapons," came over the intercom from their pilot. "We are going to Dateland."

With no control towers and only a few fuel vehicles and shade tents, the sparse alternate field at Dateland barely accommodated practice take offs and landings.

Kempinski and Kelly opened the receivers of their 50 caliber machine guns and withdrew the ammunition belt from the feeder. Kempinski viewed out his window, but the combination of their plane's bank and the AT-23 maneuver meant he could no longer see the other aircraft.

"I can't believe it. How could they shoot the tow bird?"

"I don't know, Bobby, but someone is in a heap of trouble."

"Forget it. Let's hope the pilot can land it with one engine."

The crew remained quiet on the flight to the diversion field, wondering if the AT-23 would make it. Upon landing, the pilot radioed for disposition from the Yuma control tower. They were told to wait for further instructions. Inside the smelly aircraft wearing the cold weather gear, Kempinski and Kelly started to cook.

"Geez, I'm taking this Eskimo suit off," Kempinski said, "it's getting to be over a hundred degrees in here."

The two men peeled off the thick sheepskin-lined leather overcoat and pants. Once down to their utility uniform, they sat down and settled against the inner bulkhead.

"Yeah, Bobby, we may be hot, but that top gunner, he is really going to fry for nailing the tow plane."

"Can you imagine?" Kempinski said pulling a pack of cigarettes from his shirt pocket.

"Hey, what are you doing? No smoking in the bird."

"Yikes, the whole thing has got me rattled, I lost my mind." Kempinski placed his hands on his forehead next to his hair patted down with sweat from the leather helmet and the desert heat. "I mean, Tom, I saw him rake the AT-23. If there were gunners back there like us, we would have been history."

"Yeah, we'd be sitting ducks. I wonder what they will do to him. He has to be crazy or maybe, I hate to say it, but maybe a sympathizer."

"Do you think so?" Kempinski pondered the idea of a traitor among them. After a few seconds, he shook his head. "Nah, he's probably just a dumb oilcan. Still, he could have made some Gold Stars in mom's window. Let's see what comes back from HQ."

Kelly nodded. "I hope the crew lands safely."

Their B-17 remained at Dateland for two hours waiting for instructions. To pass time, the copilot ordered them to practice loading and unloading the machine guns. As they went through the motions for the twentieth time, their headset crackled; the pilot ordered the trainees to prepare for takeoff. They were headed up to continue their mission.

"Well, what do you know, this man's air corps must fight on," Kelly said into the mike.

The pilot replied, "Cut the crap, the AT-23 made it to the ground, but not too smoothly. It's our turn to put some rounds down range, and let's hope I don't have to remind you trainees, you shoot at the target sock, not the tow plane. Got that?"

The six gunners replied in unison, "Yes, sir."

The engines roared once again, filling the aluminum tube with a deafening sound. Kempinski and Kelly braced for takeoff as the Flying Fortress left the ground. After a quick climb, it was back into the cold weather gear, much appreciated now, as the temperature was well below freezing. Like arctic travelers bundled in their thick protective clothing, the men found the target sock and started firing. As at the firing range, it was hard to determine hits or not, even with the tow plane flying level. Kempinski and Kelly burned through their practice ammo, filling their plywood floor of the gun-ner's station with spent brass cartridges.

"Did you get any hits, Bobby?"

"I think so; it's hard to tell. The sock doesn't give any indication."

"Well, the AT-23 sure did earlier."

"No kidding. Let's be glad we weren't inside it. There's

nowhere to go."

"What the heck did we volunteer for, anyway?" It was a rhetorical question and Kempinski gave his mate a downward glance and twisted his eyebrows and lips simultaneously. The two men sat silently for the remainder of the flight, pondering their mission and the bizarre situation of the morning.

Training progressed over the next few days and the men's proficiency improved as they entered their last week. Command assembled the men in formation outside their orderly room. Levette announced to the platoon, "Listen up trainees, Yuma's AAF instructors team just returned from a regional gunnery meet and we finished in first place. To celebrate, the CO has allowed an extra beer in this week's ration."

The platoon let out a holler.

Levette continued, "Just think about that next time you are aiming your weapon. This is business." He next snapped to attention and commanded, "Atten-shun!"

The platoon braced in unison. After a few seconds, the squadron and school commander appeared in front of the training squadron, followed by a Staff Sergeant and a Sergeant First Class no one recognized. The Colonel, never before in front of the squadron, wearing the tropical khaki uniform with obvious sweat spots under his arms, snapped to attention and ordered, "Adjutant, read the citation."

From the side of the formation, a Second Lieutenant Staff Officer, read a Distinguished Flying Cross citation for the Sergeant First Class and the Staff Sergeant. Both had returned from Europe after achieving the maximum combat missions, and were being recognized for bravery in the face of fierce combat. As Kempinski watched from the corner of his eye, he was impressed by the effort the two awardees must have made to earn medals for aerial combat gunnery, especially reflecting on his experience yesterday in the thin aluminum tube. He wondered if he could perform in a similar manner in the same circumstance.

After the award ceremony, the squad was dismissed and ordered to the camp's classroom building. There, the commander had reappeared with an adjutant holding a stack of papers. The commander stood in front of the group.

"Class 245, you have one week of training left. Most of you have enough points already to graduate, and those a bit short still have one week to collect more points. The time has come to decide where you would like fight; you can take on the bastard hun, or the animal jap. Either way, I am sure you men, like those two gunners we honored this morning, will do Yuma Flexible Gunnery training proud."

The men stirred in the seats, and a few let out a war grunt.

"However, today we have a special situation. Before selecting your next assignment, I have an announcement." The Colonel paused while the troops stared at their commander. "We have need for five gunners who are willing to volunteer for an important mission. I can't say anything more other than it is a secret mission. So, don't ask questions. Volunteers for the secret mission, raise your hands!"

This unexpected event took Kempinski and the rest of the trainees by surprise. Over the last few weeks, the whole concept of the military and fighting the enemy was taking a different turn and the risk of the mission tempered his enthusiasm, making the decision about which combat theater to choose difficult. But then the prospect of a secret mission lit a spark rekindling the same excitement as when he dreamed about flying a fighter. Kempinski glanced around and saw no one had yet raised their hand. His eyes met Kelly's, revealing a twinkle; Kempinski raised his hand while making a head nod to urge his friend.

Someone muttered under their breath, "Are you kidding me? 'Never volunteer' is what my mom told me."

A small chuckle rippled through the table.

Kelly scanned the faces of the other men in the room, and

then twisted his face into 'what the heck?' He shot his hand into the air. Soon three other hands joined them.

"Excellent," the Colonel boomed. "You men report to the orderly room; the rest remain here with the Adjutant. Sergeant Levett, take charge and get these soldiers assigned."

"Yes Sir, each man take a form," Levette said as he and the other volunteers left.

After about thirty minutes of waiting outside the commander's office, a lean captain appeared, tall with a sophisticated and dapper appearance in his khaki uniform, with fresh starch lines despite the heat.

"Okay, you guys, I'm Captain McDowell. I will be your aircraft commander. Report to building 455 tomorrow morning for further orders. Meanwhile, remember you volunteered for a secret mission. Say nothing to anyone about this."

Kempinski and Kelly turned toward each other.

"Tommy, what will we talk about? We don't know nothing," Kempinski said under his breath.

"Exactly the way the Air Corps likes it."

As they returned to their barracks, Sergeant Levette was waiting. "You guys have twenty minutes to get your gear packed up, out of my barracks, and onto this truck. You're moving out."

"But Sarge, we ain't finished gunnery school," Kelly moaned.

"Well, boys, just think of it as ya'll moved to the head of the class. All ya'll consider ya'llselves lucky."

"What about our promotions? Do we make corporal as if we finished school?"

"Don't ask me, Private Kelly. Ya'll now are 'classified.'"

Chapter 7

As he packed his bags, Kempinski recalled the time a few months ago when he washed out of flight school, but this time he didn't feel disappointment, and the other soldiers weren't ignoring him and Kelly. They gathered around their bunks and said,"Oh boy, you'll be sorry," and "What will you guys be doing?" Kempinski and Kelly kept their mouths shut. After more haranguing, Kelly finally said, "We ain't allowed to talk about it, so no matter what you guys ask, we ain't saying nothing."

"Oh boy, big shot secret mission," one of the troops said, "Remember, never volunteer; that will get you by in the U. S. Army." And the men dissipated to their own bunks.

Kempinski and Kelly boarded the truck, introduced themselves to the three others and speculated about what their mission might be.

"What do you think?" Kelly said with his voice revealing excitement. "Maybe we will be helping infiltrate behind enemy lines?"

"I doubt that; they didn't ask us if we spoke German or Japanese. Knowing Uncle Sam, we'll be headed for a train somewhere to some other hell hole," said Bill Callaway, one of the self-selected men.

"Where's building 455?" One of the guys asked.

Kempinski, sitting on the side bench of the two-and-a-half-ton truck nearest the cab, yelled over the front slats to the driver. "Hey Corporal, where are we headed?"

The driver said nothing.

He tried again, "Come on fella, where to?"

"We can't talk about it, so be quiet. You'll find out sooner or later."

Giving up, he leaned back against the wood slats on the sides of the truck motioning with his thumb toward the driver as if hitchhiking. "Geeze, get a load of that. I guess that's how they keep it secret, whatever it is."

"Well, whatever it is, it could be real interesting," declared Kelly.

Kempinski nodded and rubbed his hands together. "We may get to kill some krauts after all."

To their surprise, and a bit of dismay, the truck dropped the team off at the barracks assigned to the permanent party personnel at Yuma AAF.

Kelly plopped his green duffle bag outside the barracks, a two-story structure like all the others the Army had built in a hurry the last few years: a wood frame building with simple box windows and a red asphalt shingle roof. "This is where we are going, right here in Yuma?"

As he spoke, Captain McDowell exited the building to meet the troops. "Listen up men, you are now assigned the 438th Training Squadron. You will each get your gunnery school promotion and your silver gunner's wings. The Air Corp's newest corporals in MOS M 0757-Radio Operator Mechanic-Gunner."

Kempinski stuck out his chest and beamed at Kelly giving him the thumbs up.

"Pair up and pick a bunk on the first floor. Tomorrow, report to building 455, like I said earlier. Take the rest of the day to get used to your new surroundings."

At sunrise, the secret mission started inauspiciously. They met their new platoon sergeant, SFC Goodwin, a fireplug of a man from Maine. He seemed to be as wide as he was tall and spoke with a heavy New England accent that moved his butch crew cut up and down with each long A sound.

"Today, you troops belong to me. Here is the assignment list for the day." Kempinski and Kelly were shocked to see they had kitchen patrol, or KP.

"KP, that's our secret mission. What are we going to be peeling, classified potatoes?"

Goodwin shot back. "I don't like your attitude mister."

"Sorry Sarge," replied Kempinski. "We were just wondering what we were going to be doing."

"Is that so? Well, the Army will let you know what you need to know when it sees fit. Meanwhile, you will execute this duty roster in the most proficient manner you know how. Got that?"

"Sure do, Sarge."

"You all finish your detail, then at 1500 hours report to the company orderly room in clean duty overalls."

The contingent stirred from foot to foot with the prospect of learning something, anything, about their next assignment, but then moved to their assigned tasks for the day. Kempinski and Kelly used kitchen knives to reduce a big pile of potatoes to a smaller pile. "Jeeze, what a waste, peeling potatoes with a knife," Kempinski said pondering the army issued blade. "My mom has this nifty peeler that would take the skin right off."

"Well, you heard Sarge." Kelly twisted his face to resemble the elder New Englander. "Do duh jaahb in the most praah-fishing mahhnahh."

"You crack me up Kelly. That's a Boston accent for sure. Let's finish up these last spuds and get back to the room to change into clean overalls. These are covered in sweat and potato slime."

"Yeah, maybe the real mission starts at 3PM."

At 1500 hours, the five men milled around the orderly room smoking and waiting for the next step in the army's grand plan for them. When the minute hand hit 12, SFC Goodwin strode into the room. "Put out those cigs, and take a seat in the classroom."

The team did as instructed. Goodwin checked his watch and then Captain McDowell entered the room.

"Attention," bellowed Goodwin, louder than necessary for the room.

The men quickly stood at attention next to their desks.

"At ease, take your seats," McDowell said as he faced the team.

"Today we are conducting a security briefing about your roles and responsibilities in dealing with classified material. We are about to embark on a classified program, and that means Uncle Sam is entrusting you to keep your mouths shut."

Kempinski inched forward on his seat. He had never heard of anything classified and the idea made his imagination scurry with notions of spies and coats with fedoras, like in a Humphrey Bogart movie.

McDowell continued, "First off, you will be signing this disclosure form. If you reveal any of this information in the future, you will be subject to the Articles of War and penalties, up to and including a firing squad."

Kempinski gulped and glanced at Kelly who made a motion like closing a zipper across his lips.

Kempinski made a small smile as he absorbed the gravity of Captain McDowell's words. He vowed to himself not to mess up and reveal anything.

McDowell's talk continued as he explained various levels of classified marking. He concluded the briefing by having each man fill out their non-disclosure forms and several army forms necessary to get a security clearance.

"It will take some time for the army security to assign your clearances. Meanwhile, we will continue the base duty assignments. When the clearances come in, we will start aircrew familiarization training. Any questions?"

Kelly raised his hand. "Err sir, what type of aircraft will we be flying?"

"That type of information is not classified, but let's get in the practice of keeping quiet. For now, you have no need to know. In due time, you will see."

The briefing ended and the men returned to their barracks.

"What do you think Bobby?"

"I don't know, Tommy. I guess we keep our mouths shut and see what happens."

"Carter heard a rumor McDowell flew B-25s over Italy."

"The B-25, the Mitchel--how many crew members on that?"

"Er, six, I think: pilot, co-pilot, and navigator combined with bombardier, radioman and two gunners."

"Yeah, the radioman also serves as a gunner. Supposed to be a nice bird." Kempinski rubbed his hands together. "I wonder what kind of missions we will be running."

While waiting for their security clearances to be processed, the team endured typical quotidian tasks such as more KP, charge of quarters, policing detail, and guard duty with World War I vintage M-1 rifles, yet no ammo.

Two weeks later, Captain McDowell assembled the group outside the orderly room. "Gents, we still need some clear-ances to come through, but we are starting training in the aircraft today. We have been assigned aircraft 6829; it's a swell Mitchell.

Due to the nature of this mission, we will not be using a full crew complement on the bird. For today's flight, we will have myself as commander, First Lieutenant Ritter as co-pilot, First Lieutenant Schwagger as navigator/bombardier, Corporal Kempinski at radio, and Corporal Kelly as gunner. Uniform for the day is flight suits with parachutes. No side arms." McDowell proceeded to brief the crew on the upcoming mission, a low-level familiarization flight, the first step in an accelerated process to get the assigned crew members working as a team. "Get with your jeep drivers and go to the bird; get familiar with your posts."

Kempinski turned toward Kelley and gave him the thumbs up sign. "Better than KP; finally some action. This is the cat's meow!"

"I'm sure they'll figure out a way to make it miserable, though."

"No baloney there, but I've never been in a Mitchell. I'll need to review the radio manuals."

"No, you don't, Bobby. It's like riding a bicycle; once you do it you never forget."

"How do you know, you gink?"

The two friends jokingly pushed each other. Then Kempinski went to the equipment bench and donned his parachute pack, leaving the straps loose around his torso, and adjusted his olive drab duty cap. He left the briefing room where two Willy jeeps with drivers were waiting to take the men to the flight line. The pi-lot and co-pilot, wearing the round saucer-shaped service hats each had molded to suit their personality, grabbed the front passenger seat in each jeep and the navigator and two enlisted men squeezed in the back with their legs hanging over the edge.

The jeeps approached the east side of the field, the opposite side of where the gunnery school aircraft parked. To their front stood a bevy of bare aluminum B-25 twin engine bombers.

"Hey, how hep," Kempinski whistled, "the B-25J model, the newest one in the Army's inventory."

Kelly rubbed his head, wiping away some sweat. "Yeah, not some recycled jalopies. Maybe they won't reek like the training aircraft."

The crew assembled around Captain McDowell, "This is the B-25J. The Army's newest 10-ton aluminum master-piece; it isn't something you just wander out and get in. Over the next few days, we are going to learn all there is to learn about this bird. So, pay attention as we take a walk around the aircraft."

As Captain McDowell briefed the men on the various external aspects of the plane, Kempinski listened closely with his ears perked to the side. He noticed it was much smaller than the B-17, his arm span was almost as wide as the fuselage. Meanwhile, Kelly lingered behind, trying to stay in the shade of the aircraft whenever possible.

"Prior to each flight, we check oil and gas, the struts, tires, and the controls. Normally this is the pilot's job, but we will be working as a team, so I like to have all my crew participate with me," McDowell explained. "Once we check the outside, we then go to our stations and do assigned checklists."

Kempinski nodded. He liked McDowell's approach; teamwork seemed like a good thing.

McDowell led them to the front gear strut. "The last thing we check prior to boarding is this shimmy damper. It has a little nubbin that sticks out of the top. If it doesn't stick out at least three-eighths of an inch, we don't fly. On airplanes as big as the 25, if the shimmy damper fails, it can destroy the airplane. I saw a Mitchell over in Africa that lost the damper on landing roll-out; it sheared rivets and buckled sheets back into the wings, completely wrecking it."

Kempinski couldn't believe such as small part could affect the aircraft, but it doubled his resolve to learn as much as he could.

McDowell continued, "Just below the shimmy damper is a knurled cap screwed onto a rod that goes through the strut. Under the cap is a pin that can be pulled out, allowing the nose strut to turn freely for towing. The cap has to be finger tight or we can't taxi and take off. Following the checklist is critical for safe flight. You follow your checklist and we will get along just fine." McDowell, while only a few years older than Kempinski, was an officer and a combat veteran, something Kempinski admired. But more importantly, McDowell's command presence filled Kempinski with confidence.

McDowell raised his round pilot's hat. "Alright, that's it for the outside, now climb in and run through your station's checklists. Make sure you wear your headset and intercom. We will stay below 8,000 feet, so you don't need to wear your oxygen masks."

Kempinski watched as McDowell, Ritter, and Schwagger climbed a ladder through a hinged hatch, located in the belly of the airplane, about in line with the propellers. The crew chief motioned to Kelly and Kempinski. "Gunners use the rear hatch."

Kempinski nodded and moved to the rear opening where a metal ladder protruded from under fuselage. He climbed up. "Check this out, Tom, plenty of room," he said as he entered the largest compartment in the aircraft. "There it is, the radio station." He pointed just aft of the bomb bay bulkhead. The radio operator's seat was against the right wall, facing the left wall was a complete set of radio equipment.

Kelly climbed in and softly whistled, "Yeah, it's not stinky like those Fortresses. Smells more like hydraulic oil."

Kempinski studied the interior familiarizing himself with the layout of the communication gear. The crew chief stuck his upper torso in the bottom hatch and started pointing out some of the equipment, including the oxygen bottles, fire extinguisher, fire ax, and a bright red crank handle next to the bomb bay bulkhead.

"If the captain orders it, the radio operator uses this red crank to manually open or close the bomb bay doors. It's a real job, so hope you don't need to do it someday. The rest of the gear you should know."

Kempinski nodded and took a seat facing the radios. He adjusted his headset and opened his checklist book.

Kelly took a seat opposite him.

"Hey, aren't you supposed to be the tail gunner?" as he pointed to the rear tunnel.

"Yeah, but the captain said to stay here during takeoff and landing. Plus, we ain't going to see no jerrys on this flight. So, what difference does it make?"

"You better get used to doing your job as well as possible. We may need it someday. And I got a feeling Captain McDowell won't take slack effort from anybody."

"Yes sir-ree, he sure seems hard boiled."

They fastened their seatbelts and cinched them tight.

McDowell announced they had finished the flight checklist and asked the crew if they were go for flight.

"Yes sir, radio mission ready," piped Kempinski.

"Roger, fire engine one."

The 16 radial cylinders, arrayed in two banks of eight, roared to life. Even wearing his headset, the deafening roar and vibration surprised Kempinski; it was much louder than the B-17s. When the second engine fired up, the sound seemed to more than double, and reminded him of a New York subway car screeching along the IRT line, only worse.

The pilot taxied the plane while Kempinski listened to the radio headset. 3,600 horsepower in the two big radial engines shook the ten tons of airplane gently, but noisily, such that Kempinski took some time to get used to distinguishing the Morse code from the engine racket. As soon as they took off, McDowell asked for a liaison check with the airfield tower. Kempinski keyed the microphone and reported take off and heading to the tower. The plane banked west toward the open airspace over southern California.

"OK crew, this is McDowell," the pilot said over the general intercom. "Since this is a familiarization flight, we will each get to cycle a couple of times through our typical mission tasks. Lt. Schwagger, set a heading for San Diego."

"Yes sir," came Schwagger's voice over the intercom.

"Corporal Kempinski, when set, report heading to liaison."

"Roger sir."

Tailgunner Kelly, report any contact to the rear, friend or foe."

"Yes sir," Kelly said as he unstrapped, giving his friend Kempinski a 'I know you told me so look,' then scurried hunched over to fit through the rear tunnel to the tail gunner station.

McDowell was true to his word, as the Mitchell flew over the barren desert, he had each of his crew members practice their tasks again and again. Kempinski was particularly busy sending reports to the ground, logging each station, and assisting the navigator by taking radio location checks at each mission set point. Before he knew it, McDowell announced it was time to prepare for landing by stowing gear and strapping in. The pace of activity kept Kempinski's mind active and he had little time to worry about his anxiety clouding his mood prior to take-off.

As the bird touched down, the wheels made a satisfying screech and Kempinski blew a sigh of relief. The return to ground brought a smile to his face.

"Hey Kelly, that was something. I can't believe how much stuff I had to do. I could barely keep up."

Kelly, now sitting next to him in the rear compartment,

replied, "Maybe for you, but I got a darn headache searching for bogies in the desert sky. Hopefully the enemy will be a little more forthcoming on the next mission."

"Well, you never know." Both men cracked up laughing

The next day big news arrived. Captain McDowell announced their security clearances had been approved and the crew would start the secret mission as soon as command notified them to fly. Meanwhile, there would be daily training missions.

McDowell led his crew in a week of intense drills only broken up by physical fitness and sports activities. With each takeoff or basketball game or baseball scrimmage, the team started to gel. In the air, they all worked on their jobs taking orders from McDowell. But on the ground, the officers stayed in their BOQ away from the non-commissioned officers' barracks. It was a time-honored tradition of no-fraternizing between the ranks.

On their seventh mission as they prepared for landing, Kelly hunched over toward Kempinski and removed his headset. "Hey, did you see those irrigation ditches about 15 minutes ago?"

"No, I was at my post."

"They really shimmered from the air. And the water seemed so inviting. What a break from this blasted heat. I'd love to dip my toes in that."

Kempinski twisted his lips. "Yeah taking a swim would be awesome."

"Why don't we try to get a vehicle and drive out there?"

"I don't know, last time I drove a car, it didn't end up too well."

"No problem buddy, I can drive a car. A jeep is a piece of cake. I had a delivery job in the city before Uncle Sam requested my presence."

"You know the company has a daily supply run to the Dateland field. Maybe we can tag along," offered Kempinski.

"Nah, we need our own set of wheels."

Kempinski could tell by Kelly's expression a different set of wheels were turning in his mind.

Upon landing, Kelly talked to the ground chief about borrowing the maintenance jeep for a couple of hours. The chief agreed as long they brought the vehicle back in good shape. Meanwhile, Kempinski scrounged around in the company orderly room and found a map of the Yuma area. Together, he and Kelly figured out the general directions to the ditch.

"Look here, Tommy, it seems we can get to the ditch without having to go through the main gate."

"Yeah, I see, that way we don't need a day pass from the charge of quarters. Good thinking."

As they readied some towels and canteens of water, Kelly bemoaned. "Sure would be nice to bring some beer, instead of this water."

Bill Callaway, one of the other enlisted man whom had volunteered for the secret mission, was sitting on the steps outside the orderly room. When he heard the word beer he stuck his head in the door. "Hey guys, what's up? You are getting some beer?"

"Oh no," replied Kelly swinging the map behind him as if to hide it from Callaway. "We were just talking."

"Like heck you were, about not needing a pass. What are ya'll doing?"

"Well, Cal," Kempinski offered, "we were thinking how to beat this heat, and we're taking a ride down to this irrigation ditch we spotted from the air. I'll bet the water is real cool."

"Yes, it is." Callaway paused and made his face take on a mock officious sneer. "And off limits too." He gave Kempinski and Kelly a comical sneer, then added. "Jones and I are coming too. We all need to cool off."

"Well, they are building a swimming pool over by the PX," offered Jones with a promising tilt of his head.

Kempinski waved off the comment as if he was shooing away one of the ever-present desert flies. "Which will be done when we transfer to some other post."

"Ain't that the truth," bemoaned Kelly.

After a moment of silence, Kempinski begrudgingly agreed. "Well, alright. You meet us out here in ten minutes, and not a word to anyone else."

Jones and Callaway shook their heads enthusiastically and jumped up faster than Kempinski had seen them move since assigned to their secret mission.

After reassembling near the orderly room, the crew climbed on the jeep and rode towards the back of the Yuma Army Airfield. Thirty minutes from the barracks past acres of countless Creosote Bushes and Beavertail cacti, they found the irrigation ditch. It paral-leled a dirt trail that seemed infrequently used.

"Oh my, water," beamed Kempinski, "and not dirt."

"What are you waiting for?" Kelly stripped off his t-shirt and utility trousers.

"Well the edge is pretty steep," Callaway hedged, with concern creasing his forehead. "How will we get out?"

"Hmmm, we'll just use the tow rope off the jeep and tie it to this fence post."

"Good idea, Bobby!" With typical Kelly aplomb, problem solved, he turned toward the canal and, wearing only a jockstrap, jumped. "Last one in is a rotten egg. Whoopeee."

Kempinski took the time to tie off the tow rope and dangled the end over the edge, then he dropped his kahkis and shoes, rolled up his underwear to make it function as a bathing suit, and jumped in like a cannonball. He planned his trajectory to land near the other guys already horsing around in the water.

The group splashed and swam, laughing like school kids, the stress of the ongoing war seemingly forgotten. They took photos of themselves carousing. Kempinski felt the urge to take a smoke break, so he swam to the rope and climbed out. As he lit his cigarette and leaned back against the jeep, he yelped, "Yikes, that's hot." His involuntary reaction to the sun-cooked fender turned him back towards post. There, he could see a dust trail following a vehicle towards their position. He squinted and thought he saw a Jeep with siren mast and the MP lettering.

"Holy crap, guys, quick everybody, out! MPs are heading our way."

"What the hell," Kelly gurgled with water spouting from his mouth.

"Get out now; we have to get away."

The three guys in the water at first didn't know what to think, then Kelly figured it was a joke. "No way, Bobby, you are trying to bust our stones."

"You guys can't see over the berm – get over here now or I'm leaving without you." As he said it, he frantically pulled on his trousers and utility shirt. His wet underwear hadn't dried, even in the desert heat, and made a wet ring around his pants below the waist. He stared towards the dust clouds, and figured they had about five minutes.

"Is that so; you can't drive the jeep, remember!"

"Listen, you flat tire, we have less than five minutes before they are here."

Callaway meanwhile swam over to the side and climbed up.

"Damn, Kelly, it does look like MPs. We gotta go. These ditches are off limits."

"Oh, crap," spit Kelly as he and Jones did the Australian crawl like Johnny Weissmuller toward the bank. They scurried up the steep sandy edge past the scrub sage brush and, in their underwear, jumped in the jeep. Kelly pushed the clutch, shifting the gears to neutral, pulled the choke halfway and stepped on the starter button underneath the accelerator pedal. The jeep, fortunately kept in A-one condition by the maintenance platoon, started with one try. The others piled in, a jumble of arms and legs, onto the passenger seat and rear compartment. In a burst of gravel, sand, and dust, Kelly pulled the jeep away with about an 800-yard head start. But, in his haste, he and Jones had not picked up their clothes off the sandy berm. Only Kempinski, who had hastily dressed, and Callaway, who was attempting to put on his pants in the back seat, had clothes. As their utility vehicle's suspension chattered with acceleration, Kempinski glimpsed to the rear and saw they had a chance to get away. Then he turned around and realized his friends were semi-nude.

"I think we might get away, but you guys are about to set a new fashion statement for YAF."

"Really, Bobby, and this seat is burning my rear. I can't believe I left my utilities there. Let's try to shake these guys before we figure out what to do next."

Kelly bounced the jeep faster than the road conditions allowed. As they took a turn to follow the irrigation ditch, Jones, in the rear compartment with Callaway, shouted, "Slow down, Kelly, they have stopped where we were swimming."

"Oh great," as he swung his head rearward.

Kempinski used his hands to shield his eyes. "Nah, I don't think so, it looks like they are heading the other way."

"There's so much dust, it's hard to tell."

"Geeze, we need our clothes."

"Well you have to admit, Tommy, it's pretty funny."

"Not funny, Bobby, if they are MPs and they find my wallet in my pants, we are in big trouble."

Kempinski turned to Kelly. "Your wallet is back there? Oh Lord."

"Well, I left in a hurry, or did you forget?"

"We have to go back."

"Yeah right, you think my clothes are still there," he said more as statement than question.

"Maybe, at least we can find out if the MPs, or whomever was in the vehicle, stopped at our swim hole."

"He's right Tommy," pleaded Jones, muscles in his face taut. "We can't go back to base in our underwear."

"Alright." Kelly slowed the jeep and made a circular turn in the scrub desert. Kempinski held onto the windshield frame as he strained to see where the other vehicle was headed. "Listen Tommy, whoever it was is pretty far gone. Maybe they didn't even know we were there."

"In this desert, it's hard to tell. I mean it looks like there is a lake between here and there."

"That's just a mirage." Kempinski pointed down the road, "Just take it slow and try not to kick up so much dust. We might be able to slide in and out."

Kelly followed their track to the irrigation ditch swim site by stretching his neck to scan over the steering wheel. "Hey, I think I see my utilities where I left them."

"Yeah, mine too," added Jones with a relief that relaxed his face.

"Well, Kelly, you pull up and Jones and I will grab the stuff. Be ready to drive off, just in case."

"What are you worried about? Coyotes?"

They all laughed, then Kelly slowed to a creep, as Jones and Kempinski jumped off the passenger side and scurried to get the lost items.

"Ouch, ouch, this sand is burning my feet," Jones piped as he did a strange tip toe dash to his pile of clothes. "I don't think the other vehicle came here."

"Probably not, but we were better safe than sorry."

As the jeep idled, Kelly donned his uniform and tied up his government issued shoes. "Well, close calls like that we don't need."

"Yeah, let's head back, this might not have been a great idea."

"Are you kidding, Bobby, I had a great time; I got cooled off,"

"Yeah, and almost thrown in the cooler."

Kelly and Kempinski dropped off Jones and Callaway at the barracks and returned the vehicle to the maintenance platoon. The maintenance sergeant showed them where the vehicle wash rack was and the two friends hosed off the desert dust and sand off the olive drab paint. They parked the jeep on the motor pool line and returned the log book to the maintenance sergeant along with a pack of Chesterfield cigarettes.

"Pleasure doing business with you boys." The sergeant took the log book and fags with his grease stained hands. "Wasn't sure if you got hung up in the accident."

"What accident?" Kempinski said dropping his chin at an angle.

"An Army bus loaded with troops got nailed by a freight train at the crossing in town. A big mess, lots of casualties."

"Holy shit, those poor bastards," Kempinski and Kelly exclaimed in unison.

"Yes, it stinks. But you know they just sent out a call, they need blood at the dispensary".

"Let's go, Kelly, maybe we can help out."

"Ah, not me, Bobby; I'm afraid of needles."

"Well get over it. If it was us needing the blood, you know the guys in the bus would do it."

"I guess so."

"And on the bright side, the infirmary is loaded with nurses – we could use the female company."

News about the war always spread through the camp like wildfire, rumors usually, but the bus accident was local and hit home hard. Troops all over YAF were talking about it in hushed tones, reminding them of the random nature of their military fate, and many of them may not be going home.

After returning from the blood donation, Goodwin informed the men in the barracks Captain McDowell had summoned a special evening formation. The air crew rambled out of their whitewashed wood building on the dirt assembly area between the barracks and the company orderly room.

The troops' posture and lack of chit chat confirmed their somber mood. McDowell strode to the front of his men, wearing his service cap and khaki dress uniform with his impressive fruit salad of service ribbons. He addressed the troops in his deepest command voice. "All right soldiers, we've had a bad day. 28 good men. Gone. That is the price we pay to win this God forsaken war."

Kempinski was taken aback by the number 28. 'What a disaster,' he thought.

"To lose men in non-combat is something we can't afford. It's our duty to focus every day to prevent accidents. Do your job and keep an eye on your fellow crew. If you see something wrong, stop and take a minute to assess the situation. Look out for each other and execute your post in the best of your ability." McDowell paused a few seconds to let the message sink in. "Now listen up, tomorrow we start our first test mission. I want everyone on the flight line a half hour early for our morning flight to review the aircraft checklists and safety procedures. Study your checklists tonight and be ready to go. It's a bad day and we will pay respects to our lost comrades, but we still have a job to do and a war to win. Dismissed."

Kempinski and his crewmates broke formation with a little more vigor than they had at assembly, then shuffled back to the barracks. "Geez Kelly, 28 guys killed."

"I can't believe it Bobby, and not even in a flight."

"This whole thing is ridiculous. There's flight accidents all the time. You kind of expect at the pace they rush us through this training, but to get killed by a train. It's hard to accept."

"Well, we made it this far."

"It's a numbers game, I guess. We all think the next guy is going to get it, and you know what, a lot of people are getting it. I can't count how many people from my neighborhood aren't coming home."

"Yeah, Bobby." Kelly paused rubbing his chin. "You know, I could really use a beer."

"Forget that, Kelly; we have to review our checklists like the old man said. Plus, we used up our weekly quota."

Chapter 8

McDowell's flight crew and crew chief assembled before daybreak at Mitchell tail number 6829. Each wore a jump suit and parachute, with a kit bag containing their cold weather gear and oxygen mask. All smoked while they waited for their commander to arrive.

Soon, a pair of headlights streamed down the flight line toward the crew. As it got closer, the men could see it was a jeep. McDowell smartly exited the vehicle as it pulled to a stop.

"Hey Captain, you learn anything about the mission?" Lieutenant Schwagger yelled.

"Snuff the smokes men and gather round," answered McDowell.

Each man ground what remained of their cigarettes against their boots and placed the butts in their pocket to avoid foreign object damage. They formed a small semi-circle around their pilot awaiting orders as the first ray of sunlight cracked over the desert floor.

"Here's the scoop; we are flying a test mission today with a new piece of classified gear that works in conjunction with the Norden bombsight. We'll fly a routine circle track at 10,000 feet over the Colorado Desert while the test engineer calibrates the device. He's a civilian and he'll tell us what to do once calibrated."

"Geeze, boss, a civilian?" bemoaned Ritter, the co-pilot.

"Yeah, I met him; he's alright. Some kind of whiz-bang scien-tist. He'll be setting up it up for BTO."

"What's that?" Kelly joked. "Big Time Operator?"

Kempinski sneered at Kelly, as if he was saying to cut it out and be serious.

"Negative, it stands for Bombing Through Overcast, BTO. You know how the military loves acronyms. Anyway, its sounds like it could be a real improvement in our bombing. It will allow us to drop our package on Jerry even if there are clouds or at night."

"Wowzza," whistled the crew. While the flying weather was typically excellent in the desert air, all the men understood the elements played a big role in mission execution in the combat theater. Night flying would also reduce the threat of dealing with enemy fighter aircraft.

McDowell continued, "BTO will allow the brass to up the operations tempo and keep the heat on the enemy."

Kempinski nodded, thinking it could be a real advantage to the USA. If he couldn't be in the real action, at least he was doing something important.

"They should be arriving soon with the equipment, so get ready to man your positions."

The crew started to move to their assigned positions when two Army panel trucks painted olive drab approached the Mitchell. A bespectacled rail thin and balding man wearing dark slacks, with white shirt and stiletto tie exited the first vehicle. The other truck pulled off at a slight distance from the crew and despite the heat, a colonel and a major in pink and green uniforms exited, but did not approach the plane. Kempinski had never seen these officers before.

McDowell motioned to the engineer. "Mr. Donald, this is the crew. Crew. This is Mr. Ernie Donald."

The crew members half waved - half saluted. Donald returned the greeting with a smile, but his austere facial skin turned it into a smirk. He hitched his pants above his waist and strode to the back of his vehicle. Throwing open the barn doors of the truck he

withdrew a rather bulky canvas bag was stenciled "TOP SECRET."
He struggled to carry the bag and making it more difficult was his
apparent attempt to keep it from the crew members' view.

Kempinski could see McDowell frown and the captain
quickly directed, "Lieutenant Schwagger, help him get set up.
Remember, this is a classified system, so no horsing around or
bullshitting about it."

"Yes sir," Schwagger replied and moved toward Donald
just in time to help prevent the secret system from falling to the
tarmac. They carried the bundle to the front crew hatch.

"All right, crew, mount up. We'll be flying as soon as the
equipment is set up."

Kempinski, Kelly and the others went to the respective stations on the Mitchell. Kelly took his usual take-off seat near Kempinski at the radio compartment.

"That's strange, Bobby. They don't even trust us to see
what the thing is."

"And with all that brass watching."

"Never seen those before, but McDowell sure seemed
keyed up."

"Yeah, I know. I guess there can be spies or sympathizers
anywhere. But, I like the idea about improving our bombing missions. Anything to kill more krauts seems like a good idea to me."

"I'm keen to that."

The men drew silent and waited, as typical in the Army, for
what seemed a long time, then the pilot called over the headsets,
"Prepare for engine start."

"Finally, hurry up and wait is over," said Kelly as he settled
into his seat.

The engines roared to life and were as noisy as usual, like

someone banging two steel pails next to each ear. Kempinski finished his radio operator's checklist and notified the commander.

The plane took off toward the west away from the sun and heading toward the Colorado Desert, the southeastern most portion of the California desert bordering Arizona. It was bleak and hostile terrain, getting only about eight inches of rain per year with no evidence of human presence.

Once at altitude, the mission seemed normal to Kempinski, except the navigator kept calling out course changes. He figured it must have had something to do with the calibration procedure. All the steering activity kept the crew busy, so when the pilot announced they were ready to land, it seemed like they had just taken off. Kempinski stored his gear for landing and sat back in his seat. Kelly sidled up next to his friend.

"Hey Kelly, so far this secret mission seems like no big thing
."

"You got that right. I felt like a drugstore cowboy on the rear gun, but with no broads for targets."

"Who would have known a secret mission could be so boring." Kempinski reflected flying these planes seemed exciting at first, but lack of action was dull, yet not without danger. There were regular plane crashes and the crews needed to stay focused. Still, he felt like the war was passing him by while he was stuck in this hellhole desert.

Once the engineer had the bugs worked out of the system, the crew flew daily, sometimes two missions per day over the Colorado Desert. In the second week of testing, McDowell announced they were going to try a new twist to see how the system worked on detecting coastal targets. Kempinski immediately could see how that could be a big advantage when attacking the Japanese mainland, as many soldiers seemed to feel was inevitable.

At their morning brief, McDowell explained they would fly from YAF and head due west to the Pacific Ocean. There they would follow a pre-cleared practice course, so no coastal defense would mistake them for a kamikaze, and line up the B-25 on the southern part of San Diego. The system, which Kempinski deduced was some sort of radar, would identify the boundary between the ocean and the city. To truly test the crew, the test engineer would not accompany the flight. Schwagger would have to operate the classified equipment to see how an actual crew member would perform.

With an early morning take-off, the plane quickly ascended to 20,000 feet requiring the crew to wear their cold weather gear and oxygen bottles. Kempinski disliked the mask as it hindered his task accomplishment and gave him a claustrophobic tightness. 'Get over it', he reminded himself, 'focus on the task at hand, block out the unease'; but sometimes his mind raced and a distorted pattern of black and white geometric shapes would pierce his vision, followed by a throbbing headache. Kempinski found sipping on coffee in his government-issued thermos helped, even though most crew avoided drinking, so not to urinate during the mission. High altitude cold could wreak havoc on exposed skin, especially skin most men viewed sacrosanct.

As the crew left the confines of the continental US, Kempinski had to try radio fixes using transponders on land at oblique angles. He found the task challenging and was a bit slow in calling the position to the pilot.

"You keeping up back there, Bobby?" McDowell queried.

"Roger, sir, we are at the turn point."

Navigator and bombardier, Schwagger, confirmed and the plane banked into a 180 degree turn.

Schwagger announced the system was ready and McDowell turned control over to the bombardier. Schwagger's voice, with an edge of surprise and a bit of trepidation, announced he had just put on blinders blocking all view out the front window of the Mitchell.

McDowell queried him on the open crew channel. "Do you have to use those blinders? As the bombardier, you are in control of the plane."

"I don't like it either, Captain, but the procedure says we need to be sure we are only responding to the radar screen input. This will be the same as if we are in clouds or at night."

Ah ha, Kempinski thought, it is some kind of radar device. He had gone to the base library and had read up on it, but only found a few references in some Army manuals and in Popular Mechanics.

"You know there are mountains just beyond the coast."

"At 20,000 feet, we will be fine."

"I'll be watching, anything looks strange from up here, and I'll pull her up."

"I'm with you there all the way, sir, procedure or not, I want to get home someday."

"Roger," replied McDowell, but Kempinski had flown enough with his pilot now to tell he was not happy with the situation. And rightfully so, it seems once a month a plane would smash into the mountains around Yuma, taking the whole crew with it.

Schwagger called out the distances to the coast as they neared San Diego, and McDowell said nothing meaning the radar device was working well. As they neared one mile out, the bombardier hit the bay switch and announced, "Open bomb bay doors."

Kempinski knew this was simulated for test purposes, but was surprised when he heard the bomb bay motors operate as they were just in front of the radio operator station. The air passing the open bay added to the cacophony in the aircraft. A shiver, not due to frigid air, but the idea of what they were doing, made him refocus on the nature and extent of the war.

"Zero point," Schwagger exclaimed with excitement.

McDowell confirmed. "Roger, we are over land."

"Bombs away."

Kempinski knew this time it was certainly simulated as they had not loaded any kind of ordnance. Good thing, as the folks just waking up in San Diego might not appreciate their special delivery.

Once the mission had finished, Schwagger said he had photographed the screen and bombsight per the test procedure. McDowell announced they were turning 180 degrees and to get ready for another test run. Kempinski logged the turns, called in their position and took radio fixes. Soon he heard bombs away again. This time McDowell did not announce a return to the test run. Instead he said, "Schwagger, give me a bearing to Carlsbad."

"Carlsbad, skipper?" queried the navigator, "that's 30 miles off the test course."

"According to the test plan, we are done and I need to do an aerial reconnaissance of Carlsbad."

"Aerial recon?" There was a pause. "Whatever you say Sir."

Kempinski eyed Kelly in the tail gun. Kelly shrugged.

Schwagger gave the compass heading and Kempinski felt the plane bank to the port side. He was getting ready to call in his checkpoints when McDowell said, "Bobby, we are in a new drill. Go to radio silence."

Kempinski sat back in his chair, shrugged his head to the side and confirmed over the crew intercom, "Roger, radio silence, Sir." He logged the turn, then just listened to the radio to see if they would pick up any messages.

As the Mitchell approached the Carlsbad area, Lieutenant Ritter called out a low altitude warning, "1,200 feet."

"No problem, Ritter, we got this," McDowell seemed almost giddy. Kempinski figured the officers were up to something, but he wasn't sure what. The plane seemed to go nose down, which at 1,200 feet surprised Kempinski, then he felt the plane bank hard to starboard.

"Wahoo, did you see that?" Ritter whistled over the intercom.

"Yes I did," replied McDowell. "I got an eyeful."

"Your girl's built like Hedy Lamarr. Has she been waiting all day for you?"

"Nah, I told her to be outside around now."

"Should we make another pass? I want to see if she is really topless."

"Nope, too much time down there and someone is bound to pick up our tail number. Plus, what do think she was waving? It wasn't a towel."

"That was her shirt?" Ritter gave his commander a leer. "You lucky dog."

"All right the party's over," McDowell said with a certain smugness. "Schwagger, give me a heading back to YAF."

"Roger sir, back to a rally point or direct?"

"Make it direct; we've been up long enough."

Schwagger gave the heading and a warning about having to cross some high mountains so be sure to gain altitude. McDowell raised the nose and increased the throttles, and trimmed the bird for hands off flight. Since they had a long flight ahead, he engaged the autopilot, setting the servo controls, matching the various flight control cards, and switching the on-off switch. Gently, he made manual adjustments and observed the plane's response after nudging the controls. McDowell and Ritter settled in for a smooth transit through the desert air passing over the vast and unpopulated southeast California desert.

About thirty minutes later, Ritter called out a warning over the crew intercom "Fire indicator – engine two."

"McDowell keyed the intercom microphone. "Kempinski, check outside the gun port. See if you can see anything on engine 2."

The fire warning spiked Kempinski's adrenaline. He nearly tripped on his kit bag as he hurried to see outside the gunner port, "Err sir, the engine is smoking."

"Do you see any flames?"

"No sir." Kempinski was surprised at how calm he remained. He figured the training and drills McDowell had run them through paid off.

Ritter announced with a voice revealing mounting concern, "Oil pressure dropping in number 2. Perhaps a supercharger failure, sir." Ritter twisted his head to glance outside his side window, just above the armor plate, toward engine number 2. "Flames now, number 2."

A chill ran through Kempinski. He subconsciously snugged up his parachute harness. This wasn't a drill. "He's right sir," Kempinski added over the intercom, "Now flames coming out the cowling vents."

"Set the number 2 fuel valve to off."

"Roger," confirmed Ritter.

"Props at Increase RPM; that should blow out the flame."

"No dice, sir," said Ritter with a lump in his throat as he watched the engine through the co-pilot's window.

Screeching and grinding vibrated through the Mitchell's frame; the engine's horrendous metal on metal contact indicated its demise.

"It's not the carburetor, Ritter, feather the prop."

McDowell grunted as the right propeller came to a stop, its blades edged into the wind. He diddled with some trim wheels and sat there, holding the wheel, boring along with only one engine going.

"Open cowl flaps, and set selector to engine number 2," McDowell mouthed the commands to reflect the checklist training. "Pull the CO2 handle."

The CO2 bottle, a last resort for extinguishing an engine fire would dose the engine nacelle with the inert gas, the goal to starve the fire of oxygen. "Pulled sir." After a minute passed, he craned his neck out the side window. "I can't see any flames."

"Roger," McDowell replied with a voice as calm as if talking over dinner. "Listen crew, we've had an engine fire. We shut it down and are flying on one engine. We can make it back on single power, but I'm not sure I can trust it. The Mitchell is a tough bird, but if it was an oil fire, it can still flare up and, if we have damage to the controls, we may have to abandon ship. So, for contingency, all crew prepare for possible bail out, get your 'chutes cinched up tight. And grab an emergency kit and your canteen."

When Kempinski heard 'bail out' he subconsciously fingered the rosary beads he kept in his pants pocket.

"Ah, sir," Schwagger chimed in. "We are way off the planned course."

"Shoot, that's right. Give Kempinski a position and bearing. Then call it in. If they ask about our location, say we diverted to fly around some weather."

Ritter, scanning the various cockpit gauges, suggested they gain altitude as they lost a bit during the engine shut down. McDowell nosed up the aircraft and applied a bit of power, adjusting the trim dials.

"Go to one-engine checklist. Double check emergency

gear."

While the pilot and copilot were busy with the one-engine procedures, Kelly left his tail gunner position and neared Kempinski, sitting on the jump seat for the side gunner.

"What do you think, Bobby?" Kelly said off the crew intercom with an ashen face beset by an expression Kempinski had never seen on his happy go lucky friend.

"I'm not too keen on bailing out," he replied flatly, but inside he was quivering. Nothing but a piece of silk cloth above him was not how he envisioned taking on the Jerrys.

"Me neither, but I think our odds would be better joining the Caterpillar Club than a crash landing."

"We'll see. Turn around and let me check your 'chute."

Kelly did so, "Looks good."

"Let me check yours, Bobby."

Schwagger's voice came over the intercom with the current location. With the information, Kempinski tapped out a Morse code aircraft distress call on the control tower liaison frequency trying to pace the dits and dahs accurately despite his nerves. He also sent a message with their position. The tower responded with an acknowledgement and request for more status.

"Sir, HQ wants to know more information on our status."

"Tell them engine 2 oil fire, likely supercharger failure. Plane is flyable, no structural damage noted but engine still smoking."

Kempinski keyed the message at 25 words per minute, as fast as he could. Listening with his brow tensed in concentration, he jotted down the reply, then relayed. "Sir, tower acknowledges and recommends diversion to alternate field. No other planes in the area for support."

'Yeah, no kidding' thought Kempinski as their pilots probably weren't buzzing their girlfriend's house.

"Another message, Captain. Tower says if smoke doesn't abate, recommend abandoning ship."

There was a pause and Kempinski could sense McDowell's consideration.

McDowell replied, "Schwagger, where's the nearest airfield?"

"Not much out here. Since we are north of our course, let's see." The navigator paused as he scanned his map. "The nearest is Thermal AF, but it's way north, even on our current course. By the way, sir, it was turned over to the Navy a couple of months ago."

"A Navy landing strip is still a strip. Bobby, do you have their radio frequencies?"

"Negative sir," chipped in Kempinski. "We were only issued Army fields."

"Then Schwagger, what's the next nearest airfield?"

"That would be Welton Auxiliary Field, just northwest of YAF. About 95 miles away. It would save about five minutes of flying versus going to YAF."

"That's a good field; they have firefighting equipment. Give me a bearing to Welton."

"Roger, sir, errr, let's see, head 105 degrees about 95 miles."

"Making 105 degrees."

As McDowell banked the plane, Ritter called out "Engine 1 temperature rising."

"Is it overheating?" McDowell's voice remained calm.

"Hard to say sir. Probably."

"Radio, call in our position. Crew prepare for bail out."

Kempinski hastily did a radio locate trying hard to concentrate on getting the position keyed accurately. If they bailed out in the middle of the desert, the last known coordinates would be critical for a timely rescue. While he calculated the ship's position, Kelly pulled the two pins on the aft emergency hatch. The tail gunner stood examining the tan desert floor slide by underneath. Just then the plane shuddered. Kempinski wasn't sure if it was turbulence or another engine failure.

"Crew bail out." McDowell's voice sounded firm.

Kempinski raised his gaze off the message key to see Kelly's eyes wide with uncertainty.

"Go," Kempinski mouthed as he finished transmitting the bail out status to tower.

Kelly pinched his nose and fell through the hatch.

"Kelly out," reported Kempinski nearly yelling into the headset while his heart raced in his mouth; the idea of jumping quickened his pulse and raised his blood pressure.

"Schwagger out," Ritter added, "I'm out."

"Kempinski, status."

"Sent position." Then as he raised off his seat he paused. "Er sir, what are you going to do?"

"I'm going to try to fly this baby home. It's a risk, but the test equipment is too valuable."

"Then I'm staying with you."

"Roger, then send a status report and get the location of the crew to the tower for rescue."

Kempinski did as ordered, telling the tower on the liaison set the area the crew bailed out. The tower replied they would start a search mission.

"Bobby, grab a flare gun and get up here. I need help flying this beast."

Kempinski stood, and shook his head in disbelief as he knew nothing about flying the Mitchell. He set the radio selector to command net which would allow voice communication with the tower when in range, then grabbed the flare gun. To get to the cockpit, he would have to crawl through a D-shaped tunnel between the bomb-bay and the top of the aircraft. While slim, Kempinski could not fit into the narrow passageway wearing the parachute, so he released the harness and held the folded up silk canopy in his hand. The idea of bailing out might have terrorized him, but taking off his insurance policy had an equally debilitating effect. He pulled himself up and into the corridor then shimmied along the aluminum panel with the flare gun in one hand and his escape harness in the other. Popping out into the navigator's area, Kempinski re-donned the straps and silk, pulling the canvas a little extra tight.

"What do you want me to do sir?"

"Sit in Ritter's seat and watch the temperature gauge on the right-hand side of the yoke. Tell me when it goes into the red."

"Roger." Getting up into the copilot's position seemed almost impossible to the radio operator. The cabin roof was low and the seats close together, which meant he had to walk on the row of knobs and levers that covered the space on the floor between the seats. He did it as gingerly as possible and plopped into the canvas covered chair. For a moment, he was taken aback by the view in front of him; the dials, switches, levers and gauges were much different and more complicated than the Kaydet he flew back at Gulfport airfield, but then the reason he was on the flight deck hit home.

"Now, here, take the wheel, and push hard on the left rudder, I need to give my leg a break and check the fuel in the tanks at the engineer's stations." Kempinski took the wheel, and a slight out-of-trim condition caused the nose to drop. McDowell told him to pull the nose up. Kempinski heard and pulled with his right arm while the other rested on the throttle controls.

"Pull hard," McDowell suggested. With only one arm, Kempinski could hardly pull the wheel back. He released the throttles and grabbed the wheel firmly with both hands, and slowly the nose rose. McDowell turned the trim wheel.

"Wow, these controls are heavy!"

"We have it trimmed out. Don't make any turns, and I'll be back in a minute."

As McDowell climbed out of his seat, Kempinski felt his heart in his mouth. He couldn't tell if he was shaking or if it was the control's feedback. He concluded his nerves were misfiring, but the control pressure was so stiff his quivering did not affect the flight, and he certainly wasn't going to make any turns, at least not intentionally.

In a minute, McDowell was back. "I rebalanced the fuel tanks since we're only burning one engine. Should be good until we get back. How's the oil temperature?"

"High but pretty steady, sir."

"Alright, let's find Welton field."

Kempinski followed McDowell's directions as they flew across the barren desert and soon they lined up on Welton. As they approached the field, the command net was in range and McDowell received verbal confirmation the tower had cleared the runway for their emergency approach. When directed, Kempinski fired the flare gun outside the sliding copilot's window toward the runway. The floating flash would normally signal wounded airman, but in this case, they just needed to get the ground's attention, and having an ambulance ready wasn't a bad idea.

McDowell asked Kempinski to hold deployment of the landing gear. "The airplane will stall with only one engine and the gear hanging out, so pull the switch exactly when I say."

As McDowell brought the plane down, Kempinski could hear him grunt and strain against the controls. "Geeze this is a monster," he said "the slower we go, the sink rate increases and the controls seem to lose some of their effectiveness. This thing is pulling my arms off."

Helpless, Kempinski just watched the ground appear closer and closer. The Mitchell flared and McDowell called for gear down. Kempinski pulled the lever and the aircraft dropped and bounced on the runway. Once the plane rolled out, McDowell called for flaps up, cowl flaps open, and boost pumps off. Kempinski scanned the instrument panel, but had no idea what to switch, so McDowell reached over and followed a checklist he had memorized long ago. They coasted to a halt just off the edge of the runway.

"Phew, that was interesting."

"Good job, sir." Kempinski removed his flight cap and wiped his brow.

"You too, Bobby. That took some guts to stay with the plane."

"I don't know, sir, bailing out didn't quite seem right. And speaking of that, I wonder how those guys are doing."

"We called in a good position. They'll be plenty of planes out searching for them."

Somehow Kempinski didn't feel so positive; his friend Kelly and the others could be in real trouble.

"Is there anything we can do to help find them?"

"Nah, we have a load of debriefings to do regarding this mission. The Air Corps knows what to do." McDowell quickly threw a slew of switches, then undid his seatbelt and nearly jumped out of the seat. "And I want to check that engine. That could have been a bad day, but we weren't ready to buy the farm, not this time." Then he disappeared out the front hatch.

Kempinski pondered the comment for a second, then started to climb out of the seat.

McDowell scolded, "Don't dilly dally, Bobby, when a plane has a fire you get out quickly. Even on the ground."

The statement startled Kempinski and he hustled out the opening in the floor.

After securing the payload and ride back to Yuma, they had debriefings and maintenance checks, Kempinski made a beeline for the company headquarters. He paced the floor of the orderly room waiting for news about his fellow crewmates. Finally, Callaway, the corporal on duty, answered the phone. "You found them, oh, two of them. That's good."

"Who?" Bobby mouthed leaning over the desk, the veins in his head emphasizing his intensity. "Who did they find?"

"Schwagger and Ritter, Ritter has a bum leg."

"What about Kelly? Where's he?"

"Nothing yet, but don't worry, Bobby, they'll find him."

"Yeah but it's getting dark." Kempinski visualized the desolation he saw from the air, and the idea of his friend in the desert with no water.

"They said Ritter saw two chutes, so his chute worked, he can't be that far away."

"You know what it's like out there. I wonder if he has his canteen." The last statement came almost as an afterthought, and he retreated to an armchair across the room. As he pondered, he became more and more despondent. The concern for his friend surprised him, and he realized he valued his friendship more than the idea of fighting the war. What was his role in this war anyway, he thought? How can a devout Catholic want to kill Krauts? Sure, it was kill or be killed, but the way the events were turning out, the war would probably wind down before he even saw action. Then the notion of invading Japan crossed his mind and the futility--guys were talking maybe a million casualties to take over the island nation of fight-to-the-death fanatics. As these dark thoughts came and went, he fidgeted in the wooden seat.

The hours crept by with each phone ring jerking Kempinski to attention, then resignation as Callaway would shake his head.

"No news, Bobby, why don't you go to bed?"

"You know I can't sleep, I feel like we should help find him."

Then, near midnight, the phone rang again. Callaway picked it up and announced the unit identification, then he beamed. He covered the mouthpiece half of the u-shaped device with his hand. "They found him Bobby. A ground unit stumbled on to him, but didn't have a radio. He's a little scratched up, but OK."

"Hot dog, that's great." He rose and shook Callaway's hand. "I tell you, now would be a great time to have a beer."

"Yeah, well, I'm on duty."

"And I don't have any beer rations left." Kempinski scratched the side of his head, then ran his hand through his premature receding hairline, which had the effect of clearing his mind of the darkness it had just harbored, "But we'll figure out a way to get some when Kelly gets back."

Kelly and the two officers that bailed out returned after spending a day at the Kingman Air Field infirmary. Other than Ritter's sprained ankle, and some dehydration, they survived their initiation into the Caterpillar Club. For their return, Captain Mc-Dowell managed to find some beer, and, in a slight violation of the

Army's no fraternization rule, shared a drink with the crew outside the orderly room.

"Ah, shoot," slurped Kelly as he chugged his cold brew, "I now have some silk for the future Mrs. Kelly."

"You flat tire, you don't even have a girlfriend," chided Kempinski while smiling and sipping his drink.

"We can fix that," McDowell chimed in, "while they re-place the motor on the plane, the CO has given us a three-day pass. Maybe you can find some women willing to give you handsome aviators a second look."

"No bullshit, sir?" beamed Kelly, a bit emboldened by the beer and his recent harrowing exit from their aircraft. "Well, Bobby, I know where we're going. Carlsbad! To find that topless dame."

The crew all smirked and checked McDowell to see his re-action. The commander winked and raised his beer towards Kelly. "Watch out there, Kelly, she is more than you can handle: worse than flying a smoking, overheating, one-engined Mitchell." The crew burst out laughing, yet Kempinski knew it was black humor and a thought about how the mission could have ended sent a shake through his psyche. A quick hit of a beer hid his inner frown.

As the enlisted men returned to their barracks, Kelly of-fered, "The only way I am going to find the future Mrs. Kelly is if we head to San Diego. You know as well as I do from flying over that desert, there are no dames for miles."

"What'ya mean, we have the WAC barracks on base."

"Come on Bobby, there is so much competition for the two real women over there. We need to find some new targets."

"Two women? Ha, there's a whole company of WACs."

"Depends on your definition."

"Definition of what?

"Women."

"Geeze, Kelly, you are something." Kempinski crossed his arms in front of his body. "Listen, the maintenance chief isn't going to lend us a jeep to go to San Diego."

"No sweat, old buddy, we'll hitchhike." Then Kelly spread out his arms and moved them like a general explaining the grand strategy. "We get lucky and catch a ride, and we can be in San Diego in about three hours."

Chapter 9

Kempinski and Kelly talked Callaway and Jones into accompanying them to San Diego for the weekend. Three of them, like proper military men, laid out a plan. First, they collected other ideas from YAF permanent party that had already made the trip. They figured they would get a room at the USO hotel and then hit some swanky bars and shows. Kelly, however, seemed uninterested in the planning.

"Guys, our best bet is to catch the Army bus to the downtown Yuma train station, there we head west on Depot road." Kempinski extended a piece of onion skin paper he had borrowed from the orderly room. "I made this itinerary for how we can get there and back. I even added some time in case we have trouble catching a lift."

"Hey Bobby, that's no fun," Kelly butted in across the barracks aisle while he lay in his bunk reading Life magazine. "Let's just go."

"Kelly, if we don't have a plan, we won't make it. San Diego is all the way across California."

"I know that, we been flying over it for three months."

"Yeah, but facing backwards must have messed up your concept of distance."

Callaway and Jones laughed at their goofy tail gunner, while Kelly just smiled and turned a bit red.

"Listen, grab your flight bag with what you need for two days and meet me at the PX in 10 minutes."

Kempinski gathered a change of clothes and his shaving kit. He felt for his rosary beads, and decided to leave them in his locker. Won't need them for this type of trip, he thought.

Outside the barracks, he linked up with Kelly. They both wore simple khaki uniforms, GI issued ball caps and loafers.

"Listen Kelly, I'm glad you made it back from the desert."

"You're not kidding, Bobby. As I floated down, I searched the sky for the other parachutes and didn't see any. That was a weird feeling." Kelly shook his head and his eyes offered a distant stare, as if recalling the event. After a second, his expression changed to a smile. "But darn, you made it back with the plane. I made it back, with only a few cacti thorns up my ass, and we're on our way to San Diego."

Kempinski laughed, "Yeah, booze and shebas, you know a cure for anything."

"Indeed, and the way the war is going, it might be the only action we are going to see."

"I know, according to the newsreels, the Krauts are about done. We should be in Berlin soon." Kempinski almost sounded remorseful.

"Those Japs, now that is a different story."

Kempinski bit his lower lip. The specter of a Japanese invasion loomed, and the seriousness of their undertaking had made itself clear. "Well, this weekend we forget all that in an ossification festival."

The four airmen met at the PX and took the government bus to the train station in downtown Yuma, a handful of low framed buildings with the assorted businesses necessary to support a rural farm town.

"Some downtown," Kelly commented. "This can't compare to the Big Apple."

"Yeah, but how do we catch a ride?" offered Kempinski, new to the hitchhiking fraternity.

"It's easy; you hide your bags and stick your thumb out." And sure enough, no sooner had Kelly stuck out his thumb then a black 1938 Chevrolet 4-door sedan pulled over ten yards past them.

Kelly ran to the passenger side where the window was already rolled down. The driver, a middle-aged woman with a curled brunette coif, wearing a light-yellow blouse with padded shoulders and a grey skirt, reached over and said, "You men need a lift?"

"Yes ma'am," Kelly replied in his most sincere voice. "We're bound for San Diego."

"Well, I'm heading west; I can get you to El Centro."

"That's about half way," said Kempinski as he walked up to the car.

"Swell," beamed Kelly."

"Well hop in. I can use the company. I'm visiting my Mom; she's not doing too well."

"Sorry to hear that, Ma'am."

"I'm Gladys," she smiled and waved the troops in.

"Howdy, Gladys, I'm Tommy and this here is Bobby, Cal, and Ed."

The men nodded, then Kempinski reached for the rear door

and piled in behind the driver, then Callaway and Jones followed. Kelly took the front passenger seat.

Gladys put the car in gear and pulled off.

"We are you from, Tommy?"

Well, Bobby and I are New Yorkers. Cal hails from Wisconsin, and Ed, err, where are you from?"

"Atlanta, you oilcan," replied Jones. He and Kelly had a running, friendly redo of the civil war.

"I'm from El Centro, a farm girl, but the Army needed workers in the repair shop in Yuma. So, while my husband's in Europe, I'm working here."

"What's he doing in Europe?" Kempinski asked, wondering if Gladys was telling them she was married, or if she was available. He figured it wouldn't eventually matter to a self-made sheik like Kelly.

"He's in the Third Army, a Captain in Patton's charge."

Kempinski whistled. "We wish him well." After a pause, he said, "We're airmen, out of YAF."

"Oh, I can tell," and she smiled.

After a few minutes, Callaway squirmed between Kempinski and Jones. "Well, since Gladys was so nice, I wonder if you all would be interested in what I have in my pack?"

Kempinski and Kelly turned their heads to the man in the middle.

Callaway bent over and fumbled with the cover of his flight bag. He pulled up a bottle of Old Crow Kentucky Bourbon. "Where'd you get that?" Kempinski exclaimed.

"Oh, I picked it up a few weeks ago, in exchange for a little favor for the supply sergeant."

"Well, that's keen," slobbered Kelly, his mouth already watering for a hit.

"Gladys, do you mind if we pass the bottle to start our weekend?" Callaway held up the bottle so she could see it in the rear-view mirror.

"Why, sure boys, I might even take some myself. It calms my nerves for driving," and she gave a mischievous smile that convinced Kempinski her prior comment was about being alone.

Callaway broke the paper seal and twisted the top off the fifth. He took a quick swig straight from the bottle, then gave it to Kempinski who wiped the top and took a drink. "Woah, some strong stuff."

They each took a turn, and the bottle still had plenty left, so they passed it again. Each time Gladys took her share as the bottle made its rounds.

"Do you guys like to sing?" the driver offered.

"Oh, not me," Kempinski quickly replied. "But Cal's a real darb. He has a great voice."

"Oh, not that great, Bobby."

"Come on Cal, don't be shy. Sing us a tune," chided Gladys.

"Well...OK. This one is for Bobby and Tommy." Callaway took one more swig in an apparent attempt to bolster his nerve and started to sing the Ry Cooder song 'Coming in on a Wing and a Prayer.' He snapped his fingers and started.

"A one and a two and a three, Comin' in on

a wing and a prayer Comin' in on a wing

and a prayer With our one motor gone

We can still carry on

Comin' in on a wing and a prayer"

They all laughed while Callaway sang the popular Air Corps tune. Then Gladys challenged Callaway to sing something not so militaristic.

"Oh…, what do you suggest?"

The rest of the car started offering titles, "How about 'Danny Boy'."

"Nah, something from Glen Miller."

Gladys lifted her eye to the rear-view mirror and said "I like 'Heart of my Heart' by Ben Ryan."

Gladys kept her view in the mirror while Callaway tried to recreate the song in his head.

"Come on, Cal, do you know the words? You can do it," she said encouraging him. Just as she said it, there was a terrible crash, like a bolt of lightning. The Chevy was thrown laterally by an impact to the front driver's side of the car. Gladys' sedan plowed into a farm truck approaching the only intersection for ten miles. Kempinski was thrown forward, then as the car spun and flipped, forced into the shelf fronting the rear window.

Two days later Kempinski awoke in the Kingman Army hospital. He had a tremendous ringing in his ears. "Whe….where am I?" He mouthed, but the words barely came out due to dryness and confusion.

"Oh, you're awake, Robert. That is swell," said a face fuzzy around the edges to Kempinski. "You been out for two days."

"Oooout, I don't…." Kempinski tried to shake his head but it made him dizzy.

"Relax, stay still." The voice soothingly offered. "Here's a cup with some water."

The face seemed to firm up, and while still a bit blurry on the edges, was one of a pretty young lady wearing a white paper nurse hat. She offered Kempinski a ceramic cup to his lips. The water helped relieve his parched lips.

"Thanks," Kempinski said as he lowered his head back onto a pillow, then a sharp pain shot up his back. "Ahhh," he exclaimed as he slightly arched his back.

"I'm afraid you have a broken bone in your spine, Corporal Kempinski."

"Broken bone, what the…?"

"You were in an accident."

"An accident." Then a memory of the car and singing songs popped in his mind.

"Never mind that now. Just stay still. It is the best for your injury."

"What happened?"

"You were hurt." The nurse raised her gaze around the ward at the other patients. "Can you please wait a moment?" She rose and left the room.

Several minutes passed, then the double doors into the room swung open and the nurse returned, followed by an Army Captain dressed in khakis. The officer, holding a bible in his hand approached Kempinski's bed. He gently placed his hand on top of the injured airman's. "Good morning son, glad to see you finally awoke. I'm Father Callahan, the Chaplain."

"Hello Father," responded Kempinski, the words barely coming from his mouth. Then, after a pause, "Am I dying?"

"No son, you should recover just fine."

"What happened Father? How are my buddies?"

"Well, there was a car accident. Your friends, Corporals Bill Callaway and Ed Jones, were hurt, but they have been released from the hospital with some cuts and bruises."

Kempinski, though groggy, processed the information; he seemed to remember the impact and being thrown about the car. Then he realized the Chaplain did not mention Kelly. "What about Kelly, is he okay?"

"Robert, the Lord has a plan we don't always understand."

Upon hearing the priest's answer, Kempinski averted his gaze then shut his eyes.

"Corporal Thomas Kelly is now in the Lord's hands."

Kempinski sucked in a deep breath that caused his back to ache. "Oh no, oh no, not Tommy."

"I'm sorry, my son. I understand you were close."

"No, it can't be."

"It was a viscous impact. The driver, Gladys Smotherton, was also taken back by the Lord."

"Oh no," moaned Kempinski.

The priest took a small vial of oil and with a dab anointed Kempinski's forehead, saying

"Per istam sanctam Unctiónem

et suam piíssimam misericórdiam, ádiuvet te Dóminus

grátia Spíritus Sancti;" The nurse replied, "Amen."

Then the chaplain anointed his hands, saying:

"ut a peccátis liberátum

te salvet atque propítius állevet".

The nurse again uttered, "Amen."

"Now let us offer together the prayer our Lord Jesus taught us:

Our Father who art in heaven,

hallowed be thy name..."

The nurse also recited the Lord's Prayer and, after a second, Kempinski opened his eyes and softly joined in the recitation.

"Give us this day our daily bread

and forgive us our trespasses,

as we forgive those who trespass against us,

and lead us not into temptation,

but deliver us from evil.

Amen."

Epilogue

Kempinski's recovery took six weeks. During his hospitalization, the war in Europe ended and his squadron disbanded with the individuals reassigned to assorted units. His hospital discharge led to a new assignment of convalescent duty at Williams Field in Chandler, Arizona. Limited to office work, he watched and celebrated the Japanese surrender with the other men in his holding unit. Kempinski didn't make any close friends in this post-war period as most soldiers were just passing through as their terms expired. Despite everyone striving to head home, Kempinski was grateful for the medical care the military provided and he felt he needed to do something to absolve the grief of the death of his friend. To this end, he reenlisted on November 1945 with the agreement to spend a year in Germany as part of the occupation army.

The Army authorized six days for him to travel by train virtually across the country to the embarkation port in Charleston, South Carolina. He dutifully accepted his orders from the adjutant's clerk whom he didn't know, as all the members of his unit had been reassigned. He grabbed his aviator pack and in his khakis with canoe cap, started on his journey. The trip to Phoenix station was made quietly in the back of an Army taxi as he reflected on the anonymity that can happen in such a large army, especially in one where you lost your best friend.

The Pullman car of the Southern Pacific's Argonaut leaving Phoenix for New Mexico was crowded with soldiers and family members heading east. Kempinski ignored the mass of travelers and retreated to his thoughts. He rubbed his rosary beads in his pants pocket and stared without looking out the window. He lost his chance for action, but that strangely didn't bother him. Peace was better than war. He was pleased to be assigned to the 8th Air Force. The auto accident that claimed his friend still lingered and he hoped the change in scenery would help him refocus on his duty.

As the miles passed underneath the steel road wheels, Kempinski thoughts converged like train tracks in the distance; the regimen and discipline of the military was good for him. Yes, he had a few disappointments and some tragedy, but for the most part he toed the line. The few times he got into trouble, it was usually just a manifestation of Hall's storm and stress, after all they were just teenagers placed into a man's role and thrust into a variety of difficult situations. Still, he did well. Maybe the Air Corps could be a career.

These thoughts faded like the smoky exhaust of the locomotive as it wended its circuitous route through a variety of western towns and stations. His train frequently had to pull over on a siding while other higher priority freight missions with important military cargo, mostly cattle, passed. One stop after another, transfer after transfer, then again; the country certainly hadn't gotten smaller, yet he was glad to be near terra firma, as his enjoyment of being a passenger in an aircraft had passed.

By day three, he had had many sitting hours to ponder the accident that cost him his friend and a bad back, on flying in Air Corps planes, on the global war, and the changes it wrought, and finally on his upcoming assignment in Europe. What would Germany be like after such a massive conflict? What would he do in the Occupation Army? What would he do for a profession? As the Pullman neared the Crescent City, he had somewhat formulated a plan: he'd give a military career a go, but perhaps try for another job, maybe air traffic control.

The train crossed the mighty Mississippi River and soon slowed to a stop. The conductor announced they'd continue in three hours after the locomotive received a service and new crew. Even though it was November, the steamy air of New Orleans at first seemed like a wonderful break from arid Arizona, but hanging out at the train depot, he soon felt warm and thirsty. Spying a few airmen heading away toward a trolley, he shouted, "Hey fellas, where are you going?"

"Bourbon Street, that's where the action is."

"Can I tag along? I could use a drink."

"Sure," it's just a short hop this way."

Leaving the trolley, the ad hoc crew boisterously rambled down Canal Street and took a turn on Bourbon Street. They grabbed a beer from the first bar they found, finished it and then moved further east on the street. As they pondered whether to enter a new establishment, two bouncers threw a drunk soldier out the doors of a saloon right in front of Kempinski. The New Yorker did a double take.

"Varchek, is that you?"

The soldier stood up and dusted off his trousers.

"Yeah, who wants to know?" Then he made eye contact.

"Dommie, it's me, Bob, from the East Side!"

Varchek adjusted his hat, set his jaw, and through alcohol glazed eyes said, "Well if it ain't Bobby Kempinski, a corporal even."

Kempinski noticed Varchek was still a private.

"Yes, it's me. I'm passing through on my way to Charleston for overseas deployment."

"Holy cow, if I wasn't drunk I'd say this wasn't possible, but you know booze makes anything happen."

"What are you doing in New Orleans?"

"Hah, you mean 'Nawhlens.' I'm almost a local now. I work at the Michoud Tank Assembly factory in East New Orleans, the Army couldn't pass up on my mechanical ability."

"You've been here since New York?"

"Oh, no." Varchek laughed then his face turned cold. "I spent time slogging through Italy until I got this." He pulled up his pants leg revealing a viscous scar across a now deformed knee and calf. "It hurts like hell, a piece of an 88 is still in there."

"Geeze. Makes my broken back appear lame."

"How'd you break your back?"

Kempinski was going to say something, then said, "Nothing like yours. Let's go have a beer."

"We can't go in there. The owner is still sore at me for my last visit." He placed his arm around Kempinski and half-dragged and half-stumbled with him to the next bar down the street.

One shot, then another followed by a beer chaser, the two New Yorkers celebrated their chance encounter in grand style taking on a two-day bender with the airman missing the train and staying in Varchek's apartment in a drunken stupor. It seemed they tried to wash away their experiences more than celebrate the future. In one drunken moment Varchek admitted his drinking was the reason he was still a private. He kept missing formations and reporting late. The impact of that was lost in Kempinski's alcohol-induced haze. When Kempinski finally came to, he convinced Varchek he had to head east.

Varchek accompanied him to the train station. "Well, Bob, it's been fun, really good to see you."

"Yeah, we made it to here. Can't say that for everyone in the neighborhood."

Varchek shook his head. "I know. Anyway, I have one more month in the Army, then I'm heading back to the City. When I get home, I'm going to open a service station on Staten Island. It's something a gimp can do. I'll live in my Aunt's house. She passed away last year."

"Sorry to hear that, Dommie."

"Hey, what can you do? I just can't wait for the Army to let us go."

"Ah," Kempinski paused, wondering if he should say anything. "I don't know, I just re-upped."

"Are you kidding?"

"Nah, the Army Air Corp suits me."

"Well, from my knot hole, the Army sucked and I got a leg to prove it."

"I know."

They made the rest of the trip to the station in silence. As Kempinski boarded the train he told his hometown friend. "See you in Manhattan."

The mechanic waited at the train station, then as the loco-motive started to pull away, he yelled to Kempinski seated at the window. "Hey how is the Model A doing? You still owe me $10 bucks."

Kempinski threw his hands out to his side and then to his ear like he couldn't hear, and soon the station was a memory.

Due to the unplanned activity in New Orleans, Kempinski arrived two days past his report date. The replacement depot commander had a strict view of the Army regulations and cut no slack. Via a commander's Article 15 proceeding, the captain busted Kempinski to Private and put him on a troopship to the old country.

With the threat of U-Boat attacks gone, the grey vessels sailed in a straight line to Bremerhaven, a six-day trip of rolling waves, seasickness and lousy food.

His first German assignment was as B-25 radio operator on the Squadron commander's plane. The General took a liking to Kempinski, and not wanting a Private on his personal crew, gave him a field promotion back to Corporal. Part of this might have been to help keep his mouth shut as the B-25 made regular milk runs between Germany and Italy, dropping off mail and bringing home contraband such as liquor, nylon stockings and cigarettes for the General and his girlfriends.

In the Occupation Army, Kempinski took on other assign-ments such as air traffic control and VD patrol, a routine job of rounding up German women desperate for money, and having the medics check them for venereal disease. It was a much different role than what he had joined the Air Corps to do, but the remnants of war in Germany made him grateful the events passed as they did, even if it had cost him a friend. But he also realized, by wit-nessing firsthand the destruction wrought on Germany and seeing the reclamation of US soldiers' remains, that Kelly was only one of many lost due to the war.

As the VE Day approached its one-year anniversary, the mindset among the airmen surrounding Kempinski changed; they now all focused on going stateside. The troops in Germany were worried good civilian jobs were all taken by the soldiers already on the home front. Despite reenlisting a few months earlier, he decided he too needed to go back to New York, and so he counted the time until his commitment ended. On November 11, 1946, he returned to the United States. After a two-month terminal leave, the US Army granted him an honorable discharge as a Corporal.

Kempinski's brother, Teddy, and his friend, Frank Gustav, survived many merchant marine trips across the Atlantic. Gustav reunited with Kempinski in New York where they remained life-long friends.

Private Robert Kempinski after basic training.

Robert Kempinski (left) and Tom Kelly in the desert of Yuma Flexible Gunnery School.

Robert Kempinski (front) and buddies pose after swimming in an irrigation ditch.

Robert Kempinski learning to play golf in the occupation Army in Germany.

Robert Kempinski (left) with three other crew members in front of their B-25J bomber in Yuma AAF, 1945. Note the different uniforms and parachute harnesses.

Yuma Flexible Gunnery School incident where a trainee shot the target tow plane. The B-17 "Misfit" (right) survived the Japanese attack on Pearl Harbor and 1,300 combat hours in the South Pacific before being assigned to Yuma. (Artist rendition)

Tom Kelly clowning in front of the WAC headquarters in Yuma.

Robert Kempinski (holding mop) doing typical GI tasks.

Robert Kempinski's crewmates under their B-25J. The streamlined shape is an automatic direction finder antenna.

Robert Kempinski (back) and Frank Gustav (center) after WW II with lady friends.

Julian Maxey (center) in layers of cold weather gear with fellow soldiers near their bunker in Korea, 1953.

Unidentified members of Julian Maxey's squad in front of a bunker in Korea.

Julian Maxey wearing light body armor in Korea.

Rob Kempinski calls in a position on the jeep AM radio in Korea near the Chinese Tunnel, 1983. Note the gas mask and chemical decon kit on the web gear.

44th Engineer Battalion S3 shop. Rob Kempinski with pistol in back. PVT JH Kim on back right. PVT Jang lower left. Note, the 5 ton Tactical Operations Center truck covered in camouflage netting. Kempinski and some other soldiers are wearing the charcoal-lined chemical defense clothing.

Rob Kempinski's men of Second Platoon, 902nd Bridge Company, 11th Engineer Battalion unloading a ribbon bridge segment at Fort AP Hill, Virginia, 1980. Note, operators wearing life vests for over water operations.

Second Platoon, 902nd Bridge Company, 11th Engineer Battalion deploying a ribbon bridge segment at Fort AP Hill, Virginia, 1980. The bridge boat on the left controls the deployment and directs the floating segments. Operators remove helmets when over water. This was the segment from which the platoon initiated Second Lieutenant Rob Kempinski.

Members of the Engineer Center Brigade march in the 1982 George Washington Day Parade in Alexandria, Virginia. Rob Kempinski is second from the right, first row.

On the first weekend off in Korea, Rob Kempinski took a group of soldiers to a Korean national park in the mountains. He's wearing a hat with Broken Heart Battalion' symbol.

While working on a project inside the DMZ, Rob Kempinski took this photo of the "Bridge of No Return" into North Korea.

Rob Kempinski in summer class A uniform at the Seoul House in Korea in front of bonsai trees.

A Direct Order

2 Kilometers from the 38th Parallel, Korea 1952

Mine fields are the most indiscriminate weapon – once placed, anyone or anything that steps into it is about to have a bad day. During the last year of the Korean conflict, with the battle bogged down into virtually trench warfare, minefields sprouted everywhere. That was what Private Y. H. Kim appeared to have discovered.

"Don't move, Kim," Corporal Julian Maxey commanded. "Stay still."

Kim stared back at his squad leader, his pathetic expression revealing he did not understand.

"Don't move! Mines." Maxey shouted again, motioning with his hands to stay put.

Kim's face contorted into a fear-based half-grimace half-scowl. "*Ai guh*, mines, where?"

"All around you, in the frozen mud." Maxey adjusted his steel helmet pondering how he was going to get the hapless soldier from the rancid mine-filled mud, fetid mud that oozes in the daytime around boots and then as the boots retract, sucks on legs straining knees until one can barely walk; mud that freezes each night forming hidden ruts, treacherous and hard, but not hard enough to protect from a mine blast. Viscous mud that can hide a mine and can swallow a blown off foot. Putrid mud for burrowing under to live, to hide from death. Mud in uniforms, mud in teeth and mud in every pore. Mud surrounding the hapless Kim and a score or more of mines. "Don't move, Y.H."

The halt in the platoon ignited Lieutenant Cooke, the platoon leader, and he worked his way forward to Alpha team, "What's the holdup, Corporal? We have a time table."

Maxey pointed with his gloved hand to his left. "Over there, Private Kim found a minefield."

"How did he get off the trail?" Cooke shouted.

"It's dark, Sir. Who knows, Kim is always fouling up."

"Well, get him out of there now and get this patrol moving." Cooke turned and headed back to the patrol's main body.

"Yes, Sir." Maxey motioned for Staff Sergeant Ho to come over. Ho and Kim were Korean citizens assigned to the US Army. KATUSA, they were called, Korean Augmentation to the US Army. While Kim spoke some English, Maxey told Ho, "I'm not sure that jack soldier Kim understands, so tell him in Korean not to move. Tell him we are going to clear a path for him back to this position."

While Ho relayed the instructions to Kim, Maxey signaled to Private First-Class Maxwell, his friend and fellow draftee who attended the same Advanced Individual Training in Kentucky. Having similar last names meant they were assigned in the same alphabetic group as replacement troops to the 223rd Infantry Regiment, 40th Infantry Division, California National Guard.

"Hey, Maxwell, get over here."

Maxwell squatted over to Maxey. "What's up Jigger?" using Maxey's nickname.

Maxey took off his helmet, then load bearing harness and rut sack. He removed his bayonet from the end of his M-1 Carbine and gave the rifle to Maxwell.

"I have to clear a path back for Kim. Hold my stuff and keep the squad here."

"But, Jigger, the LT says to move out."

"I can't risk Kim hitting a mine. It'll only take a few minutes to clear a path. Have the rest of the squad pull security."

"You're going to clear the path for Kim." Maxwell said it like it wasn't worth it.

"Yeah, Kim is no soldier. Deer have better sense than him. He doesn't have a chance."

Maxey high crawled over the frozen mud to a broken barbed wire strand indicating the border of the mine field. Then creeping on his stomach and using his bayonet, he probed the icy soil inch by inch, feeling for anything hard under the crust. Faint moon light illuminated his way but his eyes had adjusted to the night and he could see the knife penetrate the hard soil. Sweat beaded on his temples despite the cold night temperature as he worked his way to the stranded soldier. As he moved he marked the path by disturbing the soil. When he finally reached Kim, 15 minutes had passed.

Maxey stood up and grabbed Kim by the shoulders. "Alright Kim, follow me and stay directly behind me. Go slow and stay right behind me. Got it?"

Kim shook his head up and down with vigor.

When they got back to the waiting squad, next to Maxwell was Lieutenant Cooke with a horrible glare on his face.
"What the hell is the holdup, Maxey?"

"We had to clear a path."

"Damn it, Maxey, next time just let him step on a mine. It would serve the dumb shit right." Cooke motioned to the main body of the patrol and shouted over his shoulder. "Let's move out."

Maxwell curled his eyebrows as he handed Maxey his weapon.

Maxey shrugged on his load bearing harness and rucksack, replaced his bayonet, then motioned with his hand for the squad to move out.

The squad started again snaking its way up the steep mountain terrain into the night, another numbing patrol in a conflict soon to end.

Three hours later

The patrol neared its objective rally point and the first squad started to assume assault positions. The mission tonight was to engage and destroy an enemy position suspected of lobbing mortar rounds into the US lines. Corporal Maxey was crawling into position when an artillery-fired flare ignited overhead, lighting up the narrow valley the patrol had entered. In the flicking flare light, Maxey could see a line of movement about 100 yards to his front. He whispered back to the next man in line, Maxwell. "Movement to the front, a lot of movement. I can see a platoon-sized patrol."

Maxwell's voiced tinged with energy. "I see it."

"Get the squad's machine gun in position," Maxey directed. Just as he did, Maxey could hear Lieutenant Cooke order fire. Several rifles and machine guns opened fire from the main body of the patrol.

"They're too far in the draw to see the all the movement," Maxwell shouted to Maxwell. "We need to get our machine gun in position."

Maxwell pointed. "The machine gun team is behind that rock there."

"Never mind, open fire."

Maxwell laying prone started to fire across the valley. The movement of the approaching Chinese patrol intensified; shapes started to run towards Maxey's position.

"There's hundreds of them," Maxey said as he aimed his rifle and took a well-aimed shot. "The rest of the platoon is too deep in the draw to see all the charging Chinese. Keep firing." Maxey's squad lay down a base of fire and took down several of the enemy soldiers, but the shapes continued to advance on the patrol.

After another minute of the firefight, Maxey scooted back to the machine gunner. "What's the problem? We need more fire power."

"The gun is jammed. Some brass has fouled the ejector," said the gunner as he fumbled with the receiver cover.

"Get it fixed right now and engage to the front. The Chinese are charging and getting close." Maxey high crawled back to his firing position as the flare light faded away. Just as he arrived at his position, he could see a Chinese soldier jump into his squad's neighboring position.

"Chinese inside our position," he yelled back to Maxwell. Maxey grabbed a grenade off his load bearing harness, pulled the pin and lobbed it just in front of his squad's position. The explosion brought a flash and a sharp scream. Next, a Chinese soldier appeared directly in front of Maxey. The soldier raised his arms holding a thick stick with two hands, screamed some sort of war chant and charged. Maxey raised to one knee and screamed back, then raised his M1 with bayonet and buried it right into the Chinese soldier's chest. He fired a round whose impact blew the soldier back off his bayonet.

Maxey rose and moved to his left and saw another Chinese soldier approach Maxwell's position. "Maxwell, watch out!" Maxey raised his rifle and shot. The round hit the enemy in the head, throwing him violently to the side.

As Maxey took a prone position, the squad's machine gunner dove next to him. "I got it cleared. Where are they, Maxey?"

"Right down the ridge. Let them have it."

The Browning M1919A6 machine gun spurted into life – laying a withering arrow of fire marked as a red line by a tracer every five rounds.

"Good work, keep it up," encouraged Maxey over the roar of the machine gun.

As the machine gun fired to the right, another Chinese soldier appeared to Maxey's left. The soldier was screaming and running. Maxey leveled his rifle and tracked him, and took him down with one shot.

By now, the main body of the US patrol had reached Maxey's position. The combined fire of the whole patrol put out a powerful wall of lead stopping the initial Chinese assault. Another flare went off and Maxey could see the remaining Chinese soldiers falling back. Many of the rear Chinese soldiers had no weapon - only the soldiers leading the charge were armed.

"They're pulling back. Take well aimed-shots only," he ordered.

One by one the weapons stopped firing.

"Hold your position," Maxey said as he went from squad position to squad position. The soldiers of his squad remained alert. Some were reloading their weapons and Maxey was pleased to see they had no casualties. Then he moved up the draw to the patrol main body. Lieutenant Cooke was talking on a radio as Maxey found him.

"Status report?" asked the Lieutenant.

"All accounted for. We managed to hold off their first charge."

"Move it out. Headquarters says to pull back. They are going to shell the other side of the valley."

Maxey rubbed his forehead. "That will be close. We better get out of here."

"Tout suite," replied Cooke.

Maxey ran back to his squad position. "Everyone up, pull back. The Lieutenant called in an artillery strike on the other side of the valley."

The squad members passed the word, then picked up their gear and moved rearward. As they did, the first barrage of 105 mm artillery rounds flew over their heads and impacted the hillside with a tremendous roar about 200 yards away.

"That's too close. Move out, move out. To the rear everyone, now."

"What's the LT trying to do kill us, too?" moaned Maxwell. "We had them beat back. He didn't need to call a strike on our own position."

"Just keep moving and shut your trap." Maxey pushed Maxwell. "The sooner we get back the better."

Near the Slate River, Buckingham County, Virginia

I'm sitting next to a Hickory tree with my son-in-law, watching the Saw Pile. My family and I have been hunting these lands for so long all the areas have nicknames: The Saw Pile, Old Man Marshall's, the Horseshoe, Wilson's. Hunting is my favorite past time and a good reason to get away from the demands of the farm. Today my son-in-law has joined me. He's a former army officer, a New Yorker, but not much of a hunter. He likes to go with me with his camera to take pictures, except for today. I talked him into taking one of my shotguns. Maybe he will get his first deer. It's cold and the trees have lost their leaves, making the overcast day reminiscent of a day on ridge 612 in Chorwon Valley Korea.

Looking straight ahead, I tell my son-in-law. "In Korea during the war, we had KATUSA. There was one Private Kim, heck they were all named Kim; anyway, he annoyed the new Lieutenant. I don't know why. In combat, it's easy to get mad. This

LT, he was new to our unit. He was a reserve officer from California. We had lots of new officers showing up in the battalion as
the rumor was the war was going to end soon. They seemed to be
coming over in droves, notching combat time to enhance their files,
couldn't be any other reason. I mean, who would want to be where
we were? They came over because they thought the war was going
to end."

My back itches, so I adjust my position against the back of
tree and scan the field for any sign of a deer. In the distance, I can
hear the dogs barking. I love the sound of the dogs; the best part of
hunting. I turn to my son in law. I never told anyone about this, but
he spent a year in Korea with the Army; years after the war, yet
still he might understand. I continue.

"I was the squad leader and we were getting ready for our
evening patrol. So, this Lieutenant Cooke, called me into his bunker. I gathered my rifle and helmet and left our bunker, telling the
guys to make sure they clean their weapons and get enough ammo
for tonight and to fill their canteens."

"Crouching along the trench I'm careful to keep my head
below the revetment—no need to give a Chinese sniper an easy
shot. The LT's bunker was a bit better than ours, but still it was
nothing more than a dug-out room with rough lumber walls
surrounded by sandbags and topped by frozen mud."

"I saluted the LT and reported. The LT's fatigues looked
amazingly clean and he was close shaven. Compared to me, I
hadn't changed clothes in three months and was wearing practically everything I had. It was frigid that winter."

"Lieutenant Cooke told me. 'Corporal, this is an import-ant
mission tonight. We need to learn what the Chinese are doing
beyond the ridge.'"

"This was baloney. It was the same patrol we had done
night after night for the last few weeks. I didn't say anything, and
the LT continued, 'Put Private Kim on point tonight.' He seemed to
pause to see how I would react. I stood still. 'And have him tie

a live grenade to his bayonet and tie it such that the pin is out. If he gets ambushed, the grenade will slide off the bayonet and go off, warning you there is an ambush."

"I wasn't sure I heard him correctly, so I asked. 'Tie a live grenade with the pin out? That doesn't make sense.' Lieutenant Cooke's face turned red, and he glared at me and said, 'That's a direct order!' I didn't know what else to say, so I saluted and said 'Yes sir."

"Walking through the trench back to the squad bunker, I kept trying to understand the LT's intention. Best I could figure it was a real stupid idea, or he was trying to get rid of Private Kim. Back at the bunker, I told Sergeant Ho, our KATUSA translator, Private Kim was to be on point tonight. I didn't tell them about the grenade, yet, as I was trying to think of a safe way to do it."

It sounds like the dogs are turning toward our position, so I stop and listen, scanning the field. I remind my son-in-law not to move, so as not to scare any deer heading our way as they run from the yapping hounds. We wait and listen. After a few minutes, nothing seems to be happening, so I drop the barrel of my shotgun and continue.

"As we assembled on our side of the opening in the perimeter wire, I told Sergeant Ho and Kim to take some parachute cord I had scrounged up and to have Kim tie a live grenade to the bayonet. Ho eyes widened and he tilted his head forward. I said it was the LT's order. He nodded. I think Ho didn't care for Kim either, but I always thought he was a simple kid and who could really tell. I mean, the Koreans seemed so different from us in many ways. It was their country, their war. But they were also like us. They could get blown up just like any American.

It was getting dark by then, so I explained to Ho and Kim how to tie the grenade to the bayonet and Kim didn't seem to understand. Sergeant Ho screamed at him in Korean; I don't know what he said, but whatever it was, Kim wrapped the handle to the grenade and then tied the cord around the bayonet base. Ho then removed the pin. I tested its security, then we formed into teams and started out the wire counting off to the sentries at the opening. The path through the wire rambled back and forth, so there was no straight shot for an infiltrator. To each side were randomly strewn mines and debris from the remains of regular mortar shelling of our position. Kim led Alpha team out the opening and we waited for the signal to follow. Sergeant Ho raised his arm and Bravo team moved out. There wasn't much moonlight and the terrain was steep and rough, broken tree trunks and limbs everywhere. We walked about fifty yards when there was a flash of light and an explosion out front."

I pause and recall the night as if it was yesterday.

"I knew what happened immediately. Kim's grenade went off. He must have tripped and the grenade flopped off the bayonet or the cord got loose, or was cut. I'm not sure—there wasn't much left. He didn't have a chance."

The wind seems to have changed, blowing the sound of the dogs clearly to us. They appear to be heading back in our direction. I ignore them and turn to my son in law.

"The next morning, we waited at a rally point until the sun started to rise. We gave the sentry the password and worked our way through the wire dragging Kim's battered body behind us on a stretcher. At the opening of the trench lines, one of the GIs told me Lieutenant Cooke wanted to see me as soon as I returned. The medics took Kim and I sent the rest of the patrol to the chow line while I went to the HQ bunker. Lieutenant Cooke stood there next to his olive drab field desk. He was clean and well rested and appeared to be working on some paperwork, perhaps an after-action report. He said to me 'So, Corporal Maxey, I heard you took artillery fire as you were leaving the perimeter last night.' He gave me a glare. I gazed at him for a few seconds and then slouched with my palms raised up at my sides. 'Whatever you say, Sir.'

His face lightened a bit, and after a few seconds, he dropped his gaze and signed his after-action report."

We're quiet for a few minutes. My son-in-law doesn't say anything, which is unusual for him as he likes to talk. I guess he gets it. There's still no sign of deer. The dogs seem to have stopped barking and it's getting late so we head back to the pickup truck to call it a day.

US Army Processing Hall, Charlottesville, Virginia 1951

"Next," bellowed a sergeant behind a table to the line of draftees in the converted basketball gymnasium.

Julian Maxey, a slightly built man, whose small size disguised he was several years older than the other draftees, sidled up to the table.

"Name?"

"Julian Maxey."

"DOB?"

"December 10, 1928."

"What can you do in the Army, son?" The NCO scanned Maxey from head to toe, giving him the once over.

"Well, I was hoping for supply or transportation."

"What did you do in civilian life?"

"I'm a farmer…"

The NCO cut him off. "The army doesn't need farmers. We need infantry. Can you handle a rifle?"

"Sure, I've hunted since I was a kid."

"Hmmm, you're a bit small, but you look tough." The NCO shuffled a form and checked a box. "Welcome to the Infantry, Private Maxey." He stretched his hand across the table.

Maxey took the beefy hand and silently shook his head along with it.

The NCO said, "Form up in group A over there and wait for more instructions."

Forty Years Later and a Few Miles Away, Mary Washington Hospital, Charlottesville, Virginia.

My son-in-law visited today. Nice to see him even if he had to drive a few hours. He asks how I feel.

"OK," I say. "I just had some chest pain. Nothing serious."

He nods and sits down next to the hospital bed. The Redskins are on TV, so we both watch some of the game. We talk a bit about Joe Gibbs and how John Riggins seemed unstoppable.

I say, "You know over in Korea, one night my Lieutenant gives me a direct order. That's right, he said a direct order to tie a live hand grenade to Kim's bayonet."

I shrug and let my head fall back into the pillow. I feel sleepy and maybe not sure what day it is. It must be the medicine.

"He says it was a direct order. To tie a grenade with no pin to a bayonet. Heck, I wasn't even sure how to do it. Later, as we leave the wire, the grenade goes off. Kills Kim."

Feeling really sleepy I nod off.

After a while, I wake and my son-in-law is still there quietly watching the football game. He asks me if I want some water.

I shake my head no and say. "One night in Korea, we were going on patrol." My voice is a bit unsteady. "The Lieutenant tells me to have Kim walk point with a live grenade tied to his bayonet. He says 'if the grenade goes off, you"ll know you are being ambushed.'" My son-in-law is biting his lip. He knows. He was in Korea, too. "He said it was a direct order. Then in the morning he

asks me "I heard you took some artillery fire as you left the wire."
I shrugged and replied, "Whatever you say, sir."

USS Telfair - Middle of the Pacific

Corporal Maxey seemed to have gotten over his queasy
stomach after a few days at sea, but the rough weather today was
making him feel ill again. He left the sleep bay – an array of bunks
densely crammed into an airless, windowless cavity in the middle
of the fast attack transport ship. Packed like the chickens Maxey
kept at his farm prior to the surprise arrival of a draft notice, he felt
like he could no longer tolerate the smell and cramped quarters.
Wearing only utility green fatigues, he found respite on the deck
between groups of seasick soldiers hanging their heads over the
railing. Next to him was Private Maxwell, a round-faced kid from
Kentucky, leaning on the railing. Maxey and Maxwell were in the
same training platoon at Fort Campbell.

"I feel like I'm getting poor again," Maxey told Maxwell.

"Me too," replied Maxwell, wiping the spray off his face.

"Too bad, I was on a roll last night; I cleaned out those men
in poker."

Maxwell edged closer to his friend, "Yeah, I think you won
so much because you were the only one not ready to puke from
these blasted waves. I mean, they all turned yellow." He pronounced 'yellow' in a strange way due to his Kentucky accent.

"How do you spell that?" Maxey asked Maxwell.

"Spell what?"

"Yellow."

"Come on, I can spell it."

"Well go ahead," Maxey egged him on, ribbing his friend
made him feel better.

"Y-E-L-L-O-W," Maxwell said with defensively, then

pronounced the word in his deep Kentucky accent, "Yallar."

Maxey laughed. "Well if Y-E-L-L-O-W is pronounced yallar, then spell mellow."

Maxell stood spreading his legs indignantly. "I ain't spelling it. You talk just as funny as I do. Your Virginia accent, if that's what I can call it, sounds just as weird."

Both soldiers laughed, then silently watched the waves passing the ship.

Maxwell turned toward Maxey with a hint of concern on his face. "How are you going to protect those poker winnings? The Sarge seemed pretty upset and I hear he aims to get back his money."

"He won't find me."

"What do you mean?"

"I plan to hide out the rest of the way until we get to Japan."

"Where are you going to hide on this ship?"

"Let's say I found a good spot and I'm not telling anyone." Maxey threw Maxwell a mischievous grin. "Not even you."

Later in the evening at 3rd platoon roll call, Maxey was not present.

"Where is he?" boomed his platoon sergeant, still green around the gills.

Someone piped up, "I saw him by the main deck gunwale this afternoon."

"He didn't fall overboard, did he?"

"Not that I saw, so your money is still dry if that's what you're worried about."

The rest of the platoon laughed.

"Knock it off," bellowed the Sergeant. "Anyone sees Maxey, let me know. Let's hope he hasn't fallen overboard, so I can throw him overboard myself."

Five days later, near the coast of Japan.

Maxwell watched over the ship's railing as Japan appeared closer and closer when Maxey sided up to him rested and relaxed. "Jigger, where have you been?"

"I told you I've been hiding," Maxey replied sheepishly.

"How could you hide on this ship? The Sarge is mad at you."

"Why? Because I won all his money or because he couldn't find me?"

"Both, probably," Maxwell laughed. "Anyway, we got our orders. We are going to be assigned to the 40th Infantry. Your luck is holding out as I hear they are a reserve unit stationed in the rear."

"Maybe so, but I'm not counting on it."

Cattleman's' Association of Virginia Recognition Ceremony

The Maxeys are a modest group. We produce chicken eggs and breed Black Angus cattle, keeping to ourselves and doing what we can to help our community. That's why it was such a surprise to win the Cattleman's Association of the Year award for our work in breeding Black Angus cattle. I mean, we have a good farm, and we work hard moving with the ebb and flow of the economy, but we simply do our work as good citizens. I suppose I should be proud of the award, but still, it doesn't pay any of the bills. My family, all girls and my wife, need providing for and I have done a good job for them over the years.

The Uniform Code of Military Justice

When an enlisted soldier joins the Army, they take an oath to obey the lawful orders of their commissioned officers. Army training instills discipline and strict adherence to obeying orders, yet the adjective, "lawful" orders gives soldiers a theoretical recourse. If a soldier chooses to disobey an order, the Uniform Code of Military Justice, Article 90 applies:

"(2) Disobeying superior commissioned officer.

(a) That the accused received a lawful command from a certain commissioned officer;

(b) That this officer was the superior commissioned officer of the accused;

(c) That the accused then knew that this officer was the accused's superior commissioned officer; and

(d) That the accused willfully disobeyed the lawful command."

In combat, such disobedience could be punished by death. Soldiers that choose to disobey an order take a chance. In court martial proceedings, other military members determine whether an order is legal or not. In the heat and stress of combat, the definition of lawful is not always clear. In Korea, it hardly seemed to exist; but the law and what is right don't always coexist either.

Dillwyn Virginia, Thanksgiving Day 1993

Every night for the past 30 years, I took a bath at 8 pm. Tonight, my wife draws my bath, but I just don't have the energy to get up. My breathing has become labored and difficult. The doctor suspects COPD, but I haven't taken the tests yet. As much as I hate to admit it, years of smoking, working in the dusty fields and the dander-laden chicken house has taken their toll on my lungs. It might even be emphysema. After filling the tub, my wife helps me down the hall and I start my bath. Each night I get in the water, I think back to the trenches in the Chorwon Valley. Four months without a bath – now I will take a bath.

Chorwon Valley, January 1953

Private First Class Maxwell entered the primitive bunker with an armload of torn tree limbs, broken ammo cartons and blasted lumber.

"What are you doing?" Corporal Maxey asked from his sleeping bag on a crude wooden bunk.

"I'm building a fire and going to boil some water, so I can get clean."

Maxey, fully clothed, jumped out of his bag. "Are you nuts? The smoke will draw artillery fire. We'll get blown up."

"I'll take the chance. I can't stand it. I haven't changed my underwear in months. Nor have I cleaned myself. I have never been this filthy."

"You can't build a fire."

"Why not?"

"Because we'll get killed. And dirty is better than dead."

"At least I'll go to my maker clean."

Maxey put his hands on his hips and assumed a defensive pose with his legs. "You're not going to make a fire. We're all filthy. I haven't changed my clothes either."

"I'm doing it."

"You're not. That's an order."

"You can't order me, you and I were drafted together." Maxwell argued but he was losing his enthusiasm.

"I'm a corporal, and you're a PFC." Maxey felt miserable pulling rank on his friend but he didn't seem to understand the risk it would be. "No fire. You take a whore bath with a sponge and cold water."

Maxwell dropped the wood in a heap. "Damn Jigger, the water's frozen. A sponge won't work."

"I know," Maxey put his arm around the taller Maxwell. "The Sarge says we get relief in a week or two. Try to hold out."

Forty-Five Years later, Martha Washington Hospital, Char-lottesville VA, Critical Care Ward.

The nurse tells me the sensor has to stay at oxygen level 3. She says it's an order. Someone enters the room – not sure who it is. I tell them,

"Oxygen 3, the nurse says it has to read Oxygen 3, Oxygen 3, Oxygen 3, Oxygen 3, Oxygen 3, Oxygen 3, Oxygen 3, Oxygen 3, Oxygen 3, Oxygen 3, Oxygen 3, Oxygen 3, Oxygen 3."

I pause "Oxygen 3, Oxygen 3, Oxygen 3, Oxygen 3, Oxygen 3. That's a direct order, that's a direct order, a direct order, order, order, direct order, direct order, Oxygen 3, Oxygen 3, Oxygen 3, Oxygen 3, direct order, direct order." Spittle forms at my lip but I ignore it. "Oxygen 3. That's a direct order, that's a direct order, a direct order, order, order, order, order, order, direct order, direct order, Oxygen 3, Oxygen 3, Oxygen 3, Oxygen 3, Oxygen 3, direct order, Oxygen 3, direct order, Oxygen 3, direct order, Oxygen 3, Oxygen 3, Oxygen 3, Oxygen 3." My voice is fading and I'm struggling to find my breath, but the words continue. "Oxygen

3, Oxygen 3, direct order, direct order," until I can't talk anymore.

Why am I here? What am I doing? ......What have I done?

"It was a direct order."

I wake up. "You know when I was in Korea, there was a patrol. I was given a direct order."

Drink Coffee, Play Golf

Chapter 1 Citizen Plain

"Hey, it's a baby killer."

"Yeah, a fascist," added the female.

The taunt echoed along Georgia Tech's Techwood Drive between the canyon-like grey steel girders of Bobby Dodd stadium and red brick walls of Brown dormitory.

I was on my way to Thursday Reserve Officer Training Corps drill, my first day wearing a US Army class A uniform. Hippies wearing semi-matching tie-dyed shirts and frayed elephant bell bottom blue jeans with greasy long hair approached me. I assumed a poker face, noticing their iconoclastic dress was no less de rigueur for their group than the Army uniform I had donned. US combat in the Vietnam War had ended about a year ago, but mean-spirited radicals still had a grudge. Many of the protesters, while raging against the US government's involvement, found it convenient to direct personal animosity towards individual soldiers, the same soldiers who would fight for their right to protest. I made eye contact as I passed, tightening my face in quiet resolve and pressed on toward calculus class.

Not that the ensemble I was wearing was the most fashionable or comfortable. A green worsted wool suit jacket with a four-button front topped straight legged pants. The upper right sleeve featured an academically inspired circular white patch. Contrasting rather fashionably with the dark green jacket was a tan poplin shirt with slim black tie. I'm glad Alexander Julian hadn't seen that color combo as I'm sure he would have suggested a more flamboyant style. On the positive side, Mr. Julian would have agreed, black goes with anything. The Army decided to change to the green suit in the early fifties because top brass believed the surplus WWII overseas jackets, worn by both veterans and civilians in a host of menial tasks, degraded the service of soldiers still on active duty.

The hat, officially called the overseas cap, but derisively called the canoe cap, or even worse, the cunt cap, wed two pieces of army green worsted wool in a multi-layered rectangular pouch shape with a leather sweat band along the inner edges of the opening. If a head contained a normal amount of gray matter, the hat would be a crude prank--something a bride might make her bride's maids wear if she knew they had slept with her future husband. It wasn't a total sartorial foppery; when indoors it assumed a flat shape that could fit between the belt and pants, thereby keeping it nearby while performing whatever task the leaders had assigned for the day.

Taking the Army Reserve Officer Training Program while attending a civilian university provided students with a means to earn a degree while giving the army access to officer candidates. The deal traded four years of college in exchange for four years of active duty, and four in the Army reserve. The reality of fitting military indoctrination into civilian life, especially one at a university in the post-Vietnam War era, set up a true dichotomy. Becoming a soldier requires assimilation into a culture attuned to devotion to duty, following orders, strict adherence to schedule and rigid attention to uniform dress code, characteristics nearly all undergraduates lack. At boot camp, the Army used the big bang theory and fully immersed enlisted recruits into the process. In the reserve officer program, it was more like Chinese water torture; slowly but steadily the military ethos dripped into cadet's brains among the constant distractions of university life.

I clearly remember how I got into this situation. As a junior at Sayville High School on Long Island, New York, I returned home one evening after class. My father, a veteran of the Army Air Corps in World War II, presented my twin brother and I with a pair of brochures. The papers outlined the details of the Reserve Officer Training Corps, in Army acronymeze, ROTC, quickly pronounced "Rot-C."

The pamphlets showed college scenes with young smiling students and a few cadets engaged in academic activity. A well-done marketing slick, it revealed none of the true military. Dad had already explained the financial reality of a policeman paying for two college students at once and my money saved up from my dairy clerk position at the A&P supermarket wouldn't stretch too far. A full scholarship sounded good, but then the next thing my Dad said sealed the deal.

"This is great. You get out of college, you'll have a job as an officer and all officers do is drink coffee and play golf!"

Dad found my weak spot. Though I loved baseball as a kid, upon meeting a curve ball, my favorite sport became golf. And my baseball swing worked well for the links, especially after a little bit of tweaking offered by a chipper Irish golf pro named Pete McConville. Pete, with a frail frame yet rosy glow to his face like a leprechaun, owned a rustic driving range in Bayport, just off Sunrise Highway. My brother and I spent two summers riding our bikes to work retrieving golf balls. Unlike now, where pickers drive a specialized golf cart with cage and automatic retriever, we gathered the balls by hand. We'd walk out on the field hovering an aluminum tube over the spent golf balls. Flexible steel fingers on the bottom end would trap the target when pushed down over it. Full tubes of golf balls ended up in a wire basket we'd load into a 1962 buckskin-brown Ford Falcon station wagon. Being able to drive a car for two summers before getting a New York State driver's license provided the most excitement working at the range. That the Falcon had a huge home-made wood frame wrapped in chicken wire to protect it from golf balls didn't dampen my teenage enthusiasm for bumping it up and down the range.

While we scoured the range locating and collecting the white orbs in our metal tubes, Pete continued to sell range balls. Most of the patrons took delight in aiming at the pickers and despite their poor individual proficiency, sent enough projectiles down range that occasionally we got hit. For protection, we wore white plastic construction hard hats with a screen over our face and neck but nothing on our bodies. Getting struck by a golf ball does not tickle, but then OSHA wasn't around. One of the other workers, Dennis, a slow fellow with an overly large head, used to brag he had a steel plate in his skull, a remnant of a prior accident and so he didn't need protection. He only lasted one season. I suppose the hard hats foreshadowed the steel helmets the Army required when in the field.

One day, Pete had three of us go into the typical Long Island scrub trees surrounding the range to "clean up the rough." I took a number eight iron into the sandy scruffy area and punched the stray balls back onto the open target area for easy pick up later. Some mean-spirited golfers decided we were good mobile targets and started launching the red and white striped orbs at us out of bounds. After yelling at them to stop it, they laughed and continued to shoot in our direction. One of them managed to hit Dennis, so the driving range maintenance engineers got mad. Instead of chipping the balls into play, we started to hit back towards the evil golfers. With the tables turned, the customers didn't like it one bit and complained to the shop. Pete came running out past the hitting bays. "What are you doing lads? Don't hit at the golfers."

I explained the events to Pete, who upon learning the facts, in no uncertain terms, asked the offenders to leave.

With my weakness for golf, and a personal defacto-Army recruiter for a Dad, we agreed to try for ROTC scholarships. After the application process, the Army scheduled me for a physical exam on Governors Island, a small Coast Guard base in New York Harbor. I took the Long Island Railroad, then subway, then ferry to get to the island. As the boat churned south, the imposing towers of southern Manhattan faded, reinforcing the feeling of leaving comfy civilization and entering "the service."

Service it was. The impersonal exam had a group of us lined up like an assembly line where the medical staff probed most of our orifices and took lots of body fluids. I passed the exam and so did my brother, leading to letters congratulating us on our award of four-year Army ROTC scholarships.

It was never quite clear if Dad was more proud or relieved about the scholarships, yet he did what he could to prepare me for the military. Not everyone felt the same. My high school guidance counselor, James McGarry, a tall man with a flat top haircut, tried hard to convince me not to join ROTC. His residual anti-war feelings led him to say my potential would be wasted in the army and he suggested I stick with New York State schools for affordability. I could sense I needed to go my own way and did not heed his guidance.

The imposing and handsome Army captain that presented the scholarships in front of our high school staff said my brother and I were two of the eleven awarded students on Long Island. Certainly an accomplishment, but it was only the beginning of a long journey starting at Georgia Tech.

Chapter 2 The Graduated

ROTC training required physical fitness and cadets were expected to maintain and improve on their own. I was active in collegiate intramural sports but didn't really enjoy the monotony of jogging; so I didn't focus on the Army's specific needs.

Captain Torino, a West Point infantry officer and Vietnam veteran, ruled over the cadets from his Georgia Tech ROTC cadre position. As one would expect for a combat arms officer, he had a brutish personality and operated on one of the lower levels of Maslow's hierarchy. He finished 501 out of 674 cadets in his graduating class--that explained the infantry branch assignment and immediate orders to Vietnam. Short dark hair, bushy eyebrows below a prominent brow and a New England Italian accent matched his broad shoulders and physically imposing appearance. He routinely badgered us to think like officers, many times in frustration. One afternoon he decided he needed to assess our fitness and scheduled a test for the incoming freshman class.

Being a self-professed 'nerdy jock', I wasn't too worried about the event. The protocol required cadets do as many sit ups as possible in two minutes. Then it was as many pushups in the same time. Next was a timed crab walk, where cadets moved "feet-ward" 25 yards while propped up on feet and hands like a crab, and quickly reversing to return the 25 yards to the start. For some reason, the Army determined this was a maneuver that prepared soldiers for combat. I didn't question Uncle Sam and got down on hands and feet and moved like shellfish. Turns out I must have had some crustacean DNA as it was my best event. Next was the run, dodge and jump, an appropriate test for a soldier as it used a couple of upright obstacles and a ditch to simulate sprinting, jumping and changing directions, something I envisioned we might have to do to evade bullets. Normally after the run, dodge and jump, there would be a horizontal ladder, but we didn't have one at Tech so the test ended with a timed two-mile run.

The ROTC cadre scheduled the physical fitness test on Saturday morning at 0700 hours. This idea had two major problems – morning and Saturday - both terrible concepts to a college student. My alarm clock signaled the arrival of the appointed time. I managed to hit the snooze button twice before the haze of the prior night's beer festival wore off, and I remembered the physical training test. Ugh, I stumbled out of bed and put on my green Army fatigues and combat boots. A glance at my watch revealed I was going to be late, something the green machine highly frowns on; so I raced off to the test without shaving. Let it be known since being a teenager, I had a heavy beard and, on this day, I had not shaved for 48 hours. While not quite a Cro-Magnon, I certainly sported serious chin fuzz in a nice dark color. While many females of the mid-seventies might have found the hirsute face appealing, Captain Torino did not. Being a good officer, he immediately spotted my poor hygiene and got his face close to my face.

"Geez, Kempinski; you didn't get close enough to your razor this morning."

"No sir." was the only acceptable response.

"What did you do, shave with a brick?" He slowly walked around me while I stared straight ahead and tried to justify my unprepared face.

"Sir, I ran out of time and did not want to be late."

"Well you were late cadet. I suggest you better plan your time; your soldiers are not going to accept such a lame excuse.

Now get out there and take the test."

Despite my lack of preparation, the first four events went well. A passing score was in hand and only the two-mile run remained, probably my worst event. We lined up on the starting line of the oval quarter mile track around Grant Field's AstroTurf football field. Lap one went without hitch and I was on pace for decent time. On lap three, my heart rate was increasing, but not too bad. As the third turn approached, there appeared to be a cadet gasping for breath on the sidelines. I didn't recognize him. The peloton of joggers passed by without hesitation. On the next lap, one mile in, Master Sergeant Gromley, one of the ROTC enlisted cadre members, was alongside the cadet who was now lying on the ground. On lap five, Sergeant Gromley was giving the cadet Cardiopulmonary Resuscitation. By lap six, most of us had slowed down but were still running, avoiding an Atlanta Fire Department ambulance on the track. The paramedics took the cadet, while I finished the test. Our scores didn't really mean much that day, as the cadet had expired on the track due to a massive coronary. No Georgia Tech cadets knew him as he was cross-enrolled in ROTC from Southern Tech, but a sad event became the first real clue of the seriousness of Army training, even ROTC.

Chapter 3 Cliffhangers

In weekly drill on Thursday, our instructor, Torino, told us about the Georgia Tech Ranger Club, an extracurricular activity that practices Army Ranger skills. Henry Stubbs, a freshman ROTC scholarship holder from upstate New York and a Techwood dormitory-mate, and myself decided it sounded adventurous and worth investigation. Henry had a sturdy body and curly black hair over a broad head that stretched his wire frame glasses. He and I wore civilian sweatshirts over slacks to the first evening meeting. It turns out this was an organizational session, but no upperclassmen had attended, only a couple of sophomores and freshmen, including one large and well-built Marine candidate named Adar Rabar. His Middle Eastern lineage, closely cropped dark hair and large-grey tinted aviator glasses sent out contrasting vibes: a gung ho marine or hippie with strange taste in haircuts.

We met in the old wood building behind the army detachment's classrooms. The room featured tables and walls painted in off-white paint yellowed with age and wear. The first order of business was to elect leaders for the Ranger Club. No one raised their hand when they asked for volunteers. This lack of enthusiasm launched Torino into a short but powerful speech.

He moved to the front of the classroom. "No matter what you do in life, if you are presented with a leadership opportunity, take it. Leadership moves the country." He glared at us with an intensity that reflected his combat experience in the jungles of Vietnam. "The Army needs you to be leaders."

While it wasn't as rousing as Ronald Reagan's Gipper speech, it transmitted the message. Stubbs and I took team leader roles, even though we'd only been in ROTC for less than a month. The club made ranger training interesting; learning the basics of patrolling, and squad tactics; and a constant emphasis on physical fitness. These Ranger standards motivated me to improve my conditioning, so I took up working out, running and doing sit ups several times a week. I even practiced pull-ups, as the path to Techwood dorm went past the old Navy annex, next to Grant Field, Tech's football stadium. Attached to the building about eight feet off the ground was a horizontal metal pole and each time I passed the annex, I did as many pull-ups as I could. A pull-up quickly builds upper body strength, and my muscles firmed with each day.

When freshman spring break rolled around in March, the Ranger Club offered an opportunity to take a four-day portion of the actual ranger school, the mountain phase, at Camp Merrill in Dahlonega, Georgia. While fellow students were packing sunblock and beer for trips to Florida, I cleaned my olive drab field gear and took a bus to the mountains north of Atlanta. The camp was the first official army base I visited, yet driving past the front gate, it more resembled a state park than the home of some of the military's roughest training. Despite the idyllic scenery, in the dark shadow of the tall pines and oaks lurked an ominous overtone, like a color version of the Blair Witch project.

First order of business, I deployed to my temporary quarters, nothing more than a primitive wood hut with two unprotected openings, one for entering and one for ventilation. I dropped off my packs. Needing to use the facilities after the long bus ride, I found the external latrine to be less basic than a pioneer's outhouse. Pointing to open pipe with an ancient valve I surmised was the shower, I tapped Stubbs on the shoulder. "Hey Henry, it's not too cold today, but can you imagine taking a shower in this hole in January?"

"My balls would shrink right up into me."

"Winter rangers. Tough," I agreed.

Next, we fell out for formation and the cadre wasted no time taking us to the technical skills area of the camp, a clearing next to an eighty-foot granite mountain cliff. As we mingled in an unmilitary fashion in the opening near the rock formation, we were startled by an explosion, followed by white smoke billowing off the top of the precipice. Two fierce camouflaged army rangers pierced the artificial brume running face-down the vertical wall shouting and firing M-16 machine guns. That someone could run down the face of the sheer slope was impressive, yet at the same time firing a machine gun astonished me. When they reached the bottom, they shrieked "hooah" and sprinted into the woods. A ranger lieutenant announced over a simple public-address system, "Welcome to Camp Merrill where we make the toughest fighters in the world. Here you will be learning mountaineering skills. Platoon leaders, split your cadets into groups."

Sixteen cadets broke into four groups with Stubbs, Rabar, Guy Clark and myself together. The instructors, all wearing starched green fatigues tailored to their athletic shapes and custom shaped patrol caps unique to the rangers, exuded confidence and professionalism. They showed us how to slide down a wall, by tying a basic rappel seat using a piece of rope and a snap link. We wrapped the climbing cord, a specialized mountaineering blend in camouflage colors, through the metal link and around our bodies. Using a leather glove, we held the line behind our back and walked backwards down the vertical surface. The gloves helped dissipate the friction of the rope sliding through our grip. We started on a twenty-foot-tall wooden wall and as the day progressed we moved to the cliff. Yet just as we climbed up a trail alongside the rock face to rappel down the eighty-foot drop, heavy rain busted loose turning the precipice into a small waterfall. Training didn't stop.

Moving backwards over the edge wasn't too hard for the seated rappel. I found it interesting and simple. With the rope wrapped through a carabineer and around my back, I secured it with my gloved right hand. My legs agile and perpendicular to the face, I lightened the grip and slid down the slope. In a few seconds, I gained speed and a flash of self-preservation told me to squeeze the line which slowed me down, but also swung me toward the face. I timed the swing and absorbed the impact with my legs then pushed off the rock and simultaneously loosened my hold on the rope. After a big bound, sixty feet off the ground, I thought I was hot stuff. A couple more repetitions and I found myself next to the safety cadet at the bottom. Luckily, I didn't need his help; so I quickly ran to the end and disengaged the snap link and headed to the waiting area. I watched as my classmates worked their way down the stone wall, all faring well.

Next came the Australian rappel. This was the technique the two Rangers had used earlier where they ran face first down the cliff. The advantage of the Australian rappel was it freed up an arm to do something important, like shoot a machine gun, if one ever had to descend a mountain in a firefight. The psychological difference between edging off a precipice facing upwards in the seated rappel and facing earthward and running down the vertical wall can fry synapses. The instructors explained, "Hold the rope in your gloved right hand as it runs through the snap link. If you need to slow down you extend your arm like the statue of liberty holding her torch. This adds friction as it passes through the link."

That was easy for him to say; he wasn't looking eighty feet straight down. Every fiber of my body was saying don't run down a cliff and yet with the first step it was move or die. So, I ran down the rock face barely using the cord sliding through my hand to slow down. I reached the bottom and ran off the edge of the line feeling exhilarated and pleased I didn't soil myself.

The Ranger cadre wasn't done. After a C-Ration lunch, the weather broke, and the instructors gathered us at the base. "Rangers never leave a fellow soldier behind. Now you'll learn the buddy-evacuation rappel. Here, a healthy soldier rappels with a wounded soldier secured to his back."

Clark was my partner and he weighed about twenty pounds less than me, so we decided to have him simulate being the wounded soldier tied to my back. The cadre showed us how to tie a bowline knot around his chest and to set up a double belay system. Using two ropes, one below belaying me and one up top for the wounded man, I did a seated rappel down the cliff with Clark strapped to me. I took more steps and shorter bounds than when doing the individual rappel, as Clark's weight added quite a bit of inertia. Yet, I made it to the base without killing myself or my buddy. After the four teams finished, the cadre directed, "alright switch around."

At the top, the instructors again checked our knots and setup with me dangling off Clark's back. With two steps down the cliff, his legs buckled and we twisted ninety degrees to the cliff, with his legs now parallel to the face instead of perpendicular. The belay man tugged hard and the bowline cinched up my chest.

"Oofff, err, Clark," I forcibly exhaled my confidence in him waning fast, "you gotta do some-thing."

I pushed off the rock with my right hand and Clark temporarily found his footing. But every ten feet or so his legs would quiver, and I'd slam against the wall, forcing the belay man to pull. We eventually reached the bottom with the bowline digging deep around my chest. I had a bruise and some soreness, but our teamwork paid off and we accomplished the exercise.

With barely time to recover, the instructors moved to the next task, the stretcher rappel. Clark, being the smallest guy, was strapped into a canvas and wood stretcher simulating a wounded teammate. Following the instructors lead, we tied the knots and set up the lines to lower him down the precipice. He kept his eyes shut the whole way but made it in one piece.

Chapter 4 Yawn Patrol

Finished with the mountaineering, we met our patrol instructor, Staff Sergeant Cunningham, a Brooklyn native sporting large biceps and broad chest with a thin waist creating a pronounced V-shape. He wore a starched green ranger cap with the top and bill custom-curved, so he truly looked more professional than our mass-issue cadet equipment. However, the most unique aspect of Sergeant Cunningham was his ability to insert the word "fuck" as often possible in a sentence. For example, "Take fuck your fucking ammo fucking out of the fucking case, fuck!" Sometimes he only used "fuck" in a sentence. For example, he once said, "Fuck the fucking fuckers." I never heard that word used as much as I did while at Camp Merrill, much to the detriment of my personal vocabulary.

For the next three days, Cunningham would accompany us non-stop teaching the main Ranger mission, patrolling. We started with basic techniques, such as how to organize a patrol into fire teams, how to write a five-paragraph field order, all the way through crossing a danger zone, such as a road or open field, to fire support. As evening broke, we didn't stop training. We used what the cadre called "Admin conditions" to practice patrolling through the night. When morning arose, we were given two hours to clean up, eat breakfast at the chow hall and return to the patrol base. Thinking ahead, I loaded my web gear and pockets with some snacks, such as raisins and candy bars then grabbed a thirty-minute nap.

The training of the prior night was done in haste to prepare us for the remaining two days, where we were to conduct a reconnaissance patrol in the north Georgia mountains. I was assigned as the bravo team leader, with Rabar as my M-60 machine gunner. As team leader, I had a small portable radio attached to my helmet that enabled me to talk with the patrol leader and the alpha team leader.

The mountain phase of regular Ranger school takes place after the trainees have had three solid weeks of fitness and patrolling practice at Fort Benning, Georgia. By the time the Ranger trainees arrive at Dahlonega, they are lean and mean. Suffice it to say, injecting college students into the Mountain Phase proves fraternity parties and chugging beer does not make lean and mean. The next forty-eight hours of climbing up and down north Georgia mountains would prove a strong test. It started with Cunningham lining up our squad and ordering. "You fucking cadets fucking jump fucking up and fucking down." We did so and all the raisins and candy bars in our ammo packs and pockets made a racket. "Empty those fucking pockets, no fucking pogey bait."

Reluctantly, I did as commanded and a quite a pile of junk food developed at my feet. Little did I know how much I would want that pogey bait in twenty-four hours, as the Ranger cadre saw fit to not issue any C-rations to the patrol.

The patrol rehearsed our mission until the afternoon, then around 1 PM, we left the camp. We were all hungry and tired and the patrol hadn't started. The first mile, the patrol climbed a stout North Georgia mountain. At our initial rally point we had our first heat casualty; the cadet carrying a box of extra ammo for the M-60 machine gun collapsed. The patrol leader decided to divvy his equipment and I received a bandolier string of 100 rounds of 7.62 mm ammunition. The only way to carry them was to drape them over my neck Poncho Villa style. The round edges of the brass cartridges dug into my exposed skin and despite constant adjustment, there was no comfortable way to lug them. We continued our march over the mountain. Within hour three, Rabar overheated. While he was our largest guy, the 23-pound bipod-mounted-hunk of machine gun wore him out. To keep him in the patrol, we rotated lugging 'The Pig' among cadets.

We pushed on until dark, steadily climbing. At dark, the patrol leader lost confidence in his route and the team leaders huddled
for a land navigation discussion. Somehow, we overshot our path
and now he decided to cut across a stern mountain slope. While
the steepness did not seem too severe on the map, the contour lines
did not give any indication of the deadfall, tree trunks and branches
strewn across the acute face. If I could only see Cun-ningham's
expression in the dark, I'm sure he would have had a demonic grin
as knowing the terrain like the back of his hand, he realized what
kind of ordeal lay in store. All he offered was, "It's a fucking
technique ranger."

Ordeal it was. Each step in the dark encountered a downed
trunk, or a rough rock, or a vertical drop. Normal vision was barely
enough to see two feet ahead. To keep from falling down the slope,
we practically had to grope over the terrain. Focusing on the ranger
tabs (luminous strips sewn to the back of our caps on the guy in
front was the only way to stay together; yet for each step lay a
trap of a jagged rock, or a fallen log or a branch to snap back into
my face. After a couple of hours of the exhausting work, fatigue
and hunger took its toll. We lost three more cadets to heat exhaustion despite the temperature being in the low 50s. We divided the
downed men's equipment among the remaining patrol members. At
one point I had the M-60, my M-16, the squad radio, the bandolier
of ammo, and an extra battery for the PRC-77 patrol radio along
with my rucksack, probably 100 pounds of gear.

To complicate matters, a storm appeared to be brewing,
but in the darkness and clinging to a steep slope, we really had no
idea of its severity. After a long tribulation, the terrain became a bit
smoother and we made it to our objective rally point. The patrol
was now down to about sixty percent strength. Rabar and I set up
the M-60 in an overwatch position while the patrol leader did a
leader's recon. He came back and informed us we were about one
hundred meters to the objective which was beyond a sharp ridge.
We deployed as stealthily as we could. Again, Rabar and I took
a tactical position on a small rock projection where our machine

gun field of fire would rake the target area, if needed. In the dark, we could see a faint light, probably the enemy smoking cigarettes. With the remains of Bravo team providing cover, Alpha team crept near the objective.

A recon patrol's main mission is to observe, and not necessarily to engage the target. The enemy, though, knowing the terrain and probably our mission, had prepared. Tripwires and booby traps surrounded their area. To Alpha team's chagrin, someone's leg or arm movement set off a trap and an artillery simulator lit up the area with a blinding flash and explosion. The bright light took out our night vision, but nonetheless Rabar and I let loose with the M-60 firing blank rounds towards the objective. He pulled the trigger and I fed the ammo belts. Even though it was only training, the Bravo team's machine guns and M-16s made quite a racket. In the dark with flashes of the weapons, the inability to see what we were shooting, and shouting in all directions, the training realistically simulated the fog of war.

When the shooting stopped, the squad radio squawked with the patrol leader's code word to fall back to our last rally point. I ordered the remains of Bravo team to exfiltrate the area and meet at our last rally point. The team grabbed its gear and on adrenaline hustled over the rough terrain to the designated clearing. After about an hour, when all were accounted for, Cunningham took the patrol to "admin" status and debriefed us on our results. Sparing all the f-words for this retelling, the patrol was a partial success, as we learned enough information about the enemy position for the reconnaissance, but detection by the enemy meant we failed the patrol. About the only thing he praised was the fire support Bravo team put out. Then he passed on the really bad news: camp HQ had radioed a major storm was getting ready to break and we were to take the most expeditious route back to camp.

The weather forecast came true. Within twenty minutes the wind picked up and hard rain fell at nearly thirty-degree inclination. It was now close to four AM and fatigue and lack of food took its toll on me. Each tree lying to my left or right took the form of a person – some sort of hallucination - and each step I took became more difficult. Struggling down the steep hill, I would take a step and drop to a knee. Being stubborn though, I'd get up, fight the sleepiness, take another step and fall again. The lack of sleep or hunger, plus the weight of the other cadet's gear pulled me down. This kept up until daybreak, where my stumbling became clear to the cadre. Each time I fell, I forced myself to go on, until we hit a muddy road, the first level terrain we had seen since the patrol started. With the rain pouring down, I still had trouble on the sticky clay trail, stumbling, with my mind falling in and out of a con-scious state. As the patrol struggled across the road, Cunningham ordered, "Admin! Fucking patrol fucking finished." A slight feeling of relief crossed my mind, but I still fell to my knees with my next step. The ribald sergeant came up to me, helped me up and said, "Fucking medevac," and pointed to a Commercial Utility Cargo Vehicle or CUCV, commonly known as a sport utility vehicle. Two Army medics grabbed me while the rest of my team collected my gear, including my M-16.

I don't recall the ride to the base, but after an examination by the camp doctor and a warm shower, they let me sleep for two hours on a stretcher. The simple prescription worked, and I rejoined the cadets and helped them finish cleaning weapons and gear. As we departed the camp, Cunningham said to me, "Good effort ranger" without using his favorite mot.

The sentence barely registered in my mind as I boarded the bus for the return to campus. I didn't last more than two minutes before launching into a sound sleep for the ride back to Tech, missing the remainder of the storm. Speaking of the storm, it turned out to be one of the worst in years and spawned a tornado that destroyed part of the Georgia governor's mansion. It also might have destroyed my motivation to continue Ranger training. Upon reflection, it became clear the main mission of Ranger training was to make a soldier as miserable as possible while learning the finer points of how to kill and, frankly, that did not sit well with my career expectations. My Catholic upbringing, especially the seventh commandant, gave me some serious misgivings.

Chapter 5 If It's Tuesday It Must be Bedlam

Cadets on scholarships had to fully commit to joining the army by the end of their sophomore year. Even if one had two years under scholarship, the army allowed reluctant soldiers to quit with no repercussions. Stubbs confided in me he decided to leave during his freshman year, but tolerated the sophomore year of training just so he'd have one extra year of free school. The army is not for everyone; in fact, I wasn't certain the army was for me, but I found it disingenuous he made up his mind to quit yet still used the scholarship. After Tech, he went on to be a lawyer!

The idea of leaving ROTC crossed my mind but the reality of paying out of state tuition with my meager bank account meant I'd continue to serve the country.

Army ROTC required summer advanced camp between a cadet's junior and senior year. I would spend five weeks in July and August of 1977 at Fort Bragg, North Carolina, the training center for all east coast college cadets. Advanced camp was the equivalent of basic training for enlisted personnel but not quite as demeaning, if one doesn't consider eight toilets in one room, four on each wall facing each other with no dividers, and a shower made of nothing more than a concrete room with four basic nozzle heads debasing. We used to joke we could play poker while taking care of nature's business. One nice aspect of summer training was my twin brother, Bern, and I would be in camp together and, while the Army had assigned us to the same battalion, we were in different companies.

The first day of camp, we met our bunkmates. The cadre briefed us that our bunkmate was to become our most important soldier and we were to look out and care for each other.

"Hey, I'm Jay Koch," he said from a round face surrounded by short dark fuzz. A buzz cut in the 1970's era of the hippies offered a clue as to his gung-ho inclinations.

I extended my hand. "Howdy, I'm Rob Kempinski from

Georgia Tech."

"Oh, you an engineer?"

"Will be, a mechanical engineer."

"I'm a business major at Indiana University in Pennsylvania."

"Indiana University in Pennsylvania?" I asked a bit befuddled.

"Yeah a state school in the town of Indiana, in Pennsylvania."

"Is that right," I blurted, "you learn something every day as I had never heard of a state university named for a different state."

"I'll take the top bunk even though my knee is a bit sore."

"What's wrong with your knee?"

"Oh, I went to jump school last summer, but I didn't get my jump wings. During tower week, my parachute collapsed, and I fell about 75 feet. Tore the ligaments in my right knee. I had a cast for two months and barely passed the physical to come to camp."

"That's a bummer. I'm going to jump school after camp this summer."

"Wow, I wish I could join you. Maybe next year."

We made up our bunks and Koch showed me a few tricks about setting up our wall locker. Then the cadre gave us a quick briefing and marched us to the mess hall for dinner. My bunkie related he did not have a ROTC scholarship but rather wanted to join the army just to be in the army, which countered my motivation.

The second day of camp was branch orientation day. The host units, the 18th Airborne Corps, and the 82nd Airborne Division had spread out on an old aircraft runway, now a large open field, an impressive array of the types of equipment associated with each Army branch. The infantry had their rifles, machine guns, and mortars; the artillery had towed and self-propelled howitzers; armor had Sheridan tanks; the Corps of Engineers had the Engineer Combat Vehicle, a modified M-60 tank with a 155-smooth bore demolition cannon, bulldozer blade, and crane boom; and lots of other olive drab equipment from the other branches. The plan for the day was to rotate the cadets to each branch display while active duty members would explain the roles and responsibilities of officers in that branch. We marched as a company to each display and in round robin format, visited each branch.

Fort Bragg resides on the sand hills of the North Carolina piedmont. The ancient dunes drain well and retain heat which leads to tremendously hot summer afternoons, with many days over 100 degrees. The sandy soil meant the old airfield surface needed reinforcement to handle the point load of aircraft wheels. Years ago, engineers had laid perforated-steel plate on the field and now grass and weeds had grown through the holes of the panels. Why introduce these two facts? Well, they have a big role in the events that happen next.

The sky was clear with only a hint of clouds. Since it was only the second day of camp, and a weekend, we had not yet been issued any field or foul weather gear. We all wore only our olive drab fatigue uniform each cadet brought to camp. My company had just finished attending the armor branch and had rotated to the signal corps branch display.

The signal corps display entailed communications, and so had a wide assortment of tall radio antennas sticking proudly into the sky and electronic equipment scattered around an elevated wooden platform. A wiry lieutenant from the 82nd Airborne Division, wearing his snappy red beret emblazoned with jump wings, stood on the wood deck talking to us through an electronic megaphone. Suddenly there was a large explosion, or perhaps concussion better described the violent sensation. Every one of us in the company found ourselves flat on the ground. To this day, I can't really explain the phenomena other than it was quick. I struggled to my feet and a few fellow soldiers were moaning. The signal corps lieutenant was face down on the ground with his left arm bent at an unnatural angle. The blast had knocked him off the elevated podium and dislocated his elbow. I was to learn later that summer while receiving training on how to do a parachute landing fall, that if you don't tuck in your elbows when you fall on your side, the joint will pop like a balloon when it impacts the ground. The poor lieutenant, not expecting the blast, obviously did not get a chance to execute a parachute landing fall, despite being a member of the US Army's elite airborne division.

My brother relayed later he was sitting crossed legged about 200 yards away at the chaplain branch display listening to the role chaplains have in keeping morale high while serving the religious needs of soldiers violating the 7th commandment. Suddenly, his left leg stuck straight out as if it had a mind of its own. Then the concussion hit.

The company cadre quickly sized up the cadets and ordered us to double time to the tree line about 500 yards away. The idea was the trees would offer protection from the rain pouring on us. As we ran through the petrichor, we realized we were struck by a "bolt from the blue," a cloud-to-ground lightning flash which typically comes out of the back side of a thunderstorm cloud. It had to have traveled a relatively large distance in clear air, and then angled down and stuck the area near the signal corps display. These lightning flashes have been documented to travel more than 25 miles. The real danger is they appear in clear blue sky. My theory is the perforated-steel plate on the ground served two functions for the bolt. It provided a large attractor for the static charge causing it to travel the long distance; however, its mass probably saved us, as the broad metal array helped dissipate the electric energy over a large area. The proof being the blast zone was much larger than a normal lightning strike extending across an area covering several branch displays, from the signal corps to the chaplain corps displays, or at least 200 yards.

Rumors swirled about a death by electrocution but were never confirmed. My company officer, Captain Blake, a 40ish year old reserve officer, had two varicose veins in his legs. The electric surge caused them to burst leaving him with two large hematomas that took most of the summer to heal.

The rest of us in the company escaped unscathed; although, some people suspect the energy level I exhibited throughout my life was due to the overcharge I received that day from the bolt from the blue.

Running into the woods offered some protection and, despite the injuries, morale was high. Once the storm ended, the branch display concept had been ruined. We marched in a soggy formation back to our home for the summer, white-washed wooden barracks built during World War II using theater of operations contingency standards. Those norms meant these barracks were designed to last only five years or so for the big war. Yet there they were, thirty-two years later, still standing.

There was a rectangular grid of at least a hundred identical buildings laid out like the matrix of New York city streets, only more orderly. These clonal structures housed the complete cadet regiment for the five-week period. Once the ROTC summer camp finished, these buildings would be vacant like a ghost town waiting for an occasional reserve army unit to visit.

Each rectangular barrack had a simple door that opened to a large room with about twenty bunk beds fronted by grey lockers and a stairway to a second floor. The crude structure featured exposed, white-painted beams and single pane windows--no climate control, no insulation, no decoration of any kind.

At one end were two small rooms: a bedroom for Sergeant Greer, our active duty platoon sergeant, and the other for storage. The other end of the building held a room that crossed the width of the floor. It contained the latrine, nothing more than an array of white porcelain sinks with old mirrors on one end, and the eight industrial toilets previously mentioned against the walls on the other. A shower room between the toilets and open bunk room had a concrete floor and four shower heads, the lack of privacy intentional, perhaps as means to build unit cohesion. Getting 40 people to shit, shower and shave in the morning within twenty minutes did take some cooperation and knowing our neighbors probably more intimately than we wanted.

It might be worth noting my platoon contained several female cadets. However, unlike Robert Heinlein's *Starship Troopers*, the army did not integrate the female and male cadets into one barracks. The ladies had separate barracks shared among women from several companies. It was the first of many concessions the army would make as it tried to figure out how to fold women into the ranks.

Chapter 6 Sergeant Milko

The day after the lightning strike, Monday, we were sent to central supply, a huge wooden warehouse with two by four racks loaded with all sorts of army gear, including thousands of trousers and shirts, where logisticians used a mere five minutes to issue us a set of uniforms and field gear. This might be why, to this day, I can go clothes shopping with one surgical strike into a department store instead of lingering like my spouse, Terry, who prefers to thoroughly check every aisle and rack searching for a deal.

Amazingly, my field gear fit rather well, with the exception of the M1 steel helmet. The M1 was two "one-size-fits-all" helmets, an outer metal shell, sometimes called the "steel pot", and a hard hat–type fiberglass liner nestled inside the shell contained the suspension system that could be adjusted to fit the wearer's head. Helmet covers and netting would be applied by covering the steel shell with the extra material tucked inside the opening and secured by inserting the liner. At 2.8 pounds, it really fit no one's head, at least not comfortably. Wearing it would build up neck muscles I never knew I had.

We also received TA-50 load bearing gear featuring a canvas web belt with strategically placed grommets for hanging assorted items such as ammo pouches, canteens, ruck packs, and a compass case. The TA-50 also had two straps that acted like suspenders helping to distribute the load of the field gear over the shoulders. We all hung a small first aid kit off the shoulder strap.

After dropping off our new gear in our lockers, we were bused to Womack Army Medical Hospital. The Army proceeded to conduct physical exams for over 2,000 cadets in a four-hour period. An orderly told us to strip down to our undershorts. We then formed in lines at various medical stations where they took blood and temperature, and conducted a variety of other medical tests, such as having us contort our bodies doing strange stretching calisthenics designed to reveal old skeletal injuries. There is nothing like bending over to touch your toes next to forty other guys wearing only "tighty-whities".

We also experienced the Army version of psychological speed dating. They had each of us sit with a psychiatrist in a small cubicle for about two minutes while the shrink evaluated our mental fitness for holding loaded weapons next to each other. I passed the evaluation, although it was nothing to be proud of; Charles Manson could have been accepted.

Next, they lined us up for inoculations. While the cadre at Georgia Tech was organized and had us receive all required shots four months prior to camp, such a small detail would not derail the mass physical exam process. Some schools did not prepare their cadets in a similar manner, so regardless of one's medical history, everyone received all the shots. The male medical specialist used a pneumatic gun to administer the injections, a first for me. The atomized jet left a little cut across my arm where the pressure pushed the inoculation into my flesh. My arm hurt for one week, especially from the tetanus shot. With all the virus antibodies I had in me, I had the potential to be a walking biological weapon.

After the physicals, Captain Blake summoned the company to the orderly room for a pep talk.

"You all should have been briefed on this at your colleges but let me repeat again how the US Army is going to evaluate you for this advanced camp," he boomed in a strong command voice.

Captain Blake, a big man, about 6 feet 2 inches with broad shoulders and large head, dark hair and tanned skin like he just spent two weeks on spring break, a prototypical tank officer. His armor branch insignia on his uniform color stood out like a beacon to me because, as a self-professed motorhead and budding mechanical engineer, the idea of a mechanized tank would be a cool way to spend my army time; but, I wondered though how such a big man could fit into a tank hatch.

"Advanced Camp will be competitive. I and Sergeant Greer will evaluate each one of you on all aspects of your training. Your scores will be a combination of the leadership skills you demonstrate when running the company or platoon, the daily skill tests including MILSTAKEs, sort of like your final exam, your physical fitness tests, and a peer rating where each of you will rank each other."

Blake continued, "Each day, we will assign a set of cadets to serve as the cadet company commander, platoon leaders and squad leaders. The positions will rotate and all of you will be given the chance to lead in each position. Your leadership skills will be assessed and how well you follow orders will also contribute to your leadership score. Remember, cooperate and graduate is the key."

The last admonition was a refrain that would reappear throughout my army career.

"Alright cadets, dismissed for chow. Wake up is at Oh-dark thirty tomorrow."

"Oh-dark thirty," I chuckled to myself. It'd become one of my favorite expressions. The army, however, meant it. As I would learn, I'd spend a lot of time doing stuff in the dark, at all hours of the night, and a lot before oh dark thirty.

The platoon broke for chow; mystery meat, corn and mashed potatoes, a mess hall staple. I meandered back to the barracks, where Koch and a few other platoon members gathered around the outside steps trying to escape the heat of the un-air-conditioned building.

"I've always wanted to be an army officer," Koch offered, "My Dad was a lifer and we moved from base to base. The army is in my blood. What about you, Rob?"

"Ha, the Army's best recruiter was my Dad, a B-25 crew member in World War II. He told me and my twin brother, 'All officers do is drink coffee and play golf.' So, we signed up. Funny thing is, I don't drink coffee."

Koch and the rest of the platoon laughed.

"Our cadre at IUP told us the scores we get at camp will determine if we get our branch and choice assignments."

I pondered that, as I hadn't thought much about future assignment. The mass induction made one feel like part of a much larger entity. And with a lightning strike, and the physicals and Koch's knee injury, it caused one to consider the seriousness and potential danger of what we were doing. I didn't really want to be here, but since I was, I figured I'd give it my best shot to see how well I could do and what I could learn.

The charge of quarters called lights out and we entered the faded frame door. Our boots shuffled across the worn wood floor planks to our bunks. I managed to fall asleep, but in two hours a cadet tapped my shoulder and said my turn for fire watch. Rolling out of bed, I took position next to the storage room and kept a sleepy eye out for a fire in the tinder dry old wood buildings. No flames appeared, so with nothing else to do in the middle of the night in a room of sleeping cadets, I reviewed the day's events. An army career was not the path I envisioned, but the scoring system Captain Blake mentioned, and the pace of activity offered a challenge, and one thing I do like is a challenge. Army life so far was pretty much a pain. Between fire watch, latrine duty, and a host of other make-work tasks, the Army found ways to fill our days, but I decided a sanguine approach would be best for the next five weeks at Fort Bragg, and three weeks for jump school at Fort Benning. An hour passed and I managed to keep the barracks safe from immolation, so I woke the next cadet in turn for fire watch, then returned to my sack. Despite it being 1 AM, the heat was still stifling, so I drifted off to sleep on top of my white sheets thinking about how to prepare for the upcoming activity while listening to nineteen other guys snore, fart and dream of the days to come.

Chapter 7 Cattle Drives

After morning chow, consisting of eggs and sausage and orange juice served army style on a fiberglass tray, we assembled outside the orderly room for morning formation. Captain Blake announced Charlie Company's first field session was to learn the basics of infantry patrolling. The ROTC Command set up an intense program where all 2,000 cadets would rotate through the same set of classes on a round robin schedule over five weeks. To support the training, the active duty resources of Fort Bragg and some reserve units from North and South Carolina set up training stations at many of the ranges over the 19 square miles of the Fort Bragg sand hills. Each day, a fleet of grey cattle cars appeared at the company formations. Each platoon would squeeze into a trailer and we would stand while an enlisted driver took us to our appointed training site. True to form the first day, we boarded the ubiquitous grey cattle car and moo-ed our way to some remote range.

The bovine transport deposited us at a series of bleachers with a small podium in front. An infantry officer of the 82nd Airborne Division stood at the podium prepared to teach us the basics of squad formation, overwatch and other Army patrol techniques. As we departed the livestock hauler, Captain Blake announced that to get motivated, the company was to make as much noise as possible. The company making the most noise of the three companies at the training range would be first at the battalion mess hall tonight. The guys and gals around me started to hoot and holler as we filled the bleachers. The racket Charlie company made was loud, but it wasn't organized and it sounded like the other companies were louder. My competitive juices surged and a brainwave hit me. I jumped two rows down in front of the company and turned to my fellow cadets. Like a cheerleader I whooped. "Let's make some noise."

The cadets responded with a coordinated yell.

Thinking what to do next, I channeled my college football game-day skills, where myself and Chip Morris, a Chi Psi fraternity brother, would lead our fraternity through some raucous cheers, although this time I was completely sober.

"Who are we?" I screamed.

"Charlie" they retorted, with good volume.

"Louder," I shouted. "Who are WE?"

"CHARLIE," this time the retort was strong, so much so the other two companies started to watch us, losing some of their vigor. The expression on the faces of my fellow cadets was one I will never forget: it leached a mob mentality mixed with a willingness to be led. Quite a reflection on human nature, I might add.

Then in a mix of creativity, and probably a bit of irreverence as I usually have a hard time taking many things too seriously, even army training, I launched into a typical college cheer, except modified for Charlie company.

"Give me a C." I tilting my body and using my arms to resemble the letter C to my side.

"C," they responded.

"Give me an H." I threw my feet wide apart and my arms in the air simulating the letter H, like a referee signaling touch-down.

"H," they blasted back.

With my palms touching over my head and my feet spread like Big Bird on Sesame street, I followed with, "Give me an A."

Now the other companies had gone silent.

"A," Charlie roared.

The intensity of the reply just egged me on. Then thinking quickly what comes after A, or yeah, R, I stood straight on one leg and threw the other out while making my right arm like the top of a capital R. I must have channeled a pregnant flamingo on one leg in the marsh. "Give me an R."

"R," screeched the platoon. It was working.

"Give me an L." I stood with one leg sticking straight out.

"Lllll." The mob stretched it out for effect.

Then for "I," I had another flash of inspiration. Stuffing my feet together I grabbed my M1 helmet with two hands, one each side, and lifted it above my head, like the dot of a little i. "Give me an I."

"I," echoed across the range tinged with a bit of laughter, with some even coming from the other two companies, who were now watching.

For the pièce de résistance I needed to quickly figure out how to make an "E". Bending over, I stuck my right arm out parallel to the ground, raised my right leg parallel to my arm, and then put my other arm underneath the leg to make the three horizontal pieces of a capital E. "Give me an E."

When the company replied, the response was the loudest, "EEEE!"

"What's that spell?" I asked jumping up and down like a dervish in front of our stands.

"Charlie." They were at least that smart.

"What's that spell?"

"Charlie."

"What's that spell?" I figured I'd ask them a third time for good measure.

They didn't forget. "Charlie!"

Then I pumped my hands up and down hollering, "Charl-leee, Charl-leee, Char-leee." I returned to my place in the stands.

My platoon gathered round me yelling, "Char-lee, Char-lee" for a minute or so until the infantry captain blew a whistle.

"All right, great spirit Charlie company, you eat first."

"Wahoo," the company roared and the guys near me slapped me on the back. Then we turned our attention to how to be an infantry soldier.

Chapter 8 The Good Book

The work of an infantry soldier would appear simple— sneak up and shoot the enemy. But the reality is more complex. Infantry tactics reflect the oldest method of warfare and span all eras, but have had to change to match the technologies available. In ancient days, warriors lined up and closed next to each other to hack each other to death. During the Napoleonic era, single shot rifles meant soldiers formed orderly lines and marched en-masse within range to shoot their enemy. As weapon technology rapidly evolved over the duet of world wars, the tactics morphed. By 1977 Fort Bragg, like the rest of the army, still reeled over the Vietnam War, a guerrilla conflict with no defined front and unclear enemies. The tactics the captain briefed reflected the basic patrol techniques done by either a squad, platoon or larger unit honed in the jungles of southeast Asia.

A large plywood table fronted the bleachers and contained a model of the terrain facing us: well-practiced topography to the 82nd Airborne training cadre who knew every hill, tree, and bush on this piece. It was as close to a text book situation the army could devise and each platoon in summer camp would try their hand at it over the course of the summer.

The Captain explained several of the key topics, such as use of terrain, overwatch, sun position and a variety of other considerations. Well trained troops could do quite a bit of damage with such knowledge, but I guess that was the idea. The company split into platoons and then squads, the basic infantry unit. Appointed cadet squad leaders assumed their leader roles and developed a patrol plan.

We set out in patrol order watching our patrol leader's hand signals while simultaneously keeping watch for the enemy off to the sides. As we did our maneuvering, our company cadre and 82nd Airborne division trainers observed. At the end, they'd give a critique of how we moved and what we did well and not so well. As an example, when approaching a "danger zone," Army doctrine preached sending a soldier out on the flanks taking defensive positions and covering the edge of the area while the rest of the patrol crossed individually when the way was clear. The first time we did this, we failed miserably - it was only a narrow jeep trail but our security was pointing the wrong way and not far enough out; soldiers crossed too soon and we made too much noise. After a few drills, though, our platoon got the hang of it and we would negotiate a danger zone crossing like seasoned pros.

Two days after our initial lesson, we did another patrol exercise and this time the patrol leader assigned me as the point. The point of an infantry patrol has one of the most important and dangerous jobs and requires some good navigational and observation skills, and confidence. After all, the point leads the patrol wherever it goes, whether to the objective or into an ambush. And as explained by the grisly Vietnam-veteran instructors, the point man had a much shorter life expectancy than the rest of the patrol.

For today's mission, the operations order called for a point reconnaissance, meaning we were to go investigate a certain location, record what we saw regarding enemy activity, and return without engaging the enemy, unless the enemy fired on us, or we were ambushed.

"Hey Rob, you're point," Cadet Kane directed in his southern drawl. "We gots to go about 1 click, to the northeast. Jay has security so you and me will take a leaders' recon."

"Got it," I said, examining the green and black camouflage paint on his skin. "Let's see the map."

Kane spread out the map and pointed to the objective.

"Hmm that's further than a click. What are the coordinates?"

He rattled off the eight-digit number and I could see he had made a mistake.

"Hey, try this." I put the projector on the map and indicated the objective, a trail crossing near Normandy drop zone. "Something was weird about those numbers," I said using the phrase as a face-saving move for Kane,

"Oh yeah, I see that. Thanks."

I pointed to a small knoll on the map about ⅔ of the way to the objective. "We should try to work our way up that hill; we might get a view of the objective if the brush isn't too bad."

"Good idea." Kane turned to Koch. "You got the patrol security back here while Kempinski and I do a leaders' recon."

Koch nodded, his face a serious mask altered by dark green and black cammo paint I had applied on him and that he scrapped on me, the mutual duties of a bunk mate. He made a hand signal around his head for the patrol to assume a defensive posture.

Kane and I moved out, and even though we were only in training, it was a bit unnerving as we knew the 82nd Airborne had aggressors deployed to ambush or worse, capture cadet patrols. The enlisted GIs were known to have their fun with captured cadets, or as they viewed them, future officers. Plus, detainment would mean we flunked the patrol, which would hurt our evaluations. We stepped deliberately and kept a sharp eye, moving from tree to tree for cover and concealment. When we arrived at the hilltop, we could only get a partial view of the approach to the objective. Kane asked, "What do you think, Rob?"

"I think we've seen enough. We can parallel the path we took to this hill, then set up security and approach the objective."

"Yeah, cool, see what's we gots to see, then skedaddle."

I studied him for a second then pointed further north. "Yeah, but we go out that way. Remember, the Sarge said 'Never go out the way you went in.' We make a rally point there, near that big tree, link with security, and head back across the other side of the field from where the main body is now."

"Man, you think good, bro. Let's do it."

"Roger."

We returned to the main body and already we were sweating like pigs in the Carolina heat. I drank some water while Kane worked on his hasty patrol order. He briefed the platoon and we set out. I led about 50 yards in front of the patrol following an azimuth Kane had given me. As we walked, I would regularly stop and raise my fist into the air. The soldiers would stop, and we'd listen and look around. Then I'd look back to Kane and he would give me a new azimuth. It was smooth sailing as the leader's recon gave me a pretty good idea where to go. As we approached the final rally point, I scanned the ground and saw an unusual bright orange mushroom shaped like a golf ball in the pine needle ground cover. I kept going.

At the final rally point, Kane dispatched a recon team that low crawled the final 100 yards through some heavy brush to the objective. It took the two-man detachment over an hour and a half to make the traverse and execute the task. Yet, slow was good and stealthy enough so they were not detected. Upon return, they reported seeing a deuce-and-a-half with a water buffalo and three soldiers wearing red berets. No contact was made, so the patrol spread the information via whispers, and we reversed our trail with me on point following the direction Kane had given.

About 100 yards short of the final rally point, I spotted the orange mushroom again and stopped the patrol. Everyone squatted down or took defensive positions. I ducked walk back to Kane to keep a low profile.

"What's happening, Rob?" Kane had a tired look with his sweat having washed off most of his camo paint.

"We have to head more northerly; we're going out the way we came in."

"No we ain't," Kane snipped.

"I'm telling you, take us 45 degree more to the north."

"How you know that?" Kane sounded confused.

"I spotted a mushroom that I saw on our way in."

"A 'shroom. Man, you're killing me."

"Let's go more to the north. Trust me."

"Roger bro, we got it." Kane took his compass and shot an azimuth. "Head that-a-way. It looks thick, but I trust you." He pointed out a dark bush off in the distance and I resumed my position on point.

After a couple more northerly jinks to climb over some rough terrain, we worked through some thick undergrowth that snagged our uniforms, gear and bare skin. Some of the cadets were grumbling until we cleared the thicket and were about 500 meters to our finish point. Then rifle fire crackled in the air. It sounded like it was coming from the rear. We were all issued blank ammunition and red blank adapters on our M-16 rifles. The adapters made weapons function as semi-automatics even though there were no rounds going downrange. The platoon returned fire and, after about three minutes, the attack broke off. Kane ordered the patrol across a tall grass field to the finish point and we double timed it.

Once we made it to the end, the cadre took us to "administrative condition." Kane did his reconnaissance debrief and we circled round for evaluation.

The 82nd Airborne infantry Staff Sergeant said, "Well ya'll did well." Then he spit out some chewing tobacco juice that countered his positive tone. "You accomplished the mission. That's the main point, but your movement was too congested. The patrol and squad leaders have to keep more space, especially in some pine type forest like this." He moved his arms around. "I liked how you took the rough terrain for the return." Kane threw me a quick smile, and I winked my left eye. "Few patrols take that 'cause it looks hard, but you know the enemy is probably thinking the same thing. By taking the difficult ground, you avoided an ambush, all the enemy got was a few wild shots at your rear element. That's a good day in my book. Now clean your weapons; you have thirty minutes before the trucks arrive."

The vibe in the platoon was electric over the successful patrol, our first for evaluation. Over the next few days, though, the missions became more complex and challenging, and the dreaded Carolina temperature kept climbing and climbing. As we prepared our patrol routes, Range Control had radioed all sites that we were in Heat Category IV, meaning the temperature and humidity had risen to a level such that physical exertion could lead to a serious heat injury, such as heat exhaustion, or worse, heat stroke. The Army's solution was to allow us to unblouse our trousers, which is to let the cuff fall over the boot top, ostensibly letting in cool air, and to untuck our shirts. You know it was serious when the army allowed soldiers to break uniform discipline. To combat the heat, we took showers and used liberal amounts of portable air conditioning, commonly called talcum powder.

In addition to the heat, the weight of combat gear added to the physical discomfort. It really strained my shoulders and neck. Holding my head upright wearing the M1 helmet, took some conditioning and soreness.

One patrol after another got to be tiresome, but each day we had a different platoon leader and so I had to give it my best. The peer rating stuck in most of the platoon's mind and helped motivate me.

Chapter 9 The Heat Was On

In the second week, I was carrying an M-60 machine gun on the patrol and the operations tempo was nearly continuous. The thermometer was nearing 105 degrees and heat category IV by 9 AM. The mission was to attack a defined defensive position. Once we neared the position, the plan was to charge the enemy foxholes, ably manned by regular army soldiers. I could feel the symptoms of heat exhaustion coming on as the patrol progressed, but I still pushed. The M-60 would have a critical role in this mission as it needed to lay down a base of fire to suppress the enemy position while our troops charged. We set up about 800 yards out and on command fired about 200 blank rounds, simulating a withering base of fire. The gun barrel sizzled heat, and spent cordite combined with the sun made me woozy. Fortunately, the assistant gunner and I were lying down behind the weapon. After our assault team took the position, the platoon leader ordered the support squad, including me with the M-60, to charge and join the attacking squad. We rose and gathered the gun. As I passed a foxhole dug by the aggressors, I felt a pull on my leg and loud explosion near my head. The retreating troops had set a trip wire attached to an artillery simulator. In actual combat, I'd been dead; instead, the training served its purpose and taught a strong lesson about taking care around old enemy positions. Something I would always remember, well that plus the ringing in my ears from the artillery simulator that probably took a few dBs off my audible frequencies.

The company went administrative to eat a C-ration lunch; however, that last charge up to my simulated death contributed to my heat exhaustion. I felt clammy and would soon be a heat casualty if I didn't get my core body temperature reduced. I placed the machine gun next to my bunkmate and took off my green utility shirt and tried to get cool in the shade of a tree. Koch helped and poured the remainder of my canteen over my head. My vision was blurry and I felt nauseous.

The trainers recognized the extreme heat and soon an olive drab tanker truck drove by the dirt trail and stopped near our platoon break area. Two active duty soldiers popped out and with a fire hose attached to the rear spigot, proceeded to spray water on anyone who wanted to get cool. Nearly everyone in the platoon volunteered. The driver and assistant had fun creating a wet t-shirt contest among the cadets, but I appreciated the impromptu bath. The water pressure reminded me of the times when we were kids and would frolic in the street under the spray of a New York city fire hydrant opened by firemen for testing or just for fun. Yet the water and subsequent evaporation lowered my body temperature enough to stem the heat exhaustion and enabled me to continue, albeit at a slower pace.

Heat exhaustion plagued me two more times that summer. On the second occasion, my symptoms were bad enough to have me sent to the medics who put me in the shade of a covered truck and ordered me to strip to my underwear. Then they soaked me with ice water. Believe me, the cold water felt great and I re-joined the platoon about 15 minutes later with the medic's admonition that heat injuries have a cumulative effect and I should be wary of getting over heated again.

In week three, our platoon took the ubiquitous cattle cars to a wooded and hilly area for orientation training. We had some preliminary map reading instruction and all cadets should have had a class back at their universities on map reading. I had mine in my sophomore year from Captain Torino. Orienteering was a test to see how well we'd be able to accurately navigate in actual terrain. The mission was simple: bunkmates were to pair up and find a series of eight stations in the woods given just the eight-digit grid coordinates. Of course, the army had to do it their way, and we were only given coordinates for the first station. That station would reveal the next coordinates, and so on. There were more than eight stations on the course, meaning a guess at a station would risk being sent to the wrong station for the next point. Each team received a different set and order of stations. To make it even more challenging, we would be timed, and the winning score would be the first team to get all their stations correct and have the shortest elapsed time.

Koch and I received our first coordinates and last coordinates and we crouched near our map on the ground.

"Rob, you plot the points," my partner offered, perhaps recalling my success with Kane on the earlier patrol. As he watched me use the protractor, he offered. "Rob, looks like if we are here, then it's almost due north of us." Koch pointed off in the distance.

I followed his arm where it indicated and with the scale measured the distance. "Hmm, almost 500 meters exactly due north."

"If we are going to do well, we are going to have to run to each," Koch said, then frowned. While I had trouble with heat, his airborne school injury had reappeared and the constant patrolling made his knee throb in pain.

"Sounds good to me, but the station is on the side of a hill about 30 meters across a stream. Let's pay attention to the terrain as we run. When we cross the stream on our azimuth, we'll be close." I folded the map so that the area we were on was on top and put the map under my shirt. Then, using the lensatic compass the army had issued each of us, I sighted a tall pine tree off in the distance making sure to account for the magnetic declination of North Carolina. "That tall tree is about 2 degrees east of our azimuth and about 200 yards, or," I paused to do a quick mental calculation, "about 320 meters."

"Two hundred yards, how can you tell?"

"Hey, I play golf and that is about as far as I can hit a 3 iron. But I use yards not meters for golf so I had to convert the units; engineers convert units all the time."

Koch shook his head.

"Let's go for that tree and then we'll reshoot an azimuth, but don't forget to count paces. Each running step is about 1.5 meters so we need to run about 210 steps."

I took off and he followed. About halfway to the pine tree, we encountered some heavy brush which made running difficult. My partner caught up to me and I noticed he was severely limping. We crashed through the brush and hit the stream. Keeping an eye on the tree, we jumped the stream but upon landing, he moaned.

"Aiiye Rob, my knee is killing me." He pulled up his pants and his scarred knee did indeed look swollen.

"Damn, let's find the station then we can decide what to do." I helped him up the hill to our marker tree. There we shot our correcting azimuth and I could barely see, hanging off a tree limb, a rectangular frame box with white fabric with the letter C. I ran to the station while Koch limped behind. Suspended on a string was a tool that looked like a staple remover, except it had a set of pins that made a pattern like the letter D. We pressed the pattern on our score sheet for the first station. One down seven to go. Written on the station for our set was an eight-digit grid coordinate. We plotted it, when we saw some other cadets running past our station. They said they had two already and that confirmed our predicament of being behind.

"Rob, I'm not sure I can run to the next station."

I pointed toward the next station and said, "I'll tell you what. How about if you wait by that fallen tree we passed about 200 meters from the start line? I'll finish the course and come back here. By then your knee should feel better and we'll cross the line together."

"Fine with me, Rob, if you can do it?"

"We don't have much choice."

"You're right. Go get them."

I headed off on a 600-meter run to the next station. On the way I passed several cadets, all headed in different directions. A couple were stopped in the middle of the woods not near a station, looking in all directions at a loss where to go.

I found the second station on a hill top. It was easy. The next one was right next to a ridge that I had just passed so I quickly backtracked and found it. Kane and his bunkmate were there, but they didn't think the station was right as it didn't match their co-ordinates. They said they had just followed another pair of cadets to the station. That was an obvious mistake and I told them they better retrace their steps to their last correct point or they'd be really lost. I shot my next azimuth and was off. On one station, I had to backtrack as my dead reckoning did not reveal any target but, redoing my steps, I found the white marker. Plotting and moving, I managed to find the next four stations. Now the last one was along the perimeter road. I found that odd, as there wouldn't be any ter-rain features we could associate. We'd probably have to triangulate the last point using two of the known stations. I picked two points, the first one closest to where Koch would be and the second the closest to the finish. I then jogged to link up.

"How are you doing, bunky?"

"I'm feeling better," he whimpered. "I think I can run a bit now. Did you get them all?"

"All but the last. It's tricky and we must work together to get it exact. The last point is 265 degrees and about 700 meters. It's along a road and I think they are trying to trick us. We will need to be accurate on our shoots as there are no terrain features near our target station. We'll follow this line as accurately as we can. Then when we can see the road. I'll run the other point. Where our azimuths cross, we will nail the marker."

"Roger that," Koch chirped with enthusiasm. The opportunity to help lifted his spirits and we headed off to find the final station. As we worked down the 265-degree line, we progressively marked interim points and continually shot the azimuth. Within 100 meters of the road, we could indeed see the finish, but as I suspected the trainers had set up a row of markers about 25 meters apart along the road. A slight error on the azimuth would hit the wrong marker. I told Koch to stay put and to draw a line in the dirt pointing at our marker. There were two targets that could fit within the error of our azimuth. When I came from the other direction off our second known reference point, he'd tell me when I crossed his line. That would confirm our final destination.

Having been there before, I found the second reference point in about five minutes. Shooting the azimuth, I spotted a decent reference target, an odd shaped tree about 3 degrees off our point only 400 meters away; however, I could not see the markers themselves due to the undergrowth. Since I knew the target tree was along a trail, I didn't bother to count pace and ran toward my target tree estimating 10 meters offset to my right. When I reached the road, I pointed to one of the white boxes on my line and he nodded. I waved him over and we punched our score sheet then headed to the finish line about 150 yards further down the road.

As it turned out, we were the first in our company to cross the finish line. We submitted our scores, then the instructors said due to the nature of the underbrush, we would have to go to a roped off area and de-tick each other. This meant taking off our uniforms and inspecting each other's bodies for the nasty blood suckers. The story, true or not, of a cadet that thought, when showering in the morning, that he had grown an extra testicle, was in fact a fully engorged tick on his scrotum, had us leery and focused on tick removal. We found no offending parasites.

Pleased to have finished, we weren't sure of our score as a simple error could throw off the whole sequence. We drank from our canteens while we waited for our company to finish. As the event progressed, the rest of our fellow cadets returned to the roped off area. The mood among most was grim, only about half the company found all the markers and, as it turned out, the last markers tricked most of the teams. The cadre had us form up for a head count and to announce the scores. Koch and I placed first by about 15 minutes with all stations found. Only three cadet pairs found all the proper points. It didn't say much about our company's map reading skills and I made a mental note of the finishers, so when it was my turn as platoon leader, I would know who to trust with a map.

Chapter 10 Risky Busy-ness

All cadets had to take anti-armor training sometime during camp. After the first week, the word quickly spread through the cadet corps that the field class started with a Sheridan tank charging bleachers loaded with cadets. The tank would slam on its brakes and stop at the last possible minute with the goal of acclimatizing the new soldiers being around armored vehicles. On the day Echo Company, my brother's unit, was to take anti-tank training, we heard a rumor that the tank that day failed to stop and rammed the bleachers. All kinds of stories spread like wildfire. I raced to Echo Company's orderly room to find out if my brother was hurt, but no one knew anything as the company had not yet returned. I waited outside his company's HQ and fretted much like my father did thirty years earlier waiting for the recovery of his friend Kelly. I paced back and forth asking anyone near the orderly room if they had news and, while nervous, I didn't have the extrasensory feeling of dread that normally connected my twin and I during tough times. I tried hard not to think of all the horrific scenarios. Near dark, the cattle cars arrived and, fortunately, he was unhurt, but other cadets were injured, including one with a crushed pelvis, although amazingly, none killed despite being run over by a tank.

"Are you OK?"

"Sure," he replied and chuckled, maybe from nerves. "I knew about the intimidation stunt and intentionally took a seat near the back end of the bleachers. You never know."

"Good situational awareness. I'll make sure to do the same." I patted him on the back and we walked to the mess hall together, while he filled in the details of the accident and how training continued after the Army medevac'd the injured cadets.

His good mood and preparation allayed my concerns, but the twin connection went through its paces that day.

Recondo training seemed like a reprieve from the graded lessons. It was an optional chance to try several death-defying tasks that, if accomplished, entitled a cadet to wear a Recondo badge, a black triangle surrounding a brass torch. The first task was the Slide for Life. It entailed climbing a 75 feet tall tower, grabbing a pulley device and sliding down a wire at a 30-degree angle. At the last minute, the candidate let go of the pulley and crashed into a creek using the water to break the fall. The obstacle was like the zip lines now popular, only the Army used no safety equipment.

As we lined up at the base of the tower, the instructor explained the task. He then asked for a volunteer to go first. I threw up my hand and off I went, not for courage so much as to get it out of the way. Four telephone poles with pressure-treated cross braces fashioned like a large ladder formed the tower. The first few braces were easy to negotiate, but as I climbed higher, I realized the cross pieces were further apart: sneaky on the cadre's part. The last step entailed doing a muscle up to get onto the platform. As I stood on the top I bellowed an encouraging "arrgh" to my fellow cadets. Then I grabbed the pulley and stepped off into the abyss. It was fun and the slide went by rather quickly. All those pull ups I did back at Tech came in handy as I held my body in an L-position. Crashing into the water seemed no worse than a high dive and I was laughing as I climbed over the bank of the creek.

For each of next obstacles, I always volunteered to go first, again to get the task out of the way. The most nerve racking was the 40-foot rope drop. Here we were to shimmy out on a thick rope over a ravine, again with no safety equipment. At the midpoint, there was a piece of plywood with the Recondo logo. The idea was to hang next to the sign, smack it with one hand, then ask for permission to drop. Once the NCO-in charge gave approval, gravity did its job. Falling 40 feet took longer than I thought and even hitting the water with some force, the event didn't faze. The worst part was being sopping wet in fatigues and combat boots.

As the summer ended, MILSTAKES week appeared. This was to be our final exam. I did well acing all the tasks except for one – setting up an 80-mm mortar tube. I performed two of the initial steps out of order and could not zero the weapon. Drat, my only technical mistake made even more ironic as I couldn't use my mechanical engineering background to figure out the sights on the artillery piece. My brother finished first in the battalion.

With my good scores in MILSTAKES and in the other areas, I was near the top of all cadets. However, the accomplishment I was proudest of was that Captain Blake informed me that I was the company's unanimous choice for number one in the peer review. Only one person didn't select me, and that was me, as raters couldn't select themselves.

Chapter 11 Twelve O'Clock Bye

After summer camp, I returned to my fraternity house in Atlanta to spend two weeks prior to going to Airborne school. My brother, having attended last year, told me it was a blast. I knew that jump school required a shaved head, so I decided to have a bald pate prior to arriving. I talked my girlfriend at the time into shaving it for me. I must have an ugly skull for as she did it, she started crying. In the 70's hippie era, a shaved head really made one stand out and it put me in perpetual pissed-off mode.

Three weeks at Fort Benning Georgia would teach me how to exit a military aircraft using a parachute. Lots of people would ask, "Why jump from a perfectly good airplane?" I'd say, "Those planes are maintained by the Air Force using equipment provided by the lowest bidder." That usually quieted them.

Reporting to the Airborne school, I was assigned a company, platoon and stick, the jump school term for squad. On my helmet sprawled a piece of tape with a hand-written number, C277. With our shaved heads and olive drab fatigues we had a uniformity craved by the military. C277 would be my sole identification in a class of more than 1,000 students.

Five mile runs in the morning, countless pushups and assorted other tasks, worked our muscles and mind. Jump school was physically demanding but not nearly as punishing as my experience at Ranger camp. Nonetheless, tip top physical conditioning made the training bearable.

Airborne sergeants wearing black caps, white T-shirts and white shorts with spit shined black leather jump boots took on the role of molding us into parachute soldiers. These Black Hats moved like greyhounds, with visible muscles, sinewy cords and ramrod posture that reeked of toughness. They would insist the proper response to everything was "Airborne." It took over a year after the training for me to overcome that brainwashed response, much to the chagrin of the civilians at Tech.

The first five days of training, ground week, focused on learning how to move our body to survive the parachute landing. The army's version of a parachute landing fall required bouncing on the balls of the feet, quickly twisting to the side and lowering the calf muscle, followed instantly by the side of the thigh, then the buttocks and finally the broad muscles of the upper back, always keeping the elbows tucked. In all, there were five points to a proper landing that, when executed properly, dispersed the force of impact over the fleshy parts of the body. With hundreds of practice falls on the ground, then progressively taller heights, we learned how to react when our bodies hit the terra firma.

We also got to experience how to survive if we were ever pulled by high wind once we reached the ground--a potentially deadly situation. The school had a large portable propeller air plane engine that would blast enough air to push a parachutist across 100 yards. The cadre had us wear a deployed canopy and turned the wind on us. The key was to pull the two aluminum latches holding the parachute to the risers. This freed the canopy. Failure to do so would cause the student to be recycled or worse, earn a broken bone or neck. My stick negotiated the task, but the realization that being on the ground could be just as hazardous as landing was an eye opener.

In the second week, tower week, where I learned how to steer a parachute after being dropped off 250 feet, there was a hair-raising accident. Two large red and white steel pylons loomed over the Benning central campus like twin clones of the Coney Island amusement ride, the Parachute Drop. The army towers each had rings that hung under four crossed arms on top. Three of the arms were in use at any one time with the one facing into the wind idled. Each arm dropped a fully deployed canopy attached to a steel ring. Unlike the Coney Island ride, these parachutes would float down freely, controlled only by the jumper. The idea was to teach students how to steer and how to land.

Each member of my stick formed a circle and each fastened a clip that attached the deployed parachute to a ring suspended by cable off one of the tower cross arms. Once we connected the canopy, a student hooked the harness quick releases to the risers. Then a cable pulled the trainee to the top of the tower cross arm under a fully deployed silk dome. Nearing the top, the Black Hat assessed the wind direction and directed via a megaphone, "Pull your left riser," which would direct the canopy to the left using the wind to move free of the structure. I saw the soldier spread his feet and close them, to acknowledge the command. The tower operator then released the parachute. In the next instant, the student pulled his right riser which made the fabric slip into the crossing wind and turn toward, instead of away, from the aerial gridwork. Within 75 feet of the top, the canopy impacted steel girders and collapsed. As it further crumpled momentum swung the jumper through an opening in the beams. The silk ripped and snagged some protrusion on the red and white painted mast and stopped the hapless soldier's fall. However, he started to swing back and forth like a yoyo in the interstices of the tower's framework.

Immediately, the Black Hat cadre sprang into action. Sergeant Gomez, working at the ring base, quickly donned a parachute harness as did another instructor. A group of students in our stick were ordered to grab a large wood reel of half-inch thick rope and pull the end with an eyelet toward Gomez. The tower operator dropped the lifting cable to the ground where Gomez attached it to his harness along with the eyelet at the end of the land-based rope. Meanwhile, the other Black Hat started to climb up the side of the grid structure without a safety device.

With Gomez connected to the cable running through the tower arm, and attached to the land-based rope, the operator started to raise him off the ground. Our stick was ordered to pull the rope attached to Gomez thereby angling him toward the tower where the jumper was stuck. We pulled hard and kept tension on Gomez while he reached the jumper and attached him to his harness. Meanwhile, the other instructor scaled to the spot where the canopy was snagged. With amazing coordination, Gomez activated the student's quick release at the base of each riser. Free of the snagged parachute, the student immediately fell about five feet, but Gomez's harness bore his load. Now behaving as tandem jumpers, the operator lowered the two men to the ground while we used the land-based rope to pull them clear of the imposing structure.

The other instructor used a knife to cut the fouled silk and risers off the tower structure. He gathered the material and then descended.

Once on the ground and free of Gomez, the Back Hat that gave the instruction to 'Pull your left riser,' got in the trainee's face and said, "What did I say?"

The trainee replied, "Pull your left riser."

"Show me how?"

The trainee reached up simulating pulling the right riser, then a look crossed his face like a kid caught with his hand in the cookie jar, and he quickly dropped his arms. "Oh damn, the other riser."

The Black Hat stuck out his chest and put his muscular arms on his hips. "Really trainee, since you were honest and admitted pulling the wrong riser, you will not recycle. Get back and prepare to go again." Then he turned to the rest of our stick. "For the rest of you dumb asses, we will make sure you know your right from your left. Form up your stick here."

We quickly got into stick formation.

"Ready, Airborne. Right arm up."

We raised our right arms.

"Down."

We lowered our arms.

"Left arm up," the Black Hat ordered.

Each of us raised our left arm, but I had a hard time holding a smirk, thinking only the army could make knowing left and right a basic lifesaving matter.

Later in the barrack's day room as we spit-shined our jump boots, we laughed about the left and right mix up, but I reflected on how professional and fearless the Black Hats were as they rescued the stuck jumper. Having them in the same army I was in was comforting. It also reinforced how a simple mistake could end in disaster. The incident recalled my summer camp bunk mate's injury and his good fortune to still be alive.

When it was my time to float, I tried to enjoy the ride up. Being close to the ground gave a real sense of height and, while cautious, I trusted the equipment. At the top, I tried to take in the commanding view of south Georgia, but there was no time; the instructor boomed, "Pull your left riser." I confirmed the command with my feet slap, and the metallic click of the retaining rings meant I was floating down. I pulled the left riser and turned toward the open plowed field. My parachute landing fall received a passing grade along with my control of the parachute, so C277 advanced to the next phase.

Chapter 12 Jumper

Jump week arrived and I looked forward to not only exiting the airplane, but also finishing the training. I had enough of evening two-hour spit shining sessions and being told to do push-ups for every minor 'Airborne' infraction. Monday morning after a five-mile run, we donned our parachute harness with main and reserve bundles in the hangar bordering Lawson Army Airfield. The instructors admonished us to cinch all the straps as tight as we could stand it. We then waddled (waddled accurately reflected our movement as the parachute harness resembled a cheap hotel, no ballroom). Next it was hurry up and wait for the Air Force to show up with our ride. And ride it was. My first jump was to be out of a C-141 Starlifter, a four jet-engine military transport. Due to the high stall speed, one doesn't really jump out of a C-141 jet, but rather is sucked out by the air stream via the venturi principle. We were instructed to get near the door and just walk out.

I boarded the aircraft via the rear clamshell cargo doors. Inside the cavernous zinc chromate-painted aluminum tube, I sat on the canvas troop seats, thoughts of the first jump bouncing in my mind. A few of my comrades tried to sleep as the plane taxied and took off. To pass time and overcome any nerves, I mentally reviewed the training we had drilled into us. 'Exit the plane. Tight body position. Count to four. Check the canopy. Bad 'chute, pull the reserve. Float to tree top level, then prepare for landing.'

We gained altitude and as the plane leveled off, the jump master bellowed, "Six minutes."

The guys dozing raised their heads looking alert, belying that they weren't really asleep. Most had a blank look with wide pupils due to either the low light in the windowless aircraft, or trepidation. I jostled in my seat and pulled my chin strap a little tighter with a few butterflies in my stomach, like first tee golf jitters.

The aircraft's rear side doors opened, and the wind noise drowned out my thoughts. Out of the corner of my eye, I could see the jump master run his hand around the door frame. Satisfied, he stood up and roared, "Get ready."

We echoed the command as we did countless times on the ground.

"Outboard personnel stand up."

That was my stick. We repeated the command and stood facing aft, steadying each other for mutual support.

From the rear, we heard. "Hook up."

I bundled the loose end of the yellow static line in my hand and pushed the steel hook over the taut cable that ran just above head height down the length of the fuselage. The physical action of setting the rip cord convinced me that we were indeed on the way. I had the thought, 'I hope the rigger did a good job packing my parachute,' but it passed quickly as I trusted the training and the system.

The check equipment command spurred me to run my hand over my front straps and the back straps of the guy in front of me. Everything was in place and the action quelled my butterflies.

Sound off for equipment check was our cue to tell the cadre everything was good to go.

In the front of the plane I heard the stick leader holler, "One OK." Then "two OK." Until I heard "Seven OK" and felt a hard tap on my shoulder. "Eight OK," I called as I poked the man in front of me. As the last member of the stick counted off,the jump master said, "One minute."

I repeated the command in unison with the others. My pulse quickened as the whole stick leaned forward. The trooper across the aisle made a quick sign of the cross.

"Thirty seconds." Even the jump master sounded a bit excited.

The first jumper in our stick handed the static line to the jump master and turned toward the door. I shuffled a half step toward the rear to fill the gap as my stick moved closer to the exit.

When the green light illuminated, the jump master yelled, "Go!"

The first jumper stepped off into the opening, his static line pulled by the jet blast to the end of the retaining cable. My stick shuffled to the door, each soldier following the person in front. There was no time to think; it was all reaction. I reached the door and passed my static line to the jump master and stepped into the port-side opening. For a millisecond, I noticed the blast deflector, a steel plate with large holes angled off the side of the C-141 skin, meant to offer some protection from the high-speed air flow. Alas, not enough protection. As soon as I cleared the plane, the jet blast grabbed my helmet and twisted it directly in front of my eyes, so much for a tight chin strap. I raised my arms breaking the compact exit position drilled into my brain during ground week, and straightened out my headgear. Then I realized I had forgotten to count to four. Fortunately, I heard a loud "thoomp," as my main opened wide filled with invisible air. I jerked a bit upward as the canopy arrested my fall. All the silk panels inflated properly, so I grabbed the risers of the T-10 parachute, the same basic design used by the airborne soldiers in Normandy during World War II. The other members of my platoon floated around me with a steady stream continuing to spew from the jet as it flew off in the distance. Soon over five hundred soldiers exited five aircraft and the military rationale for an airborne assault became clear: in less than two minutes, a formidable force of mean and armed warriors could be behind enemy lines.

Jumping at 1,200 feet, or the height of the Empire State Building, there wasn't much time to enjoy the ride. I had to keep an eye out for other jumpers to make sure we didn't tangle our shrouds. On the ground, I could see the cadre moving back and forth. One was yelling "pull your left riser." With hundreds of troops in the air it was impossible to tell who he was yelling at, though I figured it couldn't be me as I was clear of the other jump-ers.

With the prior training ringing in my conditioned memory, I scanned the horizon waiting to get to tree top level to prepare for the landing, when "harrumph," I hit the ground without doing an official parachute landing fall. Instead of the five-point landing which distributes the impact load across the whole body, I did a two-point landing: my feet, then my butt. The landing was so hard my body collapsed and the fleshy portion of my chin sticking out of my chin strap opening scraped along the top of the canvas of my reserve parachute leaving an oval-shaped bloody raspberry. As it turns out when above the Fryar Drop Zone, the trees are several miles away and it is impossible to tell when reaching tree-top level by looking at them. I didn't realize this and never assumed the landing position. To make matters worse, my torn-up chin wasn't the only medical issue, I jarred my right hip and it hurt like heck, but at least it didn't feel broken.

As my parachute deflated and fell around me, Sergeant Gomez came running up to me yelling "Why did you not pull your left riser?" With his focus on me, he didn't realize my riser shrouds were falling around him. Let me back up a second and say, training dictates that upon landing, the jumper stands and runs to the top opening of the parachute and pulls hard. This fully deflates the canopy preventing being a 'ground-blown jumper'. When I did this, I jerked on the parachute stretching the shrouds. It so happened Sergeant Gomez was not only wearing his spiffy Black Hat, but also his summer white shorts. This exposed his legs to the elements and my shrouds. Unintentionally by pulling on the parachute, I gave him two nasty rope burns and lacerations on his legs behind his knees.

He immediately cursed, "Damn, look at my legs." Then he turned up the drop zone and screamed, "Medic, Medic."

I could see he was still standing and not bleeding badly, so the Airborne training took over and I shoved my parachute with one hand into my duffle bag and used my other to cover my helmet number. Nearly finished, a topless jeep drove up with two medics. They gave me a quizzical look and asked, "What's wrong?"

"It's not for me, but for the Sarge."

They quickly assessed my condition and started laughing and giving Sergeant Gomez grief. Meanwhile, I slung my now stuffed parachute bag over my back and ran across the drop zone to the assembly area, gladly recalling the training, no one ever walks on a drop zone, double time everywhere.

That evening my hip really hurt, so I took some Tylenol with codeine left over from a dental procedure. The pills helped numb my aching joint so that I could sleep and finish the five-mile run the next morning.

On Tuesday evening, we were scheduled for our night jump. We donned our parachutes in the hangar and stood by for inspection by a Black Hat. To my left was a sergeant I hadn't seen before, and to my right was Sergeant Gomez, wearing two white bandages behind his knees. For ten minutes, I sweated out seeing which NCO would inspect me, when to my relief, it was the unknown Black Hat. I am still not sure what Gomez would have done if he were the one to inspect my gear; I'd probably still be doing pushups.

Due to my sore hip, I intentionally steered my parachute on my remaining jumps so that I would land on my left side. To prevent another hard impact, I prepared for landing as soon I had a good canopy.

On one jump off a C-130 Hercules turboprop, I got to stand in the door and watch the Chattahoochee River pass underneath. Even though I was much higher, the feeling of height was much less than I had on the 250 feet tower, but a thrill nonetheless, especially knowing that if I fell out of the plane, I had a parachute. The floating sensation, however, was tempered by the knowledge of the upcoming impact with the ground. The drop zone was not plowed like the sand around the Fort Benning towers and landing felt like jumping off a one-story building. Yet, in four days I finished the five qualifying jumps and 25 miles of running to earn jump wings.

When I returned to college with my Airborne wings and now nubby-haired head, I learned I finished number one from Tech at the ROTC summer camp. Captain Torino was not pleased. "How could such a fuck up finish number one in summer camp?"

"Come on sir, it wasn't that hard; I figured since I was there, I might as well apply myself."

"Well, you are not going to be the cadet battalion commander; you can have company A."

"Yes sir," I responded. The Battalion command went to a cadet that one could say brown nosed the cadre. Frankly, I really didn't care as being back on a civilian campus, my attitude reverted to a focus on my education and fraternity fun.

Cadet company commander was no big deal, it meant I stood in front of the cadet company during drill and led the group while marching. Did I tell you how much I hated marching?

Senior year progressed with no outstanding army events. Having a four-year ROTC scholarship, I was required to take the Graduate Record Exam or GRE. It turned out my score on the GRE placed me in the top five percent of all ROTC cadets in the nation and qualified me for an army fellowship to graduate school. My dad had already suggested that I ask for an educational delay to get a Master's degree. He said, "Everyone now has a college degree. You'll need a masters to stand out. Plus, you should do it now while school is fresh on your mind." I followed his advice and arranged the Georgia Tech Whirlpool Corporation fellowship. At the suggestion of my Professor of Military Science, Colonel Wayne Davis, I sent a letter to the army asking if they would let me take the educational delay using my civilian fellowship and use the army five percent award at a later point. To my surprise, the army agreed.

After being commissioned as a second lieutenant, the educational delay to active duty started and I attended graduate school at Georgia Tech under the Whirlpool Fellowship. This was a full ride with a summer job, all tuition paid, a $500 per month stipend, and a $1,500 research budget. With no military responsibilities, and living in the relatively inexpensive fraternity house, the stipend-enabled a brand-new, bright-red turbocharged Ford Mustang. I quickly became civilianized and, in my mind, a big man on campus.

Chapter 13 Hogan's Zeros

Twelve months later, I finished my coursework and thesis at Georgia Tech thanks to the excellent guidance of Dr. John T. Berry, my graduate advisor. I packed my belongings in my pony car, cut my hair, and headed north to Fort Belvoir, Virginia, for the Engineer Officer Basic Course, or EOBC.

Leaping into the active duty army after a year living as a free and easy graduate civilian came as quite a culture shock. Exacerbating the jolt was my attitude. A year spent doing research on high technology subjects came crashing to a halt as I now had to worry about whether my shirt opening lined up with my pants zipper line and the edge of my belt buckle. (This is such a critical topic that the army has a name for it. They call it the "gig line." It took me a while to learn the importance of the gig line. One day, I absentmindedly came to formation without my belt. My training officer, First Lieutenant Kalle, did not like that. To top it off, EOBC assumed we knew leadership from ROTC and focused on teaching us the technology of being a combat engineer. Combat engineering might be the most interesting job in the army; engineers build stuff and then blow it up. This is like getting paid to be a little boy again, making plastic models and putting a firecracker in them; however, as my Dad used to say, the army could queer a funeral.

The army had a three-month curriculum aimed at teaching combat engineering to the lowest common denominator in the class. Frankly, this was just the opposite tack taken at Georgia Tech where professors routinely answered questions saying, "That is obvious to the most casual observer; figure it out as a homework assignment." In my EOBC class, there were only a handful of degreed engineers, the rest were new officers assigned to the Corps of Engineers to fill out the Table of Authorized assignments. Some of these shave-tail lieutenants did not have a strong background in math or science, especially the Officer Candidate School graduates, so even the cookbook approach to Army engineer training was going to prove a challenge for them. What that meant was I was bored stiff.

For example, in a theater of operations civil engineering construction course, we were learning how to calculate the drainage requirements for a road and how deep to dig the ditch next to the road to carry away the water. The instructor showed us the table for expected rain volume then said to calculate the volume that can flow through a triangular ditch, first calculate its cross-sectional area then multiply by the length. He patiently explained since it's a triangle, the area is one half the height times the width. He proceeded to do four or five examples of how to apply this new-found knowledge to a triangle. While some students struggled at this point, I broke out a crossword puzzle ripped from the daily paper and started filling in boxes. Lieutenant Kalle noticed this and called me out of class to his cubicle. "Lieutenant Kempinski, what are you doing with a crossword puzzle in class?"

My civilian attitude still had several more weeks of erosion remaining, so I replied, "Sorry sir, but I learned how to calculate the area of a triangle in fifth grade. I was keeping my mind busy."

"No more crosswords, pay attention in the class."

Kalle and I did not hit it off well, but I believe what really irked him was I could pass all the classes with high scores while paying minimal attention. Despite Kalle's opinion, I did listen the first time the instructor would explain something and learned the material.

Some of the course topics did offer the opportunity to do interesting things. One morning we boarded a bus for Fort Meade, Maryland, where we were introduced to all the heavy earth moving equipment a combat engineer battalion could have. Not only were we to get familiar with each, but we were required to operate all the equipment. Talk about being an eight-year old kid again. Here we were with a complete set of full-size Tonka toys, except instead of bright Tonka yellow, they were painted olive drab green.

My favorite was the Caterpillar D-9 dozer, a large bulldozer weighing about 100,000 pounds, with a 900-horsepower diesel engine and a decelerator pedal. That's right, pushing the pedal slowed it down, otherwise the engine would rev-up and the dozer took off pushing dirt. When operating it, I had to gently caress the blade height lever taking just the right amount of soil in order to move mountains and not dig down through the earth's crust into the mantle.

Operating the road grader challenged the new officers. This device has a strange long frame with a spindly articulated two-wheeled front end and four wheels surrounding a rectangular engine in the rear. In front of the engine was the operator's cab, containing a bewildering assortment of levers to control a steel blade set midships on the contraption. Used to make final grades on roads and ditches, it required a fine hand and a good feel for the machine, something not possible in an orientation ride. Its operation reminded me of the subtleness required to smooth wood with an old hand plane.

The most popular piece of equipment that day among the new officers was the 20-ton dump truck. The reason: it had an enclosed cab with heating. While we were out in the field, a freak October snowstorm hit Maryland. The uniform of the day did not include the outer field jacket, only the utility fatigue pants and shirt. The whole platoon got soaked and frozen to the bone. The cadre could have checked the weather for us, just another Army foul up.

Topics dealing with explosives really kept my attention. Combat engineers are known for their explosives expertise and EOBC dove deeply into the subject. We learned how to deploy any type of device from TNT, to Semtex and C-4, to fertilizer, to even small atomic weapons (small is relative) to blow up whatever the mission dictated. We ran detonating cord, blasting caps in cratering charges, bangalore torpedoes, and set up claymore mines. One interesting bomb was a toilet seat made of white C-4 plastic explosive. As the instructor said, "Designed to blow the crap out of the bad guys."

Some members of my class though appeared hopeless. One day, our class was in the woods laying a practice minefield. Second Lieutenant Paul Pett, a West Point graduate, who wore a buzzed haircut and black-frame, Army-issue eyeglasses (affectionately called birth control glasses, as no girl would date a guy wearing those nerdy goggles) was next to me digging in a M-21 antitank mine. If it wasn't the blue inert training variety, it would have had about 11 pounds of composition H6 explosives in it with a pressure fuse. When placing a mine field, the idea is to hide the location of the mines. Pett did not dig a deep enough hole, so after placing his divot of soil on top of the mine, it made an obvious bump. The goofy officer recognized the problem, made a mental calculation, no doubt enhanced by four years at West Point, and proceeded to jump up and down on the mine using his 220-pound mass to compress the soil. He never considered that compression of the top activates the pressure switch. In combat, Darwin's Law would have necessitated a replacement platoon leader, but we razzed him enough that hopefully he wouldn't do that when leading his platoon.

The main explosives mission supported creation of obstacles to stop an armored tank advance. This mission came about as the US Army doctrine evolved from the post-Vietnam guerrilla warfare mindset to a combined arms battle against Russia in Central Europe. Russia believed in quantity and not necessarily quality and their armored divisions vastly outnumbered NATO's. The grand strategy taught was "active defense" where engineers were on the front-line building tank ditches, blowing road craters and abattis, and placing minefields to slow down a potential Russian tank horde before it pushed NATO into the Atlantic. Reflecting on this, it dawned on most of us that if the balloon would go up, the engineers would be in front of the infantry and armor on the edge of the FEBA or Forward Edge of Battle. Gulp.

Unfortunately, second lieutenants don't decide grand strategy, and the classes quickly left theater-level consequences to cover the tactical aspects of combat engineering. The course material covered a plethora of topics, and some of it could have been interesting, if the instruction wasn't written at 9th grade reading level. Once exposed to the content in class, I rarely had to do homework.

Instead of studying, I used the evenings to improve my physical fitness as this was one area where I was not acing the class. Each evening, I would hit the track and do portions of the Army's physical fitness test: sit ups, push-ups, pull-ups, the run dodge and jump, and even the crab walk. My physical condition improved to such a point that when I graduated the EOBC, the only decent thing Lieutenant Kalle said in my evaluation was I was the most fit member of the class.

After a five-day field training exercise at Fort AP Hill, my class of second lieutenants graduated and left for their assigned units. Most of the students were going to divisions in Germany, Korea or stateside units. My orders said 'USAECBDE, Fort Belvoir.' I had no idea what that meant and assumed it was the temporary assignment to the EOBC at Fort Belvoir and that my future orders would come eventually. However, after graduation when I showed my orders to a personnel clerk, he quickly announced, "You're staying here at Fort Belvoir and are assigned to the Army Engineer Center Brigade, the unit that supports the Engineer Office School."

That came as a surprise, creating mixed emotions. Seeing the world might have been a nice benefit of an overseas assignment, but then Fort Belvoir being near Washington DC had excellent social potential. Certainly, Fort Belvoir out ranked places like Fort Sill, Oklahoma, Fort Riley, Kansas or, egad, Fort Polk in rural Louisiana. After a long weekend, I reported to the adjutant of the 11th Engineer Battalion on the north side of Fort Belvoir.

Chapter 14 A Bridge to the Bar

Since the 11th Engineer Battalion's main mission supported

the Officer Engineer School, it did not have any of the traditional Army maneuver unit's chain of command. We were an unattached US Army Forces Command (FORSCOM) unit, part of the Army's largest command and the authority for all expeditionary elements. That meant if a contingency arose, we could be reassigned, and in the late seventies our destination would have been Germany. Until the balloon went up, however, we were to fit regular army training around Engineer Officer School support missions.

The day I arrived at the battalion, there was a vacancy in the 902nd Combat Assault Float Bridge Company, a separately numbered bridge company attached to the 11th Engineer Battalion. The 902nd had a distinguished history serving in the World War II Normandy Campaign through to the Rhineland Campaign. Now based at Fort Belvoir, the army relegated its mission to Engineer School bridge training support, meaning students would build mobile bridges and we would disassemble them.

The company commander, Captain William H. Croup, a lanky man with Howdy Doody freckles and protruding ears, who diligently wrote everything in a green army-issue notebook. I followed his example, and I wrote everything in my notebook. He assigned me to lead second platoon, a group of 54 soldiers in the enlisted specialty, 12C, or bridge builder. I suppose being an army platoon leader had the benefit of putting a recent college graduate in charge of 50 plus individuals – none of my civilian college classmates had any kind of management responsibility straight out of college. Management might be a stretch though; leader would be a better term, as the army had a culture codified to allow rookie lieutenants to lead.

That culture started with assigning an experienced noncommissioned officer as the platoon sergeant and as a mentor to the platoon leader. Sergeant First Class Robert E. VanLoo, a twenty plus year veteran, with multiple tours to Vietnam, greeted me into the platoon wearing a filthy field jacket with a cigarette dangling from his lip.

Sergeant VanLoo had a good handle on running the platoon

as he focused on the mission, but not on uniform discipline. Complicating matters, the members of the platoon exhibited several issues. The first was most of them were "short timers," less than six months remaining in the army. Yet despite their time in service, all but ten of the 54 were still privates, the lowest possible army rank. This struck me as odd, as having been in the big green machine for three years, they should have at least been Specialist 4th Class.

In the first few weeks, I took a light hand deferring to Sergeant VanLoo to get the job down. As I worked my way into the platoon, I reviewed each soldier's records and interviewed each man. It turns out that these soldiers were products of the Jimmy Carter volunteer army—men so lost in the poor economy, they joined the service for financial salvation. Note, a private's salary in 1981 was $6,000 a year. The three-year privates all joined after the Vietnam War ended, and all had been reduced in rank due to various disciplinary actions, called Article 15s in army argot.

The platoon possessed a consistent demographic. All were from low income families, less than half graduated high school, several were functionally illiterate, one of the soldiers could not spell his last name or his home town, and virtually all claimed their recruiters had lied to them. Yet they all had interesting stories.

One character, a Private First Class Winston, in his mid-30's was much older than the other platoon members, and claimed to have a master's degree in Russian. His recruiter enlisted him as a linguist, yet his records said he failed the Russian language proficiency test and was reassigned as a bridge builder. As a result, he had a massive chip on his shoulder. One day while Sergeant VanLoo and I were conducting morning inspection of the barracks, we entered the room Winston shared with two other soldiers. The ersatz linguist was lying on his bed in the nude.

"Geez, Private Winston, what are you doing naked in bed?" I said in a firm voice.

"I had duty last night, sir, and get the day off."

"Well fine but put something on. Nobody wants to see you

in your birthday suit."

We left the room and I shook my head, but something set off VanLoo. "He did that on purpose, Sir. I am going to fix him."

Most of the time, the polygot specialist put in minimum effort and served as the platoon's senior barracks lawyer, not instigating trouble as much as stirring the pot when someone did get in trouble. Yet after the nude incident, VanLoo watched Winston like a hawk, waiting for him to trip up. With about two months left in his term of service, the trooper did foul up. He did not appear for an afternoon formation at our tool room. Failure to show up for a formation is a serious offense; the official Uniform Code of Military Justice term was "Failure to Repair." While it might sound like a Maytag technician making a mistake, conviction of such a charge can have stern consequences in the military. VanLoo brought the matter to my attention, and I agreed to approach the company commander about potential punishment. Captain Croup read the statements and concurred by preparing Article 15 proceedings.

Article 15 punishment is non-judicial punishment that can be administered by company level officers. While locally administered, it can result in reduced rank, pay forfeiture and extra duty. Any soldier offered Article 15 non-judicial proceedings can elect to waive Article 15 and opt for a court martial trial instead. Such a selection ups the ante for the soldier as a court martial sentail a formal trial and the possibility of stiffer punishment than that administered at the company level.

It turns out that before my tenure as platoon leader, Winston had previously been up for Article 15 charges, and chose the court martial option. The soldier defended himself and somehow beat the charges. When we approached him this second time, he again selected a court martial trial in lieu of Article 15 proceedings. Quite an interesting tactic on his part, as we had a cut and dry case for his failure to repair. If found guilty in the court martial trial, he could be dishonorably discharged and lose his veteran benefits.

As he did in his first case, Winston decided to defend himself. For fairness, the Judge Advocate General gave the defendant access to the base's law library, and ordered that we provide him transportation to the library in the off duty hours. In the next few weeks, our linguist transformed from barracks lawyer to Perry Mason in fatigues. He recognized he was under the microscope so he kept his uniform clean, shined his boots daily, was prompt for all duties and formations and generally toed the line. In the evening, he'd take a company vehicle across the base to the JAG building and delve into the law library. In doing so, he was polite, and kept his physical appearance in good military order. The court martial research transformed him into a model soldier.

Here is where the plot thickens. Since Winston had previously beaten a court martial defending himself, no JAG officer wanted to risk prosecuting him this second time. A loss by an Army lawyer to a soldier defending himself would be a black mark on that lawyer's career. At first the lack of backbone by the active duty lawyers irritated me, but in thinking about it I devised a plan. Since the court martial would take a couple of months to prepare, it would have to be scheduled within days of Winston's planned Expiration of Term of Service (ETS. I suggested that we encourage the defendant to think we were proceeding with a court martial. A week before he was to ETS we would drop the charges and process him out of the Army on his terminal leave. Captain Croup agreed and so did the JAG.

For the last two months of his Army career, the odd ball behaved like a new recruit, doing all required of him and at night pouring countless hours into building his defense. With a week to go before his ETS, I called him into my stark tool room office. Sergeant VanLoo stood in one corner of the room as a witness.

"Well Private Winston, I have good news."

He turned his face and gave me a quizzical stare.

"The Army has decided to drop the court martial charges against you. There will be no trial."

His neck stiffened and his face flushed. "What, they can't

do that. I want to make my case."

"Well, I'm sorry about that. In the last five weeks you have been a model soldier, and that is all we wanted. Starting this afternoon, you will be out processed and sent on terminal leave. Good luck as a civilian. I hope you can find a career that uses your linguistic skills. Dismissed."

Winston couldn't find anything to say. He was either disappointed that he wasn't going to trial or realized that he had been had. He turned his head toward at VanLoo who was grinning like a Cheshire Cat, with a cigarette in its teeth,

"You're dismissed. Salute the LT and leave."

Winston raised his hand to his brow, probably smarter than he wanted as he was still in his good soldier mode, and that was the last I ever saw of him. Who knows, the incident might have spurred him to be a lawyer, but more than likely he ended up on welfare lying naked in a fleabag apartment somewhere.

Winston wasn't the only problem child in the platoon. Other short-timers made trouble, including one, Private Cruex, who burned his dress uniform one weekend night in the barracks courtyard. We skipped article 15 for him and went straight to Article 12, Separation for Misconduct. Cruex had a pattern of misconduct and during his administrative hearing, much like a civilian trial, several witnesses, including myself, were called to testify about his behavior. When I took the stand, I was sworn in and answered questions about his various offenses, including torching his government-issued Class A dress in the courtyard of the barracks. His Army-appointed lawyer cross examined me, much like a TV courtroom drama.

The lawyer, a Captain, started. "Lieutenant Kempinski, did you know that Private Cruex had a drinking problem and that was the reason for his actions."

"No sir, I did not."

"As his platoon leader, how could you not know he had a drinking problem?" he spat out insinuating that Rex's behavior was somehow my fault.

"Well sir, I don't live in the barracks. When in the area, I never saw Private Cruex in a drunken state. I never saw evidence that he was drunk, and I never heard anyone say that he was drinking. There was no reason for me to suspect he had a drinking problem."

And as fast as the defense attorney turned on me, he said, "No more questions, Sir," to the officiating JAG officer.

Cruex lost the hearing and received an other than honorable discharge about a month before his ETS. Such a discharge meant he forfeited his remaining pay, his veteran benefits and could not re-enlist in the military.

Chapter 15 The Good, the Bad, and the Smugly

Not all the platoon members were potential Hells Angels gang members. There were several motivated and competent soldiers that were enjoyable to lead. Specialist 4 Streb and Specialist 4 Arrington, both large muscular men, were prototypical bridge builders. Bridge building in the Army meant manhandling heavy pieces of steel. For example, the Bailey Bridge, a World War II British design, resembled a large tinker toy set with each little piece weighing 200 to 500 pounds. The field manual classified these parts as a one-man carry, two-man carry and four-man carry. Streb and Arrington could take on the four-man carry by themselves, an impressive feat. With few exceptions, 12C soldiers were burly men with the physiques of power weight lifters.

I received a personalized exhibition of their strength when we were on our first field training exercise. We had just finished building a float raft. The men said to me "Hey LT, tradition is the new Lieutenant has to ride the float out to the middle of the lake."

I said, "Let's go." I jumped onto the deck and Streb, Arrington and three others joined me. The bridge boat then motored the raft 200 yards where the soldiers started to hoot and holler. Sergeant VanLoo blasted from a megaphone on the land. "Alright men, initiate the LT into the platoon."

Whereupon four bridge builders grabbed my arms and legs. I thought I was pretty strong, but with each of them holding one of my appendages, I didn't have a chance. I couldn't move. I yelled, "Hey take my weapon, as I didn't want to lose my M-16."

They did and then swinging me by my arms and legs they counted, "One, two, three." Next I was under water and they were laughing up a storm.

The initiation ceremony at least had the benefit of cooling me off as carrying all that heavy gear in the summer was a burden in the humid Virginia air. The event taught me using the lake as a cooling device could come in handy.

Later that day, after my green utility fatigues and leather boots managed to dry off in the heat, I had to report to the battalion HQ for receipt for our orders. Special Lemieux and I drove down a road and past a field planted with watermelon. The round ripe orbs stimulated my hypothalamus as we had been in the field over five days eating Meals Ready to Eat (MRE. When we returned to our company I took off to relay the orders to our commander, but first I mentioned to Lemieux. "Why don't you visit that field and pick up a watermelon for the platoon."

Specialist Lemieux's eyes twinkled. He was a Vermonter of French Canadian extraction, and always very clever at figuring out the simplest or sneakiest way to get something done. "Ah sir, you mean a midnight requisition?"

"Yeah, something like that."

"Got it sir." He bounded off more enthused than he had been the whole week.

An hour or so later, before dark, I finished the staff meeting and returned to the platoon area where a couple of guys were eating watermelon.

"This is great, thanks sir," they mumbled while chomping on the juicy fruit.

Then I walked to the jeep trailer to get a piece for myself and was shocked to see, not one watermelon, but a whole trailer full. "Lemieux, what the heck?"

Sitting in the driver's seat, he gave me a sheepish grin, and amped up his French accent, "Yeaux know Sir, ze men 'err unngry."

We had so much watermelon we got sick of it. And the next time we passed the field, I had Lemieux stop and I put $20 in the farmer's mailbox.

While the majority of soldiers in my platoon were brutes, we did have one exception. Private First Class Clark (no relation to the Cadet Clark mentioned earlier. The wiry soldier from Pennsylvania tipped the scales at 130 pounds. Despite his small frame he thought he could do the same work as the other behemoths. But he couldn't, and he would regularly push himself to heat exhaustion. Whenever Clark's face would turn bright red, his Sergeant would look to me and motion toward Clark. I'd reply, "OK Sergeant White, dunk Clark."

Sergeant Ronald White, a giant among behemoths with 19 inch biceps and a 54 inch chest, would grab Clark, lift the slight man above his head and throw him in the water. Each time, Clark would scream and resist but like me in my initiation, he didn't stand a chance. Sergeant White handled him like a rag doll. Eventually Clark got the idea and realized he needed to do some of the jobs requiring less heavy lifting, but I always admired his stubbornness.

If I had to pick a favorite soldier in my platoon, it would be the massive Sergeant White, a squad leader. He had innate intelligence, knew how to get the job done, and had the respect of the men, including the short timers. One Monday morning, as we were getting ready for morning formation, Sergeant White entered the tool room office and said, "Sir, I really fucked up."

This took me by surprise. "What do you mean Sergeant White?"

"Last night I was on duty and making my rounds through the barracks. I could smell dope, so I knocked on the door telling those inside to open up. I heard laughter and could hear scrambling." He paused and gave me a forlorn look. "So I ordered, 'Open up.' They just laughed and someone cursed me out."

The image of the imposing White standing at the door with his adrenaline pumping flashed into my mind. It had to be an intimidating sight.

"I just meant to pound on the door to show them I was serious, and I as hit down on the door with both fists." He made the motion of raising both arms above his head and pounding the fleshy parts of his fists against the door. "The whole frame with door fell into the room." He paused. "Will I get in trouble for destroying government property?" His concern so genuine, yet the circumstances so funny I had a hard time keeping a straight face.

Gaining my composure quickly I said, "No way. You discovered a safety defect in that shoddy barracks construction. Good job."

His tense muscles relaxed, and he let out a sigh.

I continued. "And I bet those knuckleheads in the room got a surprise."

"Oh yes sir, too bad they flushed the weed down the drain."

"Yeah too bad. Keep an eye on them."

"Yes sir."

The other squad leader, Sergeant Issac Fiso, did not give

up much to Sergeant White in strength. Fiso hailed from Samoa and had a build like a yokozuna sumo wrestler. During morning runs he would struggle with stamina as he had a lot of girt to move, but when it came to humping bridge components he tossed them around like toys. Yet despite his massiveness I'll never forget his expression one day when we did some training the platoon had never done before.

I decided to teach the platoon about engineering route reconnaissance. This is a mission where engineers follow a road and record items that might be of use in future construction missions. The leader would mark on the map locations for good lumber, gravel, and sand pits, and any other potential building material. After a brief classroom lecture, I put Sergeant Fiso in charge of the route recon.

"You get in the cab of the deuce and half, Sergeant Fiso, I'll ride in the back with the squad."

The truck proceeded down a trail in the wooded section of Fort Belvoir. In the back, I talked with the squad and really didn't pay attention to where we were headed. In about 20 minutes the truck stopped and Sargent Fiso's head appeared at the tailgate.

"Er Sir, can I talk with you?"

"Sure Sarge." I hopped out of the truck and we walked about 15 yards away. "What's up?"

Fiso turned sideways toward me and the truck, his face reflecting a timorous expression totally out of place on such a massive man. He said in a falsetto voice, "Sir, I'm lost."

"Lost? Really?"

"I don't know where we are on the map."

By now I could feel 14 eyeballs burning in my back as the driver probably told the seven guys in the rear compartment what was going on. Talk about pressure.

"Let's see the map. Where do you think we are?"

Fiso spread the map on the sandy road. "Somewhere down this trail maybe." He pointed to spot on the map.

"How about using terrain association. We've been on this trail for about 10 minutes. We just crossed a stream and I can see where are in a bit of a draw with steep hills on each side." I traced my finger down the trail he suggested. "Hmm, no stream on this trail, but what about this one." I pointed to the next route to the east. "Look there's a stream and steep sides next to the road. That's probably where we are if the road direction matches a compass azimuth, I'd say that's it."

Fiso shot an azimuth and sure enough it matched the map.

"Just head about half a click down this trail and make a right. That should get us on track."

"That's great Sir, thanks."

"You'r welcome. Let's get back to the recon. By the way, did you see anything good by the stream?"

"Not really sir,"

"I noticed a sand bar. Could be good for dirt fill for making concrete."

"Oh roger sir, I'll mark the map like you showed us."

We kept the little navigation exercise to ourselves and Sergeant Fiso expressed his thanks later in private to me. He explained the importance of saving face in Samoan culture and was grateful how we worked out his problem.

Four times a week, we assembled at 6AM for physical fitness training in the parking lot outside the company headquarters. My platoon would make a box shape of three squads across and 16 or so men deep. We'd follow first platoon and third platoon and the maintenance platoon brought up the rear. Tracking the company's red guidon with an engineer castle on it, we'd run in step around the north post of Fort Belvoir, usually running two miles in formation. To keep the company in step, the officers would run alongside the soldiers signing cadence, sometimes called jodies. We would sing the song and the troops would repeat. Starting each verse on the right foot kept everyone in step. When it was my turn I frequently used an old jump school standby.

"C130 roll'n down the strip, Airborne daddy

Gonna take a little trip.

Stand up, hook up,

Shuffle to the door.

Jump right out and count to four. If my chute don't open

wide,

I have another one by my side. And if that chute don't

open too well, I got a one-way ticket to hell."

Chapter 16 Stripers

Army bridge builders play a crucial role in combat maneuvers in that they enable the rolling stock to cross rivers to continue the fight. Speed and mobility ruled the day. To this end, the 902nd float bridge company changed from M4T6 assault float bridge to ribbon bridge while I was a platoon leader. The ribbon bridge, based on a borrowed Russian design, enabled the company to erect a river crossing in a much shorter time than the old inflatable rubber M4T6 floats. We would build a traverse by backing our five ton trucks into the water then releasing a section much like launching a fishing boat. The section would float and when a crew member pulled a latch it would open up like a flower to reveal a 20-feet portion of road bed. Using bridge boats, we'd maneuver the pieces together to make a span capable of holding a 60-ton tank. The floating road bed would wave in the water like a ribbon hence the term, ribbon bridge.

Each platoon had two bridge boats made of two separate aluminum hull pieces. We'd launch the front and rear piece separately then join them together with two steel clips while they floated. We used to joke that if you counted our boats and bridge sections the Army had more vessels than the Navy. Proficiency with the bridge boats determined the speed of erecting a span.

One late afternoon, as we practiced rafting operations, a fierce summer thunderstorm roared in unexpectedly. Hard rain and lightning fell and the wind roiled the normally placid water of the basin into three to four feet waves. I ordered the boats to shore and we were anchoring them when basin-base control radioed that a civilian had reported a small sailboat capsized in the Accotink Bay, off of the Potomac River. The sailors were in the water.

I immediately said, "We got to rescue them." The boat operators volunteered without hesitation despite the hazardous conditions. I wanted to go but realized the boat operators were more skilled. Confirming they had extra life jackets, I watched as they quickly backed the boats into the intense surface action. The waves battered the boats as they moved up and down into the breaking surf. But within two minutes one of the boats returned to shore.

"What's up," I called as they beached.

"The boat broke," replied the soaking wet operator.

Not built to handle the rough waves, the steel clip holding the bow and stern section failed. A strong breaker sheared the bolts off the aluminum hull. The two boat halves flapped in the surface action and became unusable in the rough conditions.

Darn, now we had only one boat searching for the capsized pleasure craft. That would increase the time to find the needy sailors leading to potential disaster. I waited for 30 minutes scanning the water with no effect due to the poor visibility. Hoping for the best, there was not much more I could do as the boat did not have a radio and finding the distressed craft had to be problematic.

As the storm started to subside I could make out Sergeant Wilson steering toward our location. He waved and gave me the thumbs up. Sure enough when he beached the craft, we could see two crew members and three civilians, a father and two young boys in the boat. Not only that but Sergeant Wilson was towing their overturned boat behind the olive drab craft: a complete recovery. The father thanked us profusely saying he and the kids were not going to be able to hold on much longer. We moved the family to the basin-control building and secured their sailboat and the bridge boat. As we did, we found a smallmouth bass in the front section of the boat. A wave must have crested over the gunwale bringing with it a fish, definitive evidence of the severity of the storm.

Considering the dangerous conditions and the unflinching decision by Sergeant Wilson and crew, I wrote a citation recommending them for the Army Soldier's medal, the highest peacetime medal awarded by the military. After weeks of paperwork and review, the Army instead awarded them the Meritorious Service medal for heroism. I enjoyed the award ceremony recognizing their bravery and found it a satisfying part of leadership. Of course, times weren't always as pleasant.

As previously mentioned Sergeant VanLoo's personal appearance rarely met Army standards. He just did not keep his uniform clean and he always had cigarette ashes on his shirt. About half way through my tour as a platoon leader the company received a new First Sergeant. Called Top, the first sergeant is usually the most powerful and feared noncommissioned officer in a company. First Sergeant Johnson readily fit the bill. Built like a six-foot five NFL linebacker, he had a tight afro haircut and an impeccable military presence. He could not tolerate VanLoo's slovenly appearance and made it a personal project to rehabilitate his junior NCO.

VanLoo initially responded to First Sergeant Johnson's mentoring, but it's hard to change old ways. One day he showed up to work in a dirty uniform. Well it happened the same morning the Brigade Commander, Colonel David Rooksey, chose to inspect our company's morning formation. The Colonel examined the first squad and asked the first soldier, "What are you going to do to-day?" The soldier was not one of the brightest and he only offered a blank shrug. The colonel then asked the next man in the squad, "What are you going to do today?" Private Dunn replied, "I don't know, sir."

This annoyed me as the previous night I trained the platoon in knot tying in preparation for a training mission simulat-ing the recovery of a downed satellite on Fort Belvoir's south base. Although it was a fictitious mission, I had spent time preparing an old 55-gallon drum in the woods marked up to look like a satellite and had briefed the platoon after the knot tying training. The troops weren't that stupid, I assumed they were daunted by the brigade commander, who did have ferocious reputation. After walking through the ranks, Rooksey called me, VanLoo and Johnson to the rear of the formation. He proceeded to chew us out about why the soldiers didn't know what they would be doing today.

Still peeved, I said, "Sir, the men know the mission for the day. I believe they are too intimidated by your rank to say so."

Rooksey nearly blew a lid, but before he could respond, he noticed VanLoo's uniform. He switched topics for his rant, but instead of yelling at VanLoo he sternly counseled the first ser-geant. I knew this was going to end poorly as in the army 'shit flows downhill.' Johnson took the verbal lashing about appearance standards like a true soldier, saying, "Yes sir" at the end. Afterwards he requested VanLoo report to his office in the orderly room, in a clean uniform.

The first sergeant understood leadership by example and from then on, he had VanLoo report to him each day one hour early prior to morning formation for a personal inspection. VanLoo had to rekindle his boot camp days shining shoes and cleaning his clothes. I also brought him a new field jacket as his old one was too worn and never going to look decent.

Initially I crossed horns with the first sergeant over his singling out VanLoo, as I strove to be loyal to the platoon sergeant who I believed was loyal to me. However, the mentoring worked, and it eventually brought the First Sergeant and VanLoo closer and VanLoo's appearance improved. I also witnessed the value in leadership by example even if it meant personal hardship, as Johnson also had to get up an hour earlier every day. Top and I also came to a working agreement and in the long run, it was better for the military discipline in the unit.

Despite being a peacetime army, training still posed significant dangers. One day while we were recovering ribbon bridge sections in the basin, I got a radio call saying Clark got his hand stuck on the winch crane cable. Fearing the worst, I raced over to his truck whose rear wheels were half submerged in the water, normal procedure for retrieving a bridge section, like pulling a fishing boat back onto a trailer. Clark was guiding the cable as the operator used the winch to pull the floating section onto the cradle. In guiding the cable, Clark rested his hand against the steel cord as it pulled in. Unbeknownst to him, one of the metal fibers had snapped and was sticking out. As the cable moved, the steel fiber penetrated the base of his wrist and came out the tip of his middle finger. It was a gruesome sight, like a being snagged by massive fish hook and his blood was mixing with the grease on the cable.

We quickly lowered the cable to take pressure off the wound. Using a land phone we called the medics; however the steel penetrant was in far enough we just couldn't pull his hand free. We tried to stop the bleeding and treated him for shock as he felt considerable pain. When the medics arrived they also did not feel comfortable removing his hand from the cable, so we used a wire cutter to remove the broken section of wire rope.

The medics took Clark to DeWitt army hospital where he had surgery to not only remove the cable fragment but to clean the grease imbedded in his hand. He luckily managed to fully recover in a few weeks.

Chapter 17 Rollover

While a platoon leader, I believe I had my closest brush with death. I had staff duty one evening, an extra assignment that required junior officers in the battalion to represent the commander during the night and to go physically check the security of the battalion's assets. Between checks the officer could sleep for a few hours on a cot in the headquarters as we still had duty the next day. The sergeant on duty with the officer had to stay awake all night to answer the phone but would get the next day off. The sergeant also was required to bring his own platoon vehicle and a driver. Officers and sergeants on duty were from different platoons so each platoon had some leadership in place for the next day.

This night I had the maintenance sergeant, Staff Sergeant Kowalski and a driver, Specialist Shriver. Around 2 AM Shriver and I took off in the jeep to check the locks and doors of the battalion's assets. We finished all the facilities on north post and drove down US Highway 1 at 55 miles an hour on our way to check the battalion's buildings and equipment at the basin.

The road to the basin went down the hill, the steep, 100 foot drop over 400 yards, bane of the EOBC students. On Friday mornings the new officers would jog in formation up and down the sharp gradient as part of morning physical fitness training. For safety's sake, traffic engineering levied 15 miles per hour limit on vehicles. Any faster would probably simulate downhill skiing in a tactical vehicle with off road tires.

We approached the sharp grade and Shriver down-shifted the transmission lowering our speed to the posted limit. Just as he did so, there was a violent shudder as we lurched hard to the right. The front wheels left the payment and entered a drainage ditch paral-leling the road. As it did the jeep dipped right and quickly flipped onto the passenger side. The centrifugal force threw me into the driver. The Army did not install seat belts, in fact, this jeep didn't even have doors, just a canvas top and a one-inch strap across the door opening. The movement jarred my back, and as the vehicle started to flip, I thought 'this is it, we're going to get killed.' Then for a second the jeep teetered on its side, and I exclaimed into Shriver's ear, "Get us out of here."

He grunted and turned the steering wheel. Miraculously, the four-wheeler busted through the ditch and landed right side up in the woods adjacent to the road. We now started careening down the steep hill. As gravity took its toll the jeep gained speed with its handling compromised. Shriver would turn right to dodge a tree, yet we'd bounce and aim at another one. The headlights barely lit the path, and all I could do was to hold on to the seat frame as the vehicle rebounded over logs, dips and stones. The wild ride continued for what felt like forever with Shriver jerking the steering to zigzag through the thick boles; a head-on collision with any would have been deadly. With one last bounce the ride skidded to a stop as we found the basin bottom. We ended up in a small open glade just short of the battalion's facilities. As soon as the movement ended, I asked Shriver,

"Are you OK?"

He jumped out the driver's door and screamed ,"I'm going to kill that mother fucker."

"What are you talking about?"

"Rodriguez. He sabotaged us. He did a brake job on the jeep today and look." Shriver's finger shook as he pointed to the opening for the rear passenger wheel, or what should have been the right rear wheel. All that remained was an axle stub and a dangling brake line. The complete tire, wheel and brake drum were missing as the wheel retaining nut had backed off and left the axle when Shriver down-shifted at the top of the hill. "That bastard didn't replace the cotter pin to hold the wheel nut."

"Holy cow, such a small part. And we were just doing fifty-five miles per hour on Highway One."

Not replacing the cotter pin meant the nut would back off sooner or later during operation. If intentional, it was attempted murder.

"I swear I'm going to kill him." Shriver jumped up and down next to the vehicle.

"Look, calm down." In the chaos of adrenaline I felt a clarity and said, "We're fine. The jeep is banged up but can be fixed."

Shriver stomped and flexed his arms. I grabbed his shoulder. "You did great, that was amazing how you got us down the hill. Now stay here, I'm going to use the keys to locate a phone in the office over there."

I found a phone and called Sergeant Kowalski. He woke a couple of mechanics and they came with a wrecker and pick-up truck. We dragged the jeep back to the motor pool just as the sun rose. I started my report. Upon briefing the battalion commander called the Army Criminal Investigation Division (CID), the Army's version of the NCIS made famous by the TV series.

Rodriguez was a bad egg. He didn't get along with his platoon sergeant and while the CID couldn't prove it we all suspected he intentionally booby-trapped the jeep. The first sergeant immediately put Rodriguez in his sights and it wasn't long before the hoodlum pulled another stunt that resulted in a court martial, he was sentenced to 6 months in the stockade. After his jail time ended, he was set for a dishonorable discharge but before the paperwork was finished he returned to the 902nd orderly room to even the score with the first sergeant. Recall First Sergeant Johnson was big and strong enough to play in the NFL and Rodriguez was not a strapping 12C, but a New York City Puerto Rican punk made auto mechanic by Uncle Sam. Not only did the First Sergeant pound his butt, but the Army canceled his discharge, recalled him on active duty and sentenced him to ten years hard labor at Fort Leavenworth for striking a superior noncommissioned officer.

Chapter 18 Caught 22

The Army believed in rotating officers in and out of positions at least every year, and oft times sooner. The idea was a military unit, like a machine, needed to function with interchangeable parts, a valid point considering possible losses in combat. Therefore, after one year as a platoon leader, it was time to move so I was reassigned to a position with the Engineer School's training battalion cadre.

My first year as a platoon leader I did not take any vacation. With the reassignment, I finally found the opportunity to take a month off. I flew via an Air Force military airlift command flight to Germany to spend time with my twin brother. Soldiers could hop a spot on military flights on first come, first served basis as space was available. Heading eastward I flew on the top deck of a C-5 Galaxy, the USAF's largest cargo plane. The seats were plain and faced backwards, there were no windows and no heat but the flight crew issued us ear plugs, a blanket, and a box lunch for $9. Not a bad price for a trans-Atlantic flight.

We spent a month together in Germany sightseeing Munich and Stuttgart, including a private owner's tour of the Porsche factory as Bern had ordered a 944 sports car. We also did quite a bit of skiing in Saint Anton, Austria, and Zermat, Switzerland at the foot of the Matterhorn.

He had his white Mazda RX7, a rotary engine two-seater, we somehow managed to fit two sets of skis. It did well on the no speed limit autobahn, but in the month I was there we never passed a Mercedes or Porsche. They always zipped by well over 100 miles per hour.

A couple of evenings we spent at the Officers Club at Johnson Barracks where I met other officers from the 16th Engineer Battalion, including his Echo company commander, Captain Hungerford. Those in the know might notice Echo company was the 16th Engineer Battalion's bridge company. In cosmic-symmetry, of all the thousands of possible platoons at their disposal, the

Army assigned my brother and I to bridge units. Some of the 12C soldiers in his company had spent time in the 902nd bridge company. Upon reporting to Europe, they had quite a surprise seeing my brother and thinking I had beat them to Germany and remained their platoon leader.

The vacation zipped by and soon I headed west on another military flight, this time on an Army chartered civilian airline that was warmer but more crowded than the Galaxy.

Upon return I started as the 2nd Training Battalion headquarters company executive officer. Despite having an excellent battalion commander, Lieutenant Colonel Ron Dieter, I really disliked the assignment. While the platoon leadership did not use my technical education, working in the field with the soldiers challenged other skills such as leadership, management and tactics. In my new position, as company executive officer for a training cadre unit, I did not have an operational role. I spent most of my time counseling soldiers about personal financial distress, traffic tickets and writing the battalion's newsletter. I also had responsibility for overseeing the brigade's mess hall and the battalion's physical fitness program.

Dutifully I executed the job as best I could. Counseling soldier's personal problems really stretched my abilities as it took considerable empathy and patience to relate to some of the problems in which they managed to embroil themselves. Dieter also liked the work I did with the battalion newsletter as it was one of the main avenues we had to communicate with our soldiers who were spread all over Fort Belvoir. But of all these administrative jobs the one I dreaded most was the dining facility oversight. Although I could grill a steak, I never was much of cook. Multiply by the numbers of meals the mess prepared each day, more than 20,000, and I was in an area where I had no training, and frankly no interest, but high risk if something were to go wrong. Fortunately, the master sergeant in charge of the mess hall knew his job and I merely reviewed paperwork and inspected thermometers and labels on food. This type of work conflicted with my technical background and as I conversed with college buddies and learned about their engineering projects I felt like my talent was being wasted.

My job dissatisfaction however received an unexpected two-week reprieve. One afternoon, I reported for my annual medical exam. As the Army general practitioner examined me he asked me if I had any problems. I had just been weight lifting and mentioned as I did the Olympic leg lift, I would get a tremendous throbbing in my head. His expression turned serious as he quickly scribbled in my file.

"Here, report to the neurology department, room 212, and see a neurologist. You may have an aneurism."

"An aneurism," I squeaked with my voice breaking. I wasn't exactly sure what that was but I knew they could kill a person and I recalled my fraternal grandfather died of a cerebral hemorrhage. With concern I dressed and found room 212.

There the nerdy looking neurologist with longish blond hair examined my eyes, ears and felt my neck. He watched my pupils as they tracked the movement of his fingers around my head. In less than five minutes he said, "You don't have an aneurism, you have a deviated septum."

Now he had me stumped as I had no idea what the problem was and thought it must have been a brain defect.

He dashed a note on my records and said go the ENT ward on the first floor. Still somewhat in shock at the speed of this process I didn't ask the neurologist what a deviated septum was.

The sign at the ENT ward said 'Ear, Nose and Throat'. That was narrowing down the possibilities, but I was still in the dark as the internet on a cell phone didn't exist in those days and I could not Google "deviated septum." Dr. Taylor, a dapper Lieutenant Colonel, with grey temples fronting his salt and pepper afro, entered the examining room, took my pulse and felt my head, then examined my nose for 30 seconds. He turned his back to me and started writing. When he turned around he said, "You're scheduled for surgery in two weeks. Report here on March 18."

"Surgery? For what sir?"

"A septoplasty. To repair the geometry of your inner nose. It is quite deformed – you probably broke it at least once and maybe more times. You'll have septoplasty but not rhinoplasty. The army will not authorize straightening the exterior of your nose as that is cosmetic."

I never realized I had a crooked nose but looking in a handheld mirror I could see what the doctor meant.

I returned to my unit to tell them I was having army surgery in two weeks and would be out for two weeks on convalescent leave. Dieter was supportive but disappointed to lose my effort. During that period the Army assigned me the extra duty of being the officer liaison for the Army Emergency Relief fundraising campaign. As part of the job I had to see the Fort Belvoir commanding general, Major General Max Noah. He briefly gave me guidance on the importance of this task so I jumped in with vigor.

The AER fund office manager was a civilian, Amy Hungerford, an attractive woman with jet black hair probably four to six years older than me. She welcomed my participation and explained what we were to do. I started by developing a marketing campaign, writing press releases for all the unit newsletters, talking about the drive at unit formations, and designing a unique fundraising thermometer sign; as it filled up it would show how close we were to our goal. I used an outline of the Fort Belvoir badge, a diamond-shaped patch with the engineer's castle and a torch of knowledge through it. Every day as I drove though the main base guard gate I could see the sign and get a kick out of it.

When the time for the operation arrived, I took a break from the AER campaign and had the surgery. Army medicine is as close to self-serve as you will get. I'll spare the gory details of the procedure. Suffice it to say I witnessed the bloody process up close as Dr. Taylor would not let me have a general anesthesia due to my low heart rate. At one point, under the fog of the anesthetic, Dr.

Taylor put a scalpel between my nose and skin, like a tribal native would place a bone, and said, "Look at this."

"I replied, "Ooga booga."

The nurses in the operating room burst out laughing, while Dr. Taylor shook his head.

Staying home to heal, I watched the news as President Ronald Reagan was shot while leaving the Washington Hilton Hotel in Washington, D.C. John Hinckley Jr., a loner hoping to impress actress Jodie Foster, after seeing her in the film Taxi Driver, shot the Commander-in-Chief and three others. We recovered simultaneously although James Brady, the president's press secretary, had the worst of it and eventually succumbed in 2014.

After my convalescent period finished I went back to duty with splints and packing inside both nostrils. I was lucky I didn't get black eyes, much swelling or much pain, unless I laughed. Being somewhat happy go lucky this was a problem as I chuckled regularly. Nonetheless, I tried hard to keep a straight face as I went about my business.

My first day back I had my normal status meeting with Hungerford about the AER campaign. Her soft demeanor and body language had an extra friendly tone. She commented, "How cute I looked."

"It only hurts when I laugh," I replied.

She gave me a strange look then moved her face close to mine and said, "Can I kiss you?"

I immediately smiled and had to put my cupped hand to my nose, as it truly did hurt when I laughed. After a second to let the pain fade, I said, "I told you it hurts when I laugh."

She put her arm around my shoulder. "Oh I'm sorry, but I am serious."

Being an observant guy, and aware of Hungerford's reputation, and knowing she was married to my brother's company commander over in Germany, I said, "Not a good idea. Let's focus on the campaign."

Her expression changed quickly to a flat business look and I was glad as I didn't need a scandal to go with the nose pain.

I healed and got back to administering the physical fitness program for the training battalion. I would organize two training sessions per day for the soldiers the army deemed were overweight. These soldiers had three months to lower their weight and body mass index to army standards or they would face termination.

Captain Eileen Dougherty, my commander, was an architect and an Engineer officer via a direct commission. I don't believe she enjoyed the headquarters job any more than I did but she did have a weird way about her, at least by army standards. For example, she did not really possess any kind of military bearing. Her weight and height combo had her just below the army-allowed standard, yet I never saw her take physical training. She wore a considerable amount of black eye liner or some sort of dark makeup around her eyes when combined with her jet-black hair transformed her into the Mata Hari in olive drab green.

She also had some strange ideas. As I was getting ready one day to do the afternoon weigh-in for the overweight soldiers she said, "To give the troops a break, make sure you weigh them before they take the two mile run."

I was taken aback by the order. "Ah ma'am, I weigh them after they run. They might lose a pound while jogging."

"Oh no Rob, you gain weight when you run."

"Really, how is that ma'am?"

"It is all the air you breathe, it fills the lungs and adds weight."

Fortunately, the practice I had to not laugh while my nose was growing back together after surgery enabled me to keep a straight face.

"Yes Ma'am," I saluted and left for the athletic field where I weighed the soldiers before and after the run to prove each of them lost a little weight after running two miles, however I never confronted the Captain with the results.

Instead the successful AER campaign led to an opportunity to meet the new Brigade Commander, Colonel Joseph Dey, in his office. The commander had a fatherly yet military presence with a stately face and short grey cropped hair that reinforced his reputation as a fair and excellent officer. After he concluded thanking me for exceeding the fundraising goals, I asked, "Sir, may I ask you a question?"

"Yes, you may Lieutenant."

"Do you have any staff positions at the Brigade? I feel my potential is wasted as the HHC XO and mess officer. If I wanted to be a manager at a McDonalds I wouldn't have gone to Georgia Tech. Engineering operations would be a much better position for me."

"Is that so Lieutenant," Colonel Day glanced toward the Brigade Sergeant Major across the room. The CSM twisted his head as if impressed by my moxie.

"I'll consider it. Dismissed,"

I snapped to attention and saluted.

The next day, the training battalion commander Dieter called me into his office, "I hate to lose you Rob, but Colonel Dey has reassigned you to the Brigade Staff in the S3 shop. You report next week."

Well, sometimes it pays to take a risk I thought.

Chapter 19 The Charge of the Center Brigade

I reported to the Brigade operations shop, in Army jargon called the S3. Major Roger Stroude was the Operations officer and I was his assistant. We had a half dozen enlisted men, including a Sergeant Major Beasley. As a very senior noncommissioned officer, Beasley knew the ins and outs of the Army. If we needed to get something done, Beasley either knew someone or knew how to do it. He loved being in the Army and enjoyed every minute of the day. Being in his late forties he had a bit of a belly, rare for most young soldiers; it would heave up and down when he laughed. He had a favorite expression I expropriated and use until this day. "A short pencil is better than a long memory." Another interesting trait was his ability to delegate almost everything nearly instantaneously. I can't recall seeing him do any work.

Major Stroude intended to make the army a career, yet something about his bearing did not convey the military. While he was slim, with an average frame, he didn't possess a command presence due to his boyish face and straight blonde hair. Nonetheless we got along well and he supported my effort in the training section and he also offered some advice, acting more like an older brother than superior officer.

I took responsibility for developing the training plan for the Brigade which included the 11th Engineer Battalion, the 30th Engineer Battalion Topographic Map-making unit, the 15th Combat Support Hospital, and the 86th Diving Detachment; an eclectic assortment of units with a diverse set of missions. Setting up the training and overseeing the various budgets for fuel, ammo and operation schedules posed an interesting management challenge. I had three enlisted men supporting me, Sergeant Harrell, and Specialists Lewis and Strunk.

As a platoon leader I rarely played golf. But in a staff position more time freed up to pursue the little white ball. As the summer rolled around my game started to come back to me. In August I played in the Fort Belvoir championship and won. The victory qualified me to take a week off on paid temporary duty to represent Fort Belvoir at the TRADOC golf championship held at Fort Rucker, Alabama. In the actual tournament we all met our match against a tall field artillery officer from Fort Sill, Lieutenant Johnson. He had extreme length off the tee and his drives outpaced all of us. However, as fellow lieutenants in the after-tournament rounds, he and I teamed together to take some action against the more senior officers and the non-commissioned officers that dared to challenge us. While the week trip seemed too short, upon return Major Stroude, either consciously or unconsciously, tried to make me feel guilty for leaving work for golf. Frankly I was not too concerned about the major but made sure the troops in my unit understood. Since I played with them on the company's football and softball teams they sided in my camp and were happy for their golfing Lieutenant.

One of the missions the teaming section took on was to serve as an aggressor squadron to test our battalions' security practices when they were deployed to the field. We had a couple jeeps and would cover ourselves in camouflage paint and wait for dark. Then we'd infiltrate the security perimeter of the deployed units. Unfortunately for the different units we were never detected and usually captured most of the various battalion headquarters. One evening, conducting aggressor activity against the 30th Topographic Battalion, we uncovered an interesting aspect of integrating females into Army units. The map making battalion had about 40 percent female troops. As we crawled past the battalion fighting positions in the dark, we managed to capture several foxhole mates in mid-coitus. It didn't matter the troops were filthy and in holes in the ground, they let the birds and the bees rule and in the process compromised their unit's war fighting ability.

In January 1982, Specialist Strunk finished his term of service and was heading home. He had a flight from National Airport, so I offered to give him a ride in my Mustang. A vicious blizzard hit the Washington DC area, notorious for chaos on the roads when the ice and sleet accumulated. This major storm exceeded the local municipalities meager snow removal capacity. Nevertheless, we loaded his bags into the hatchback and headed north on the George Washington Parkway as the inches mounted. The car's rear end struggled to make any traction and snow piled on the windshield.

Crawling along in very little visibility we listened to the radio and learned the airport had closed due to the crash of Air Florida flight 90. A Boeing 737-200 had slammed into the 14th street Bridge only a mile or two north of us. Its wings lost lift due to heavy ice accumulation as the pilot made several procedural but fatal mistakes. We returned to base. The snow was too deep to head home, so I climbed the stairs to the second floor S3 shop to be greeted by Sergeant Major Beasley. "Hey Sir, great that you are here. Activate the alert rooster. We need the 11th Engineer Battalion to help with the aircraft disaster."

Everyone in the brigade headquarters moved into action and we responded with nearly all our diverse assets, which were coincidentally well suited for this catastrophic recovery. The divers of the 86th Diving Detachment used their salvage diving gear to assist local disaster management agencies in recovering victims and aircraft pieces from the frozen Potomac River. The 902nd Engineer Company installed float bridging out to the wreck site to lift the debris more readily. 30th Engineer Battalion topographic personnel surveyed the wreck site and produced a series of maps that located the site of each human remains, and each fragment of equipment or baggage on the river bottom. And the 11th Engineer Battalion built a temporary headquarters for the recovery effort. While a few people survived the crash, we were not involved in the rescue but rather we focused on the recovery of the casualties and jet pieces. It was sad and gruesome work, but our soldiers performed well.

Chapter 20 Animal Houses

One afternoon I noticed in the Washington Post real estate section there were apartments for rent for a reasonable amount. I mentioned this to two other second lieutenants in my battalion, John Fresh and Charlie Smith, and we agreed to consider renting a group apartment. The three of us had similar builds and were about the same height. Fresh was from Wisconsin and had light blonde hair and always cheerful face. Although he had a degree in mathematics he was assigned to the Corps of Engineers and led a platoon in the 902nd Bridge company. Charlie was the broadest with thick thigh muscles, well developed upper body and wavy blonde with a touch of red hair. He hailed from New Jersey and graduated from Princeton University as a civil engineer.

We contacted a real estate agent who showed us a few apartments. We found the rentals acceptable, but when she mentioned as soldiers we could qualify for a zero-down payment mortgage under a Veterans Administration program we considered buying a house. One thing led to another and the three of us jointly purchased a townhouse in Woodbridge, Virginia on Admiral Drive.

The arrangement worked well. We drew straws for the various bedrooms. John got the master suite and I picked the smallest room. I didn't care as the house was much better than the sterile room the army provided on Fort Belvoir. Parking was a bit problematic as we only had one spot but there were a few visitor spots. Sparseness defined our décor as we had no furniture. I recall Charlie in his Fiat and me in my Mustang racing down Virginia Highway One to get home first so the winner could claim sitting on an igloo cooler. It was the only kitchen furniture we owned.

Being industrious we visited the base craft shop and used their wood working tools to make beds, a coffee table, and end tables. I scrounged an old dresser for my bedroom. We each agreed to buy key items to outfit the house and we soon had a couch, a kitchen table, and a dining room table.

With three young officers full of vim and vigor, the house soon became party central. At least once a month we sponsored some social activity at Admiral Drive. One weekend we had a pizza party where we made the dough in advance and cooked pies to order. Another party had a Country Western theme where the guests arrived dressed as cowboys, or cowgirls, although one adventurous lady came dressed in a skimpy saloon girl outfit (that lady, Terry, eventually became my wife).

The wildest party had to be the Toga party where the music,

alcohol and the Roman spirit combined to cause the activity to devolve into a grand bacchanal. We wallpapered the house with butcher paper decorated with images of ancient roman artifacts and architecture. Prior to the party we borrowed a score of bed sheets from base supply. Any guest who arrived in civilian clothes promptly received a sheet and rope and instructions on how to wear a toga. Since underwear was not known in ancient Rome, men and women were required to go au natural under their togas. The affair lasted all night and I am happy to say did not end in a human sacrifice, but we got close. Somewhere in a shoebox in my closet are several incriminating photographs.

Virtually all of our social activities revolved around the hive of the brigade. Friday nights happy hour at the Officers' Club set the tone for the weekend. With scores of single officers looking for weekend fun, it attracted a variety of members of the opposite sex. Plans made at the club filled out other weekend activity.

One night as we caroused at happy hour commiserating about the sudden cold weather someone had the idea we should go skiing the next day at Blue Knob outside Pittsburgh. As it was already 10pm, that meant we'd only have a couple hours sleep. One of the Army nurses thought we were bluffing so I bet her dinner we would go. Sure enough at 4AM as we rolled out in John's Chevy van, I called to give her the bad news that she lost and had to pay for dinner. It turned out to be a win-win for me as I won a date with a cute lady and a free meal.

In addition to individual sponsored parties, the units regularly sponsored some sort of function. We had Hail and Farewell parties to say goodbye to departing officers and to welcome newcomers. One Saturday the battalion commander sponsored a "Who Shot JR party" at the Fort Belvoir Rod and Gun Club. The goal was each guest had to guess which character of the popular TV show, Dallas, would be revealed as the shooter. Myself and my roommates were at a disadvantage as we didn't watch TV but these 'command performances' required attendance if you didn't have duty. We all guessed wrong as did most of the country as the writers threw everyone a curve-ball.

Formal affairs, called Army Balls, required our dress blue uniforms, and civilized behavior, most of the times. However, there was one party where an Australian exchange major challenged any comer to become a "Pukka Sapper." Being that Oz lay on the underside of the world, the only requirement was to chug a beer while standing on your head. He demonstrated his unique skill and repeatedly downed a brew. Being full blooded American officers, we would not let an Aussie show us up so we lined upside down against a wall and chugged away. It must have been quite a sight to see us officers in dress blue uniforms spewing beer out our nostrils as we overcame gravity to force the beer up. I think I'm proud to say I qualified as a Pukka Sapper.

For a few months, we added a fourth roommate to our house, Dale Holly. Dale was a Citadel graduate and a former wrestler with a muscular build, and a strong type A personality. He was in the 11th Engineer battalion but soon became the aide de camp for the commander of Fort Belvoir, General Max Noah. Dale moved into the basement bedroom of the town house. We quickly learned roommate dynamics: two roommates mean you always know who did something. Three adds a degree of uncertainty. Four creates chaos especially when one has somewhat aggressive behavior, such as using up all the hot water and eating all the food in the refrigerator. In addition, since Dale was the General's aide, when answering the phone, we always had to assume the General was calling and had to say, "This is Lieutenant Kempinski, Good Evening sir, may I help you?" Many times, my mom would say, "I'm not a sir, Robert." And we'd chuckle about that.

Dale did not last too long as our roommate as he had applied for the Army program to attend the Uniformed Services University of the Health Services. After graduating he'd become a doctor. As he prepared to move out for medical school, he suggested to me and to General Noah that I would be a good replacement for him as the general's aide. Despite doing well and getting excellent officer evaluations, I was still undecided about making the army a career. Dale pushed it through and I reported to General Noah for an interview. In my class A uniform, I drove up to the Fort Belvoir headquarters, a massive Georgian brick building using a decorative vocabulary derived from ancient Greece. It appeared more like a university building than an army structure. I made my way to the commander's spacious wood paneled office and presented myself in front of his mahogany desk.

"Sir, Lieutenant Kempinski reporting,"

"Relax, Lieutenant, take a seat."

I sank into a leather arm chair across from his desk.

"I see you went to Georgia Tech, I went there for year prior to the USMA."

"Yes sir, I did, received my masters there too in mechanical engineering."

"It's a good school. Solid engineers, we need more in the Corps." Noah put my resume down and made eye contact. "So Lieutenant are you going to make the army a career?"

"Well sir I am not sure, I am still considering career options."

"You know engineers are special to the Army. I've heard people advocate for additional pay to keep engineers on active duty. We don't need to pay them more, we have exciting work and we do have special buttons."

"Yes sir." Obviously, I knew the engineers' dress uniforms had buttons unique from the rest of the army. Instead of an eagle on the brass button we had an image of the corner of a castle. Yet, I'd gladly switch to plain buttons for more pay. I kept the comment to myself to have a chance at the job.

The interview continued for a few minutes and then the general dismissed me. In a few days, I received a handwritten note from Noah saying he had selected another officer. Surprisingly I was not disappointed, as I didn't think I would fit in too well as an aide. The job entailed too much a politics, something in which I never had much skill or desire. What did surprise me was the next week I received a call from my branch career manager.

"Hey Lieutenant Kempinski, this is Major Samuels. I am looking at your records and it's time for your reassignment. You've been at Belvoir long enough. What you need for a good career is a maneuver unit assignment overseas and then go to the Engineer Officer Advanced Course. Where would you like to go?"

"That's a good question." I paused while I thought about this potentially serious question. "How about a tour in Hawaii. That is considered OCONUS."

"Got it. Let me check around and I'll get back to you in a few weeks." He sounded very cheerful and positive, so I hung up the phone and pondered my situation. Since I had a regular army commission and more than a year remaining on my four-year commitment I had no choice if they were to send me to an assignment for one year. However, getting reassigned to the 25th Infantry Division would mean more than a one-year commitment. If they sent me to Hawaii I might consider staying in for the duration of the reassignment which would have been three years. That evening I mentioned the call to my roommates and they said they too had heard from their branch officer but since they had reserve commissions and not regular Army commissions, they had options. Tom declined reassignment and Charlie was open. Being young and mostly carefree we let the Army see what it would do.

However, my carefree status started to change. Remember the adventurous lady in the saloon girl outfit? She was Terry Maxey, a beautiful young lady with a lot of class. A Southern belle from central Virginia, she wasn't scared of my Brooklyn New York background. We started dating more and more and perhaps some-thing serious was developing.

Chapter 21 The Branch Officer Always Calls Twice

True to his word Major Samuels called two weeks later.

"I got great news for you Lieutenant Kempinski," he beamed over the phone line.

"Wow, you got me a Hawaii slot?" I was surprised as there were not many engineer officer assignments in the 25th Infantry and nearly all young officers wanted one of those assignments.

"Close," he replied. "I assigned you to the Korea replacement center. It's a one-year assignment. Once you arrive in country they'll send you to a unit. Since you're single, it's an unaccompanied tour. It will be great for your career."

My eyebrows raised. "Korea." I had heard of the Army sending a few other Fort Belvoir officers there as the one-year tour fit in well before attending the Officer Advanced course. The Advance course usually happened after four years of service. "That is pretty far from Hawaii."

"Oh come on, I spent a tour there and loved it. You report September 4, 1982. I'll be posting your orders and you have a few months to get ready."

Phew, reassignment happened quickly. For my next step, I went to the library and read up on Korea. I asked some other officers about their assignments. All the career Army officers said they had a great time, so I kept an open mind. I had developed a groove regarding the Army plus the positive feedback from my superiors had me considering making a career, despite my disdain for the lack of technical work. A tour in Korea would enable me to see the real army in action as South Korea technically was still at war with North Korea.

Charlie also was reassigned. He was going to Saudi Arabia. John stayed at Fort Belvoir. We had to sell the house and we did. I made arrangements for my car and my household goods as part of the permanent change of station. The army had the process down like clockwork and before long I was boarding an airplane for the land of the Morning Calm.

Since Terry and I started dating seriously we had to make

plans for the year separation. I suppose I viewed it as a good test of the strength of our relationship. Right before I left for Korea we drove together to Long Island to visit with my parents. Everyone got along very well but judging from all the letters we wrote each other while I was in Korea we were sad to say goodbye.

Chapter 22 The Land Time Forgot

The plane ride to Seoul took a brutal 27 hours. I had layovers in Kansas City, Fairbanks, and Tokyo. We exited the charter flight at Osan Air Base, about 60 miles south of the Korean capital. A bus met us and drove the arrivees to Yongsan Army Base on the west side of Seoul close to the Han River. It was the largest and most central US military facility in Korea and headquarters for the 8th Army.

The enlisted personnel clerk processing my orders set me up as a platoon leader in Charlie Company of the 44th Engineering Battalion even though I told him I was a First Lieutenant and had already been a platoon leader. It didn't matter to him. He merely matched officers to openings on his list.

Next a five quarters ton pickup truck drove me 20 miles from Yongsan to Camp Mercer where my new battalion had its headquarters. The pickup truck arrived after duty hours, so the battalion staff duty officer explained the Camp Mercer officer's quarters were being renovated and they had no billets for me in the camp. He told the driver to take me to Hotel Yaja in Bucheon where the battalion had reserved several rooms.

We drove in the evening darkness to Bucheon, and I noted Korean civilian drivers turned their headlights off when stopped at road intersections. I asked the driver why and he didn't know. Theories ranged from conserving life on low quality headlight bulbs, being respectful of oncoming drivers who naturally have poor night vision, to maintaining tactical light discipline, after all

North Korea was only sixty miles away. Regardless, the pickup approached a four story, dumpy looking hotel. I grabbed my gear and the driver said he'd be back by 6 am the next morning to pick me up. I checked my wrist to see the time and realized my electronic watch had stopped working due to a dead battery.

"Roger, 6am. I'll be ready," and waved the driver off.

I spent my first night in Korea in a drab hotel room with cockroaches and no air conditioning. A warm fall night encouraged me to leave the window open and there was a constant din from the street. Vendors, workers and passersbys conducted business as if it were daytime. The galimatias coming up from below combined with my jet lag made it hard to sleep. With no idea of the time, I tossed and turned until I heard some other patrons moving in the hotel.

I arose, groggy from the jet lag and lack of sleep, but adrenaline kicked in as this was only my third time outside the USA. I put on the new army Battle Dress Uniform (BDU, a pants and over shirt combination in woodland camouflage pattern. The shirt had long sleeves and was worn overhanging cargo pants. Other than the green, brown and dark blue color of the camouflage the main feature of the new ensemble was nine pockets. The BDU shirt had two pockets over the breast, two more on the shirt on the bottom front, and five more on pants, including two baggy pockets on the outside of the legs. The bottom of the pants contained a string designed to cinch the fabric over the top of combat boots. I found the raiment very logical and comfortable. Walking down the dim staircase of the hotel I met few other officers staying at the hotel. They wore the old green fatigues I always thought belonged on a janitor not a soldier.

Lieutenant Meyer from Connecticut led a platoon in Charlie Company. His stocky build supported a round jovial head with lips that telegraphed his point of view and a hairline dangerously close to his eyebrows. Lieutenant Bucceri had a pale complexion and greasy black hair matching his short-time attitude. He was a couple of days from transferring back to the CONUS. Bucceri had a motor mouth and complained about everything. Meyer, as a second lieutenant, kept more reserved. The last officer was Warrant Officer Campbell from Alpha Company. Warrant officers are technical specialists residing in the nether areas of the Army rank structure, between a non-commissioned officer and a regular officer. Their rank afforded them a good deal of latitude as enlisted men had to treat them like officers and officers, if they were smart, left them alone to accomplish their technical mission.

Two vehicles from the battalion arrived and we rode together the several miles to Camp Mercer. The truck dropped me off by the headquarters area. I reported to the Battalion Commander, Lieutenant Colonel Stan Higgins. His assistant let me in his office, a spacious room inside a semi-cylinder Quonset-hut type building.

I came to attention and snapped a salute.

"Sir, Lieutenant Kempinski reporting for duty."

Higgins had a tall lean frame and a sagacious face with salt and pepper curly hair like something a jazz band member would sport.

"At ease Lieutenant."

I passed him my orders and personnel file. He examined my record.

"I see you had platoon and brigade staff experience. It might be a letdown, but I could use you in battalion staff. The S3, Major Robin Trababa, is on personal leave for a month but you can work with Captain Bill Lionel, the other officer in the operations office."

"Sounds good, sir."

"Are you married?"

"No sir."

"Any hobbies?"

"Sports cars and I like to golf."

"Yes, I see you were the Belvoir Champion. I don't play but there's an Army golf course in Yongsan. You should play there."

I found it interesting he encouraged me to play golf, as I considered it only a remote possibility.

The commander continued. "We have an important series of events coming up, our annual inspection from the IG and in winter, our army readiness test and Team Spirit, the largest military exercise in the army."

"Sounds like a challenge sir, I'm up for it."

"Excellent. Welcome to the 44th, the Broken Heart battalion."

I came to attention and saluted, then exited. I found my way to the S3 shop which was in a similar dark green Quonset hut next door to the Battalion HQ. Surrounding both buildings were half walls made of perforated steel plates filled with soil and rocks, intended as makeshift protection from artillery rounds. The building reflected crude theater of operations construction, with no central heat or air conditioning. Instead each room had a round drum fashioned into a drip diesel fuel heater and a couple of windows.

I checked in to the S3 shop and met Captain Lionel and the rest of the soldiers.

Lionel shook my hand. "Welcome to S3. I'm the construction officer and you'll be the training officer." Lionel stood about five inches taller than me and he had an athletic build, yet his face had a softness making him look younger than his years. "Here's your desk." He pointed to a metal desk nestled next to a wall locker. It was oriented perpendicular to his and arranged so our backs would be next to each other's. On the side of a short wall was a diesel stove and the major's desk.

Our office had an outside door and one door leading to an open bay where the enlisted men worked scheduling the Battalion's activity. We had a Master Sergeant Wheelen, a large man with a furrowed face and a full head of premature grey hair. While he was older than everyone else in the company, he appeared much older than he was. Under him were a variety of soldiers including Pennsylvanian, Specialist Stengle, the scheduler. Stengle could have easily been a 12C bridge builder. He towered over everyone other than Master Sergeant Wheelen, but unlike Wheelen, Stengle had mass. Stengle has spent two consecutive tours in Korea as he had a steady Korean girlfriend. Most of the GIs reveled in the availability of Korean women, even if they were prostitutes. The soldiers were barely 18 and many never had a date, yet here were women trained by their culture to be subservient to men. And men, even buck privates, appeared rich when they came from the land of the big PX.

Private Jang occupied a desk across the room from Stengle. Jang's face barely required shaving and his high-pitched voice suggested he hadn't finished puberty. He was Korean augmentee to the US Army commonly called KATUSA and handled our various accounts for fuel, ammunition, and supplies. Since every Korean male had to serve two years in the Korean military the ROK army had a plethora of soldiers. KATUSA soldiers filled out US Army ranks reducing the expense to Uncle Sam. Individuals selected for these positions had to be fluent in English and possess a higher intellect than the average draftee meaning the majority of these guys had a mental upper hand on the typical US enlisted soldier. However, the requirement to interact with us in English didn't mke them seem so smart. I also suspected these selectees came from families with some influence in the Korean political sphere as an assignment to an American unit meant a much easier time than if they spent two years in a regular ROK unit.

In addition to training, I had responsibility for overseeing the battalion communications section. Led by Staff Sergeant Bronkly, this section had ten men who would set up the various radios and communication gear to enable operation of the battalion. Bronkly hailed from Virginia and spoke with a bit of a southern drawl combined with an earnest look and blond hair receding rapidly from his forehead. The other section I oversaw was the surveyors' section, a typical part of a combat construction battalion. Specialist Dumphries led the section. Dumphries had a serious approach to life and focused on doing his job as best as he could. Part of this I think came from his implied responsibility, as unlike the rest of us single guys, he married a local lady and needed to decide how he fit in with the Korean society.

Private JH Kim, another KATUSA, was assigned as my driver. Since nearly half the people in Korea had the name Kim we always used their first two initials when addressing the dozen or so Kims in our company. He had a slight build and a youthful face and like every other KATUSA, stiff-straight jet-black hair cut in the standard ROK "bucket cut," high and tight. Although JH passed the written English exam, his spoken language skills did not match his book knowledge. Prior to joining the 44th Engineer Battalion he had never driven a car. JH's lack of driving skills didn't bother me, but his total inattention to the roads did. I never yelled at anyone the way I did at JH as he was oblivious to the danger and care required to drive especially on the congested roads in and around Camp Mercer and Seoul. On many occasions if I did not warn him we would have been crushed by a truck or bus.

One aspect of my job as the assistant battalion S3 required traveling through large parts of the countryside in the US army sector of operations. I'd visit our remote companies as Camp Mercer held only three, HHC, Alpha and Charlie, of the five companies in our battalion. Delta company resided at Camp Indian, near Uijeongbu, north and slightly east of Seoul. Also, in Uijeongbu the Combined Field Army had their headquarters near the site of a major battle in 1951. Further north, Dongducheon, near the Demilitarized Zone, hosted Bravo Company in the small Camp Nimble. This camp sat across the river from Camp Casey home of the Second Infantry Division. Frequently I would travel with Major Kim, a Republic of Korea Army officer assigned as a liaison to the 44th Engineer Battalion. We'd visit terrain assigned to ROK units to secure permission to train in their geographic areas meaning JH and I spent a lot of time in the rural areas of northwest Korea.

The Korean countryside reminded me of rustic West Virginia supplemented with low density slums and lots of flooded fields for rice. The Koreans farmers were poor, very poor. They applied their industrious nature to the hard work of rice and cabbage farming yet reaped very little reward. Most homes had crude concrete walls with makeshift roofs, no running water and no electricity. Many times, in the early mornings I witnessed farmers performing various bodily functions in the dirt courtyards outside their hovels.

The government had the people worked up to a near frenzy about war with North Korea. Everywhere there were indications of potential conflict. The government thrived on making sure this was the case. Adult male Koreans had to join the army for two years during which there were paid about five dollars per month and subjected to brute force army living. The army had a ubiquitous impact. Military vehicles of all types, from jeeps to self-propelled artillery, covered the roads; soldiers and sailors flooded the train stations and city streets. All civilian structures with any tactical importance, like gas tanks, water towers and bridges, etc., had camouflaged paint or netting. The airports were surrounded by barbed razor-wire fences and antiaircraft guns crewed by soldiers. Regular air defense practice alerts involved the whole populace. Major highways had road blocks every few miles and stopped each vehicle creating tremendous traffic jams. Even the golf courses, considered as possible invasion sites due to the open space, had trees planted in the middle of the fairways or cables strung across the greens to discourage airplanes from landing.

Surrounding Seoul were two rings of walls resembling levees. Interestingly these structures stood way above the river and weren't placed to stop flood waters. Rather their design goal was to stop or delay a North Korean attack, much like the Great Wall of China. Each road puncturing the barriers had a massive concrete block suspended over it with the edges of the mass prechambered with explosives. If the balloon went up and the enemy advanced on Seoul, the Korean combat engineers would blow the charges and the huge concrete block would fall and seal off the road.

When war happened, all civilians had a defined mission.

Youth would be called to active duty and women and old men would take on civil defense roles. Even the prostitutes had to move out to a designated zone.

Chapter 23 In the Army Now

My first month with the Broken Heart Battalion presented a slow introduction to Army life in Korea as my superior officer, the S3, Major Trababa, enjoyed his annual leave. The Broken Heart logo, a red heart ripped asunder appeared everywhere in the Camp. Either painted on signs or on stickers, it's ubiquity reminded soldiers of the unit's history where the men suddenly left for the Korean War leaving a beach full of broken-hearted women.

Upon the boss' return the pace increased significantly. Trababa had a slight build with a round olive face revealing his Filipino-American descent. He graduated from West Point and was single. He had no time for a wife as he devoted his life to the US Army, eating, breathing and thinking continuously how to make the battalion a better fighting force. Our duty hours started with 6 AM physical training and concluded each evening with a 7:30 PM-to-whenever staff meeting. One evening at staff meetings as we were nearing the end of the session, he mentioned reading, and said, "Bill and Rob, if you want to prepare for a military career, you need to read. Preparation is key. Here is a list of books every Army officer should read." He passed us a mimeographed sheet listing twenty books including Sun Tsu's *The Art of War*, President John F. Kennedy's *Profiles of Courage*, and Carl von Clauswitz *On War*.

I noticed a science fiction story at the end I had read by Robert Heinlein. "Science fiction included? I see *Starship Trooper* made your list."

Trababa wiggled in his chair. I would learn it was his favorite move indicating he was readying for intellectual debate. "A great book describing small unit tactics and leadership."

I didn't disagree as I found it to be my favorite Heinlein

story.

With the list distributed Trababa asked me to stay and he dismissed Lionel.

"Rob, the training section had been adrift due to having no officer assigned. We train like we will fight so I need you to fix the situation. I want a robust training program."

"Yes sir. Can do. I will lay out a plan and get back to you in a few days." I saluted and left the meeting.

I took on the boss's urging to better the battalion's training fidelity. My method was simple, follow the Army regulations and standards because much brain power at headquarters had been expended to develop them. In the next two days, I visited the various companies of the battalion, meeting the sergeants assigned to manage the training. The level of implementation varied but was lacking in all units. None of the sergeants had instruction in training management, they were all thrust in the job as a stop gap measure. This was a common situation in Korea, with unit staffing at perhaps 70% authorized level, the army just assigned extra jobs to people and hoped they got done. Even worse was the situation at headquarters, the budgets and schedule had holes and were incomplete and out of date. It would be hard to lead if our example had flaws.

In a few days, I briefed Trababa on what I found, and he agreed. To his credit that was all he said, and he let me do what needed to get done, a strong indicator of good leadership; delegate and verify, but no micromanagement. I respected the major for his confidence in me. Slowly, through oversight, guidance and dig-ging in and working side-by-side with the training sergeants, each company in the battalion increased the fidelity, accuracy and in theory the effectiveness of their training.

Despite doing a decent job as the battalion training officer, a big decision loomed over me like the proverbial elephant, not in the room, but in my mind: what to do about an army career? I had told myself that I'd give the real army a chance by observing how it operated in Korea. Yet not soon after I set my first footsteps in Korea at Osan Air Base, I sensed the army career path fading away. The lack of high-tech work bugged me the most. I yearned to be in the space, aviation or automotive fields designing and building mechanical stuff. I even had a large poster of a cutaway drawing of the space shuttle over my desk in the S3's shop. I remembered fondly doing some minor work at Tech supporting Dr. Berry with a consulting job designing the shuttle's robot arm.

Sure, the Army posed physical and leadership issues, but the primitive nature of work did not satisfy my technological interests. I needed to be pushing industry boundaries, working with new concepts and innovations. Yet, perhaps the deciding factor had nothing to do with the Army per se, but the geopolitics of how our leaders used the Army. While South Korea and North Korea never signed a peace treaty, the ominous feeling of supporting the south's dictatorship eroded my confidence in the overall strategic policy and intentions of our government. I had already witnessed how inefficient and, frankly wasteful, the military operated, but putting our collective lives on the line for a dictator irked me. I made a de-cision but neither voiced it or wrote it, just filed it away for future action.

Chapter 24 Jeremiah Gone-some

As the warm weather turned to fall, I sat next to Jang and reviewed the new budgets we developed for ammunition and fuel. I heard Stengle across the room and the other soldiers in the S3 shop talk about 'the hawk.'

"You guys are always talking about a hawk. What kind of hawk is coming?"

Stengle said from his desk, which could have been doll furniture placed in front of his massive frame. "Oh yes sir, the hawk is coming."

I dropped my hands and opened them towards him like a

beggar and said, "The hawk. What gives?"

Wheelen jumped in. "The cold sir." He put his arms around his shoulders like he was shivering. "I never froze as bad in my life as I did in the last winter I spent in Korea."

Stengle jumped in. "Hey sir, I'm from Pennsylvania, and when a Siberian front moves through, it makes home feel tropical."

"Great. I guess I'll get long underwear."

The troops laughed, and we returned to the task of planning our upcoming field exercise.

Since we weren't in actual combat, the acid test would be how the unit simulated the wartime mission. We planned a major training event for the winter. It would start with the battalion's annual evaluation, called ARTEP. This would take place in the northern US sector near Baekui-ri, famous among GIs for the "Chinese Tunnel," a crudely hacked road through a mountain cliff made by the Japanese Army in 1930 when Japan occupied Korea. I don't know why the Japanese tunnel was termed the Chinese tunnel, but it was. After ten days, we would mobilize the whole battalion to central Korea for Operation Team Spirit, the largest military exercise in the western world. After Team Spirit the battalion would relocate north to our usual operations area and perform construction activity under field conditions. All in all, we would be deployed for nearly two straight months.

Before we could take on the annual ARTEP, we scheduled each company for practice exercises. The S3 shop belonged to Headquarters and Headquarters Company, commonly called HHC, so we would take our training with our parent unit. Standard operating procedure required the soldiers don the chemical protective suit ensemble, an olive drab charcoal-lined jacket and pants worn over the field uniform. The complete ensemble included rubber boot covers, rubber gloves and a hooded gas mask. Military intelligence suggested if North Korea were to attack they would use chemical weapons so the suit offered protection against both gas and liquid agents but at a tremendous cost in efficiency. In the winter, I didn't mind the extra layer as it provided warmth, but it added significant bulk making every day movement a chore. Something as simple as bending over to pick up an item strained my back and leg muscles. Wearing the suit for hours on end made my body numb from constant struggle against the bulk of the thick charcoal lining. In the summer time, the suit could kill by inducing heat exhaustion and required careful observation and management of the soldiers for overheating.

Prior to the convoy movement, I donned the chemical protective suit, then added my load bearing harness holding my canteen, ammo pouches, compass, and first aid kit over the suit. Hanging from my right hip was the gas mask in its canvas cover with the bottom of the carrier strapped around my thigh. The rubber gloves and booties of the chemical ensemble filled most of my rucksack. Over this gear, I put one arm in my flak jacket, an oversized vest with stiff kevlar plates that pushed up against the back of my neck. I topped off my outfit with the heavy M1 helmet and my 45-caliber pistol. With all this gear I probably had 60 pounds of extra weight which made walking back and forth to check on the status of our vehicles enough of a chore that my legs and back revolted in spasms. Nonetheless when all was secure we signaled the convoy leader and moved out into the dark.

We deployed to a small valley east of the Chinese tunnel and set up above the bank of the river. Despite wearing the heavy gear, the team quickly assembled the battalion tactical operations center, or TOC, a five-ton truck with a covered box, like a camouflaged recreational vehicle except instead of creature comforts we had a small compartment loaded with AM radios in the front and an open area for maps, briefings and decision making in the rear. Attached to the box, Major Trabab a had designed and procured a locally-built custom tent using aluminum poles for a frame. This gave the TOC an attached seating area for operations activity. The troops set up a general-purpose small tent with diesel stove, a generator for the radios, antennas and topped it off with a camouflage net, a large olive drab and brown semitransparent contraption akin to a bridal veil intended to disguise whatever was underneath it.

Last, they set up barbed wire along the perimeter of the operations area.

While our set up went well, the rest of headquarters Company, set to bivouac about a mile from us, had problems and arrived at their area late with no water, low on fuel, and no time to set up the mess facilities. This posed immediate problems as the sun was setting and my guys had not had lunch or dinner. I talked it over with Sergeant Wheelen and we decided to send him with the troops to Camp Howe, about 30 miles away for food, while Sergeant Bronkly and I remained with the equipment. As the men departed, Bronkly and I set up a portable diesel burner inside the TOC tent to stay warm.

Within 20 minutes of the troops departing, snow started to fall at a fast rate.

"Check it out Sarge, pretty heavy snow. Did you bring skis?"

He laughed. "No sir, I'm a southern boy."

"I grew up in New York, and this, even by Yankee standards, is a serious snow storm. Look at those flakes."

Bronkly stuck his head and hand outside the tent. "That's a heavy one, like the storms we used to have when I was stationed in Germany."

As we watched the quiet beauty that descends with snow I wondered out loud. "Hope the troops are alright."

"They're in good hands with Wheelen."

"I suppose so, he's been around the block a few times."

We both chuckled and shut the flap. In near white-out conditions we set up our sleeping bags inside the TOC, something not normally allowed. Although Bronkly was the communications section sergeant we did not have the generator running, as neither of us were licensed to operate it, so the TOC radios sat idle due to no electricity. The crew had taken our two trucks and my Jeep. Captain Lionel was home on annual leave. The major was visiting Bravo Company and not expected until tomorrow so we were stuck at the TOC on our own in the wilds of Korea. It was a surreal feeling to be surrounded by so much military might, yet to be so isolated like Jack Nicholson's family in *The Shining*.

After a couple of hours as the heavy white flakes continued to fall, the troops had not returned. Looking at my watch I said, "Hey Sergeant Bronkly, where do you think the troops are?"

Bronkly face perked out of the opening of his sleeping bag, "My guess is with this much snow, the base commander at Camp Howe probably locked down the base."

"Yeah, we might not see them until tomorrow."

"You and I sir have to hold down the TOC."

I scratched my head and then pressed on my empty belly. "I don't know about you but I'm starving."

"Same here but we'll survive," he said as he rubbed the slight paunch middle age deposited on his midsection.

Despite the calm, security was an issue as local villagers were known to steal anything not watched, so I told Bronkly I'd pull guard duty while he caught some shuteye. Every half hour I'd walk around the TOC perimeter using my eyes' natural night vision to take in the splendor of hauntingly large snowflakes blanketing the river valley.

By morning the snow let up but our troops still had not returned.

"Still no sign of the troops," I offered from my sleeping bag.

"Wheelen probably has them holed up at Camp Howe, or in a ville with some mama-sans."

"Now that would be something, preparing for war by

shacking up with some hookers."

"It wouldn't be the first time."

Despite the cold and our hunger, we laughed, but Bronkly's normally jovial face turned serious.

"You know sir, Dumphries' five quarter has the diesel cans. The stove's can is almost empty."

"Well, shut it down. We'll have to rough it and ration the fuel by burning some every so often."

"Damn, it's going to get cold. Next time I'm telling the troops to leave the stove fuel at the TOC."

"Next time, we'll do a couple of other things differently, like splitting the guys so we can operate the TOC. The major is going to be pissed the battalion net is not up."

"Yes. When he gets here, we'll get warm enough."

"Let's not worry about that. Since the heat is off, I'm going to pile up some snow around the tent for insulation." I went outside and using an entrenching tool heaped snow against the bottom of the tent as a wind barrier and a layer of thermal mass. Visions of Jeremiah Johnson ran through my head as we faced the wilderness of Korea covered in a thick white blanket.

Soon, our stomachs started to growl and so we scrounged for food. I had some raisins I shared with the communication chief. Bronkly found some Mountain Dew belonging to one of the guys in the radio room.

I popped my can and raised it as a toast. "Too bad for whomever wanted a sweet treat."

"Beggars can't be choosy," he replied. We each drank a can, and the sugar gave us some energy.

Bronkly fired up the stove and I melted some snow in my steel helmet. Using a wash cloth, I cleaned my face, then shaved in the not so warm water. My companion's fair hair and relatively sparse chin fuzz helped disguise his skipping of the morning male ritual.

We wondered if we should try to start the TOC's 100-Kilo-watt generator, but neither of us were trained on it and we didn't want to risk damaging the equipment. All we could do was try to fend off the cold even though we were both wet and had no food and little water.

As the day passed we had no idea where or what our troops were doing. A jeep from another unit passed by and told us the Combined Field Army commander had suspended all training due to the deep snow. We figured with the jeeps being able to get through we should get some food by evening, so we each had another Mountain Dew and relaxed. By nightfall our troops had not yet returned and we both craved something to eat. We heard a diesel engine revving in the distance so Bronkly and I peered out the tent. The headlights revealed a deuce and half truck from Headquarters Company approaching along the river bed. We waded out in the drifts to meet the truck and to our delight it was from the company's mess hall. We grabbed an insulated can with chili-mac and sliced bread, a staple for the field mess. We spooned out the food into our aluminum mess kits and scarfed down the warm concoction. There was plenty as they expected to feed our whole section. The food truck driver collected the insulated containers and dropped some meal-ready-to-eat packages and told us he'd be back in the morning with breakfast and so we prepared for another night in the TOC, making regular checks on the security of the idle generator and barbed wire perimeter.

Finally, mid-morning of day three our soldiers returned to the TOC. They spent the two nights sleeping in the mess hall at Camp Howe and complained they had none of their gear. At least they were warm. They did bring some coffee and some powdered eggs and bacon and the diesel fuel. The crew started the generator and stoves providing lights and a bit of heat. Unfortunately, the snow caused the cancellation of another day of training, so we had the troops clear out the snow around the trucks and practice local patrols on foot to the nearest village.

The remainder of the field training exercise became a lesson in driving in the snow as we packed up the gear on day four and headed back to Camp Mercer. The key point learned was the tactical tires on army trucks have large scalloped cut on their sides, ideal for driving in mud and dirt, but not at all suited for snow and ice. For safety's sake the convoy crawled along the highways, taking almost twice as long as normal. While the troop's morale turned up , judging by the number of wisecracks, the early return to camp meant we had a tough road ahead of us as we would have to really work to prepare the unit for the ARTEP, meaning more field time.

Chapter 25 Breakfast at Tiffan-Lee's

Sure enough, Major Trababa decided we needed at least one more field training exercise for HHC prior to the ARTEP so when the weather cleared, Major Kim and I set out to find a training area where we could operate. To do so we drove about two hours northeast to visit a ROK infantry unit. JH and I followed the Major's jeep into a ROK army compound. Major Kim exited his jeep and waved to me.

"Ah Lieutenant, we arrive at lunch-e," Major Kim said. Like most Koreans he had a tendency to put the e-sound at the end of English words. "We eat with ROK unit. But one warning. General Lee no allow talk-ee during lunch-e."

"Sure, no problem sir. What about the drivers?"

"Ho," the Major muttered his face getting implacable. He sounded off in firm Korean to JH and the other driver. They cowered, then saluted and remained with the jeeps as we entered the mess hall.

The facility sparkled with a Spartan elegance, like a primitive Bauhaus rendition of a dining facility, but only serving officers. There were twenty round tables with white table cloths with big Korean-style lazy susans. I sat with a group of other Korean lieutenants all in fatigues. Someone offered a command and all the officers rose to attention, so I followed form. The ROK general entered and took a seat which was the signal for the rest of us to sit. Then enlisted soldiers wearing white kitchen uniforms brought us each a cup of rice and placed various meats and vegetables on the large turntable. Next, the servers brought individual bowls of soup. The junior officers at my table held stoic faces, then as if some hidden signal sounded, started to eat the soup in unison. I followed their lead. Before I finished the broth, my spoon encountered a strange hunk of orange and red stringy protein at the bottom of the bowl, something I can only describe as an alien life form. Not being able to ask the other officers what we were eating, my imagination conjured crazy ideas and caused my appetite to quickly wan. Not to be rude, I nibbled on some rice and kimchi until the meal concluded. Later, I asked Major Kim what was in the soup and he said he didn't know.

After coordinating use of the host unit's operational area, the Major and I went our separate ways. A few minutes later on the highway I asked JH, "Did you enjoy lunch?" Maybe he had the same soup and could identify it. JH did not respond.

I knew something was wrong, so I asked a bit louder, "Hey, did you eat lunch?"

He shook his head no.

"Damn." I had previously witnessed how the ROK army had appeared to mistreat their inductees, but JH was my troop and under my care. "Alright, in the next 'ville we pass, stop at a restaurant, I'll buy you lunch."

Kim nodded and his usual blank expression changed as his lips broke into a smile but only for a second.

As JH ate a simple meal of rice and beef with lettuce, I observed some civilians building a stone retaining wall next to the river. The town had assembled all the old folks, and I mean all of them, men and women, into a bucket brigade as they passed stones or bags of dirt to the river bed. Most of them had passed retirement age yet there they were sloughing heavy loads from one to the other. This activity summed up the work ethic and communal nature I had observed throughout the country.

The mindset was no unemployment, for unemployment meant starvation. I saw people do the most ridiculous things just to have a job. If someone could use an assistant, they had one. The bus drivers had high school-aged girls collect fares as passengers boarded. Barbers had a woman sweep up the cut hair and give the customer a strange back rub by clapping their hands over the guest's spine as if conjuring some sort of Asian mojo.

Korea in the early eighties still retained developing country status, with many people outside Seoul living in near primitive conditions. Yet the upcoming Summer Olympics on the Han River plain served as a tipping point to move the country into what the west called NIC, or newly industrialized country status. With their work ethic and focused management attention, the progress the country made in technology, industrialization and quality of life bordered on phenomenal and was only tempered by military threat of their belligerent neighbor to the north.

Chapter 26 The Longest Yard

When my birthday, March 2, rolled around, the whole battalion deployed for the beginning of a long field training exercise. We started with an ARTEP, a seven-day exam of our unit readiness by external evaluators. This was akin to the Battalion's annual exam. After the ARTEP, we'd have two weeks participating in Team Spirit to take part in the simulated battle combining many South Korean Army divisions with the American 2nd infantry division from Dongducheon, the 25th-infantry division from Fort Schafer, Hawaii, and the 7th infantry division from Fort Ord, California. Headquarters billed it as the "largest war game in the free world" and witnessing 192,000 soldiers moving over the area of operations I'd have to agree. After Team Spirit, Trababa planned to move the battalion back north near the Chinese Tunnel for a three-week field exercise focused on our construction mission.

For the annual training evaluation, I developed a training plan where the Battalion was going to accomplish most of its required tasks in six days. We would have each of our companies doing a variety of missions from basic field skills such as infantry patrolling to engineer tasks like building a wooden bridge over a ravine, emplacing tank obstacles, and clearing paths. The planned operations tempo would pose a challenge to the units as we adopted a simulated combat scenario.

For the evaluation, we deployed to our favorite location in the Cheongnyang Valley. We set up the company on the side of a small hill overlooking the valley giving the AM radios good line of sight.

As the battalion training officer, my job in the field morphed from training management into operations, with duties conveying higher headquarters orders to the various companies and overseeing quality control of the missions. I also monitored the work of our troops in the tactical operations center and checked the alertness of the men pulling security in foxholes around our area.

The technical operations center worked 24 hours a day for the duration of the event. Lionel and I alternated twelve-hour shifts orchestrating the battalion's missions. The major would only be around for the staff meeting. I had the night and Lionel had the day. In our off-shift time we had to supervise the troops and liaison with the battalion's companies. Sleep did not fit in the equation and within two days we adopted a near-zombie like state, taking short naps when we could.

The temperatures at dark rimed the ground with frost and turned it rock hard. At daybreak, as the sun rose, the ice would melt and transform the ground into mud made especially messy by the constant tactical wheeled traffic that churned it into a furrowed, slushy mire. My daytime duties required I traipse across this sloppy mess and with each step my boots would penetrate the muck. Taking the next step entailed lifting my foot yet the wet Korean soil's suction would fight back and only grudgingly release my leg after giving my knee a vicious tug. A few days of this assault my knee joints really started to ache, I reluctantly considered going on sick call, a first for me. On the fourth day, I could barely walk, and as I hobbled into the TOC. Lionel saw me limping and asked, "What did you do to your leg?"

"My knees are killing me. The suction from this mud feels like a bull pulling back every time I take a step."

"That stinks."

"At night, my legs feel fine because the ground is frozen."

"I tell you what, how about we switch shifts. You work the day and I'll take the night."

"It's worth a shot. Thanks. I appreciate it."

The day session in the TOC kept me away from the mud and freed me to check on the troops in the night. While it was colder, the frozen ground did not bother my knees and the soreness went away. Lionel's gracious act was tempered by the fact he managed to sleep most of the day while the unit was otherwise occupied. Win-win I suppose.

The battalion performed well and passed the evaluation. Our leaders were pleased, but the work was just beginning, the whole battalion had to redeploy about 100 miles south in the Gyeong-gi region to join Team Spirit. The Army held the war game in the middle of the country away from the Demilitarized Zone so as not to rile the always irritable North Koreans. Adding two more American divisions to the peninsula had already brought the communist nation to a near-war frenzy. Pyongyang placed its armed forces on a "semi-war" footing and conducted a media campaign for drumming up domestic and international negativism toward the exercise.

Chapter 27 Fast and Spurious

As the ARTEP had progressed, I had noticed an uptick in

military traffic on the roads in our area of operations, yet as the battalion approached the central part of the country, the quantity of soldiers and equipment on the move boggled the mind. Two hundred thousand soldiers, trucks, tanks, artillery and aircraft moved everywhere. Intersections flowed with tactical vehicles as the military dominated the arteries like salmon rushing the cascades. The civilians were either smart enough to stay off the roads or travel a different route.

Engineer units by nature of the mission have many vehicles so we had the luxury of driving to the battle. The infantry had no such luck. They walked. Loaded with back packs, ammunition boxes, radios, Dragon anti-tank missiles and all other kinds of gear, ground pounders lined the sides of the road for miles, the face of each soldier reflecting their toil.

Korean grunts particularly suffered as their officers did not practice care of their charges. At one point, we had to stop our convoy due to a mass of haggard ROK troops blocking the dirt road. They were filthy, ragged and in a variety of uniforms looking more like a gaggle of deserters than an effective fighting force. When they noticed we had a water buffalo (a 300-gallon water trailer) towed behind a deuce and a half, they surrounded the trailer and clamored in a rabble of voices. JH translated they hadn't had water in two days while they marched south. As the officer in charge I told them to fill their canteens, figuring their constitutions could handle the water, even though we considered it non-potable. After half or so filled their canteens, some junior ROK officers arrived and start-ed berating and pushing and punching their soldiers away from the spigots. I didn't say anything, but was glad at least some refreshed their drinking supply. The mistreatment of their draftees added one more consideration to my impending career decision.

For Team Spirit, we were attached to the 2nd Engineer Battalion from the 2nd Infantry Division meaning our engineers would help them accomplish their mission. The Second, as an engineer unit organic to an Infantry Division, would be mobile following the forward edge of battle while we established a position thirty-miles to the rear as combat support. I had a new role; each day I was to attend the 2nd Engineer Battalion's evening staff meeting and accept our missions. This meant each evening I'd radio their tactical operations center using codes set up for the war game and find out where they were located. With this information, JH and I would track them down.

The first time we linked up with the maneuver unit I was surprised by the size of the 2nd battalion's tactical operations center; it was nothing more than a camouflage net over an M-113 Armored Personnel Carrier, unlike our battalion which had tents, barbed wire fence, a large motor pool of earth moving equipment and even a massive rock crusher. I suppose that's why our unit was thirty miles behind the edge of battle, while the 2nd moved regularly depending on the flow of the conflict. The staff meeting took about an hour and it was dark when we headed back to our headquarters with the orders for the night and next day.

The second day, the second battalion radioed their position was up a draw at a high up altitude. The flow of the war game pushed them about a mile west from where they were for our first meeting. JH and I took the jeep up the same road we traveled the day before as it was fairly smooth. As we approached the turnoff to start on the trail up the mountain to our rendezvous point, a US Army major, wearing a white band on his helmet flagged us down.

"Hey lieutenant, where you headed?" he asked from the side of the road. The white helmet band indicated he was a Team Spirit umpire, but more importantly, meant we had to be near the action.

"Up this trail to link up with the second engineers, we are in a support role."

"Really," his said as his eyes twinkled like an amused kid ready to open a birthday present, "look at that mountain side over there." He raised his arm and pointed to a slope about half a mile away.

I could make out some movement on the side of the hill, so I raised my binoculars to my eyes. Yikes, there was a swarm of helmets bobbing up and down with orange bands - the opposing forces.

"Oh boy," I squeaked. War game or not, the idea of being captured activated my adrenal cortex, and thirty different hormones drove me to hyperarousal state.

As the umpire, he had the authority to determine our fate in the war game, and for a second, I started to dread this mission, as the opposing force was a ROK unit. I knew they'd be rough on me as a prisoner and brutal towards JH, since they had quite a bit of jealousy towards KATUSA soldiers.

"You are lucky," the Major smirked. "I'd say you're 200 yards out of machine gun range. You better get moving as the whole front is surging south west."

"Roger that sir, thanks," I saluted and told JH, "Floor it, we got to get out of here before they call for artillery."

JH pushed the pedal and the jeep jounced along the trail.

"Faster," I urged. "We don't want to be captured by the infantry. Number 10." I figured the ubiquitous GI slang for bad would most effectively convey the direness of our position.

The jeep climbed up the mountainside and turned behind a ridge in a defilade position from the enemy. "Keep going, don't slow down."

We made a few more turns as we climbed and finally found the Second Engineers' operations APC on a small rice paddy.

I told the captain, their acting S3, about the enemy whereabouts and he radioed the contact information to his units and higher headquarters. He came out of his APC. "Meeting canceled, we have to bali bali." He gave me a piece of paper with our missions and said bye.

The APC rumbled down the edge of the paddy and through the muck. The jeep could probably follow but we needed to get back to our TOC. I studied my map for a minute and decided to follow the trail we were on further up the mountain until we could catch a connecting route back south. The path should keep us away from the enemy. The higher we rose the more rustic the trail became but the trusty jeep handled the rough road without too much problem. At the apex of the mountain we had a beautiful view of the sunset over the upcoming valley, but the threat of capture tempered our enjoyment of the scenery.

JH and I made it back to base and relayed the orders. The next night I was careful to check the intel report and plan our route accordingly. I did this for several days but the inefficiency and risk of a lone jeep traveling near the front lines required a change, so I suggested to Trababa that JH and I collocate with the maneuver unit. He partially agreed saying I could spend nights with the 2nd battalion but during the day I'd have to travel south to monitor some of our unit's missions. In addition, he said switch to a five-quarter ton pickup truck as we needed a longer-range radio and to take Sergeant Wheelen for support.

"Sergeant Wheelen grab some overnight gear, we're staying up north for a few days."

Wheelen's driver was Private First Class Epstein, a mousy-faced New Englander relatively new to the unit. While he was a decent driver, he appeared remote and detached from daily activity.

"Got it Sir." Wheelen turned to the driver. "Epstein put your gear in the truck and get 12 MREs."

I grabbed my map book, the call signs and code book. We headed north making certain we had our blue helmet bands identifying which side we were on. The first night closer to the FEBA went well, we attended the staff meeting, radioed in the missions, and then found an area to catch a bit of sleep.

Chapter 28 The Bridge Over River Han

Near the end of the first week of the exercise, the blue forces were conducting an active defense, meaning they were fighting but gradually withdrawing, ceding land while inflicting heavy losses on the orange forces. As the blue units pulled back, they encountered a major obstacle, the Han River. The area of the operations lacked bridges capable of handling the heavy tanks and other military gear so the 2nd engineers had to enable a crossing with tactical bridge assets, notably ribbon bridge, just like those in my old platoon. The problem was they didn't have enough bridge segments to span the river. While they could conduct rafting operations, the number of vehicles to retrograde implied a complete span as there wasn't enough time to ferry all the vehicles and soldiers. Ferry operations posed the risk of trapping friendly units on the enemy's side of the river. This was where we came in. We had the idea to build a partial causeway of earth and gravel to shorten the span enabling the 2nd battalion's ribbon bridge to reach the far side. The commander agreed and I accepted the task to mobilize our heavy earthmoving assets to narrow the effective width of the river. I coded up the message and radioed it back to our TOC but since coding the mission meant translating words or letter into a three-digit code, I shortened the content and told the team we'd meet them at the crossing site with more instructions in the morning. The 44th TOC acknowledged the mission and said they'd have the earth moving equipment there by 0500 hours.

"Geez LT," Wheelen said, "they are going to hustle to get everything there by then."

"Us too. Look where we have to go," Wheelen and I hunched over the map using our red-filtered flashlight. The red filter enabled us to see in the dark without affecting our night vision. I pointed out the most direct route to the bridge sites. "What do you think, Sarge? The shortest way goes through the FEBA?"

"Can't go that way, sir"

"I know, Kim and I almost got captured the other day right there. Orange infantry swarming all over the place."

Wheelen traced his finger over the roads. "This is probably the best way."

I knew from experience driving on Korean roads the lines shown on the map were not always good surfaces and the route he chose went across some rough and narrow trails. "That's going to be tough in the five-quarter, especially in the dark. It will take a while."

"Yep, we better head out now and grab some sleep when we get there."

"Let's move out."

For realistic training, during Team Spirit, all vehicles drove at night under blackout conditions meaning we did not use headlights but rather a small white light with a hood on top so no aircraft could see the light beams from above. The tactical blackout meant we had to reduce our speed to no more than 15 miles per hour. Under these low light conditions, the trip to the bridge site would take a couple of hours, at least.

In very narrow areas, Wheelen and I took turns ground-guiding the truck along the road by walking in front and using our flashlights with red filters to point out the edge of the pavement as the blackout light provided little illumination. At one point, we crossed a dike between two rice paddies and the wheel-base of the pickup truck barely fit within the width of the road. We both walked on each side of the trail, giving Epstein visual clues so the truck would not slide off and drop six feet into the flooded field. We made it through the test but I could see Epstein was rattled and getting tired.

"Hang in there, Epstein, you're doing great," I said as I climbed in the middle. I gave him a gentle punch to the shoulder to lighten his mood. His face in the dim dashboards took on an especially sallow tone like he has seen a ghost, and he didn't say anything.

In a mile or so we turned onto a better road and Wheelen entered the cab. Since he was taller, I slid to the middle and let the senior NCO have the window and more leg room. Three of us inside, with the heater on, and driving on a relatively smooth road, I semi-dozed off. In about a half an hour we neared a village where the road narrowed. I was still catatonic as Epstein slowed, and barely aware where we were. The truck entered a narrow street surrounded by shoddy cement buildings typical of a poor Korean village. The mirrors missed scraping the buildings on each side by only a few inches. Wheelen jostled in his seat and craned his neck to look in the passenger side mirror. Then he half turned in his seat to look out the rear but the canvas top over the pickup bed blocked his view. He squirmed in his seat again, and his movement woke me. "What's up Sarge?"

"I don't know, there's something weird about that ville."

"Weird?"

"I thought I saw some *adashis* but not when we passed."

By now the truck had left the village and neared a field.

"Sorry, I must have dozed off. Epstein, you see anything?"

"No sir, just dark."

"Can't say what, but something didn't feel right about the ville."

I knew when a senior NCO had qualms, better listen up. "Alright Epstein pull over. Let's check this out."

Epstein stopped the truck and Wheelen and I got out and surveyed the scene. We were about 50 yards past the last house of the village. I didn't see any motion or hear anything, just the typical charcoal and manure smells of a Korean farm. Wheelen and I walked toward the village and surveyed the area for a few minutes, saw nothing, then we returned to the pickup. Wheelen unzipped the rear flap of the canvas cover.

"Holy shit, look at this sir, they cleaned out the cargo bed."

"What do you mean?" I walked up to look past him and shined my flashlight. The cargo bed was empty, no rucksack, no personal gear, nor MREs. The only item remaining was the radio as it was screwed into its frame. "What the heck, where's our gear?"

"I don't know how but the men in the ville emptied the truck as we drove through." Wheelen removed his helmet and ran his hands through his grey hair. "Damn. They even closed the zipper when they were done."

Epstein joined us at the back of the truck, "Ah sir, I had my whole combat load in my rucksack. All my uniforms and sleeping bag, all of it."

"All of it?" I asked. "I only had my sleeping bag in my waterproof bag."

"Well, when Sarge said 'grab your stuff' I didn't know how long we'd be gone, so I took my basic load."

Wheelen said, "Epstein, stay here." He turned to me, "Sir, let's see if we can find someone in the ville,"

"Forget it Sarge, we don't have any police authority. The best we can do is file a report. These *adashis* have had years of practice ripping off Uncle Sam. That stuff is probably in Itaewon by now."

Wheelen slouched from a combination of fatigue, anger and probably embarrassment from being ripped off in plain sight.

I had seen lots of cases of Korean civilians stealing from the Army. They thought of the big green machine as an extension of the 'Land of the Big PX.' If they could take it, they would.

"Let's load up. I'll file a report tomorrow."

We returned to the truck, and as I climbed into the middle of the bench seat I said to Wheelen, in a weak attempt to cheer him up, "At least they didn't get our weapons."

"Yes sir, can you imagine the paperwork."

"Forget paper, there goes your career. The Army doesn't take losing a weapon lightly. They stay in the cab with us."

We drove in silence for a few minutes, pondering our predicament of being in the field with no gear, including no sleeping bags. Thinking it would be cold without the bag, I at least had most of my personal gear back at the 44th TOC. Epstein and Wheelen were cleaned out. "After the bridge mission, we'll head back to camp and find some replacement gear."

"Yes sir," replied the two tired troops.

We made it to the bridgehead by 4 am. I tried to make a preliminary assessment of the site for the causeway, but it was impossible in the dark, so we stayed near the truck while Epstein caught some shuteye.

Our bulldozers and bucket loaders arrived right on time. We prestaged them near the shore and told the operators to grab a few minutes of sleep until day break. Along with our equipment the Commander of the 2nd Infantry Division recognized the strategic importance of the site and protective combat units appeared on both sides of the crossing, hunkering in hull defilade position like silent predators waiting for an ambush. There were several infantry companies, with at least an armor company of M-60 tanks overlooking the river and further back on some higher terrain, air defense Chaparral missiles on tracked vehicles. We'd have plenty of protection while we built our temporary dirt causeway.

As soon as the first ray of light hit the horizon, our dozers moved out. They lowered their blades and slashed into the river bank, pushing heaps of soil like behemoths playing in a sand box. The bucket loaders found gravel a half mile away and dumped the rock particles into five-ton dump trucks for transport to fill the crossing site. With each load dropped we shaped the makeshift causeway extending the bank into the flowing water. Meanwhile, the ribbon bridge started forming on the far side like an optimistic snake waiting to strike. Eventually they'd meet, making a Team Spirit version of Promontory Point.

While we piled the dirt, I wondered if the compacting was going to be adequate to keep the soil intact as there was soon to be a lot of heavy vehicle traffic traversing it. I decided to have more gravel added to the mix and headed over to the earth moving NCO when I noticed the air defense systems started to whir into action. The missiles swiveled from pointing across the river to down the river. I could hear radios crackling and all the Infantry gazed skyward.

"Hey Sarge, what do you think?" I asked Wheelen.

"Beats me sir."

Looking towards Wheelen, over his shoulder I noticed movement, a shape low over the river, about 2,000 yards away to the south. A glint off the flat shape revealed more movement behind it; two aircraft approaching. Soon the shapes enlarged, and the distinctive front profiles of two eight-engine, B-52 bombers appeared. As they closed on the bridge site they lowered in altitude so they were just above the water, their engine noise drowning out the earthmoving equipment. The Chaparrals whirled like dervishes, perhaps simulating taking a shot. I never learned if the Stratofortresses were blue or orange, but I figured they flew low enough to let all of us know we had been had. The whole episode reinforced the strategic importance of a bridge crossing and the need to make overhead cover whenever one stops, which we hadn't bothered to do, affirming the value of training.

We finished the causeway and linked up with ribbon bridge with about a half hour to spare. As we did hundreds of vehicles crossed the bridge, chewing up the hasty causeway. Although we compacted the soil as best we could, the traffic took its toll on the causeway, but the dirt lasted long enough to move the troops. We ordered our earth moving equipment back to the 44th's bivouac area, then Wheelen, Epstein and I also left the bridge site. Only a few miles from the crossing, we heard a massive amount of rifle and cannon fire. It could only mean the orange forces had reached the far side and a battle was underway at the crossing. I doubted the ribbon bridge had time to disassemble and for a second I was happy this was only training. I couldn't help but wonder why the 2nd didn't have enough ribbon units. That should be a major lesson from this exercise, get more or at least pre-stage ribbon bays.

Back at the headquarters I had to do some paper work and then convince the commander our gear was stolen. He shook his head and signed the loss report. Wheelen took Epstein further to the south to a supply depot. I managed to grab a few hours rest by sleeping in my cold weather parka half on a cot with my legs hugging our small diesel stove like a hobo around a 50-gallon drum.

Chapter 29 How We Won the War

The second week of Team Spirit blue forces took the offensive and started to move north. With the speed of battle, the 2nd battalion left us behind. The 44th took a mission to stay in the rear and clean up maneuver damage, as 100,000 troops can chew up roads and trails. While we did this, I offered the major the opportunity to try testing our unit security by taking a few soldiers from the S3 shop and probing our perimeter. We created a fake intel report advising units of enemy special operations units sabotaging rear operations. Six of us donned orange headbands and snuck up to the HHC security.

HHC had a selected a very defensible hill top position and to sneak up, we needed to cross a series of rice paddies. To avoid detection, I suggested we get in the paddy and use the dike as cover. I led the way and jumped off the divider into what I thought was a relatively solid field. To my dismay, I landed in a deep section of muck. My body sunk past my waist in the foul soup, made even more odoriferous knowing the Korean farmers used human excrement as fertilizer.

"Go around, this goop stinks and it's deep," I yelled to the troops.

Specialist Dumphries pulled me out and made an expression like better you than me, because from my chest down I was covered in dark slime.

The rest of the aggressors sprinted across the dike and reached the tree line bordering our target. Despite being in broad daylight and having warned the units about 5th column activity, we reached HHC's position without detection. To let the company commander know they'd been compromised, I popped a smoke grenade and the troops fired off a few rounds while inside the barbed wire.

We debriefed the captain about what we did and they doubled the guard. Meanwhile, Wheelen saw me covered in mud and shook his head. "Hey sir, there's a field shower about five clicks down the river. You need to get that crap off you."

"No shit Sarge, with no pun intended."

I stripped out of my field uniform and grabbed a change of BDUs. "Bring a change of clothes JH, we're going to take a shower." It would be our first shower in over two weeks.

We arrived at the field shower at dark, which was nothing more than a GP medium tent, with temporary wood pallet floor and a water purification unit hooked up to a heater and shower nozzles. Nonetheless, the warm water felt wonderful even if the air temperature hovered near freezing. The warm-cold dichotomy prevented one from lingering yet I stayed long enough to get the remnants of the rice paddy sludge off my body.

Chapter 30 A Funny Thing Happened on the Way to The Exercise

As we completed Team Spirit we once again mobilized the battalion to the north and started our construction training exercise. We planned to stay three weeks in the field tackling various projects, some with tactical value but most civil engineering jobs to benefit the small villages in the training area. The biggest project would install a soccer field for an orphanage, my favorite project while in Korea, as the living conditions in the orphanage bordered on cruelty. The field would give the children a small respite from their austere existence. A couple of us passed the hat and we bought soccer balls and supplies to make goals. The expressions on the kids' faces when they started playing on the field brought me the most satisfaction I had while in Korea.

One of the tactical projects entailed creating semi-permanent fighting positions for tanks on the sides of the mountains above a north-south oriented valley. The positions would offer US or ROK armored vehicles defilade and over watch positions, creating a strong defense in case the communists flooded the valley. We'd link these dugouts via a series of crude trails along the cliff sides. Major Trababa wanted me to oversee the project so he radioed me coordinates to meet. JH and I took off for our rendezvous.

We found the Major at the base of a steep hill.

"Hey Rob, we built one position up there." He pointed up the nearly vertical face. "I want you to examine it and put five more positions along this ridge.

"Sir, how do we check it out?"

Trababa smirked. "We drive up and see it."

"Drive up?" I assessed the imposing cliff face. "A jeep can drive up that?"

"Sure. Follow us."

Trababa hopped in his jeep and his driver took off. The jeep revved and scooted up a nearly vertical face. I could scarcely believe the vehicle could drive up a such a steep slope, but when I told JH we were following the major, his face paled three shades like he'd seen Godzilla. Obviously, JH too had never seen a jeep do such a maneuver. The problem was the major's driver had several years driving experience whereas I served as JH's de facto driver education teacher.

"Alright, JH, here's what we do. Put it in first gear and rev the engine to 3000 rpm, drop the clutch, and keep the jeep pointed up hill. Put the pedal to the floor and whatever you do, do not, repeat, do not, take your foot off the gas. Understand?"

He shook his head affirmatively.

To be certain I said, "What are you going to do?"

JH said in his broken English, "Firstee gear, big gas, straight up hill. No stoppee gasse."

"Great, let's go."

JH popped the clutch in low gear and the jeep surged up the hill.

"Follow the tracks," I suggested.

JH nodded with his knuckles white as he squeezed the steering wheel. The jeep's ability to climb up a nearly vertical face surprised me and when we got to the top I immediately started looking for a way down, as we were not reversing our path on the slope. I noticed a tank trail we could follow so I breathed a sigh of relief.

While I assessed the construction of the fighting positions I could see their value as the tanks would have a well-protected yet clear shot through the few remaining slope side rampikes on anything traversing the valley. The sparseness of trees always surprised me and reflected poorly on the husbandry of Korea's natural resources until a local explained the woods had not yet recovered from exploitation brought by 45 years of Japanese occupation.

I heard a jet engine coming from the south. A warthog, the USAF's ungainly A-10, lazily rolled along between the two mountain slopes. More impressive was that I was looking down at the twin engine jet, as the pilot practiced nape of the earth tactics. The warthog always gave me comfort knowing it was there to support us ground pounders and as to confirm my thought, the aircraft suddenly pulled up, climbed into a roll then dove. The pilot apparently lined up on an imaginary target right in front of me. I waved and encouraged him. "Go get it, man." The carnage the tanks and aircraft would bring to bear on the critical terrain below my view only became real when reports from First Gulf War showed the destruction wrought by the A-10 on the road from Basara, Iraq.

Chapter 31 Homeward Bound

We finished the construction exercise after six weeks in the field and the battalion headed to our respective camps. It was nice to get back to the BOQ, for there resided warm showers and comfortable beds.

About two weeks after returning from our prolonged field exercise, Sergeant Bronkly knocked on the wall next to the opening to our office.

"Yes, Sergeant Bronkly, what's up?

Bronkly entered the room and placed his hands on his hips somewhat in exasperation. "Sir, you're going to have to counsel Specialist Dumphries. He has beaten up the medic."

My jaw dropped. "What? Dumphries beat up the medic? He's such a quiet guy, he wouldn't hurt a flea."

"Go figure, he did."

I put my work aside and reached for a sheet of paper to document the counseling session.

"Alright bring him in."

Bronkly ushered Dumphries in my office. The lanky soldier stood alongside my desk with his eyes down and holding his fatigue hat folded between both hands in front of his belt.

"OK Dumphries, I'm told you beat up the medic after sick call."

Dumphries continued to look at his hands and softly replied. "I did sir."

"Why did you do that?"

He raised his gaze and I could see concern etched on his face. "Well sir, he told me I had VD."

I stared in his eyes for a second, pondering his response, but no matter how I figured it didn't make sense. "You punched him out because he said you had VD? I don't understand."

"There's no way I have VD." He crinkled his nose showing defiance and possible confusion. "Since returning from the field I've only had sex with my wife. I don't have VD."

I considered Bronkly who shrugged, then looked at the hapless Dumphries.

"You are dismissed pending further investigation."

Dumphries saluted and exited the room. I watched him turn the corner and heard the outside door shut. I motioned toward the communications NCO and said, "Sergeant Bronkly, here's what we're going to do. Go with Dumphries in the five-quarter to get his wife and have her checked out by the aid station. Read her the riot act and get her to admit in front of Dumphries she went back into business. Meanwhile have the medic come see me when he gets a chance. I'll see if I can smooth his feathers."

It turned out Dumphries' wife, whom he met while she worked as a lady of the night, returned to her former career while her husband spent six weeks in the field. Her lack of protection betrayed her secret attempt to make some extra spending money that despite her industriousness started a careful reassessment of his marital status. The medic, being a caring person, forgave his assaulter, and agreed not to go to the commander, so I arranged a long weekend pass for his understanding. Dumphries got some extra training assigned and a trip to the Chaplain for marriage counseling.

Humphrey's situation was really the tip of the iceberg. The

prevalence of prostitution around military bases in Korea and the cheap prices for the services made sexually transmitted disease the largest readiness problem for the battalion. At one point half of the American enlisted men in our unit had some sort of venereal disease. I never heard of a KATUSA contacting this type of illness as they had no money, and maybe more self-respect.

Each major base had a sign near the main exit ranking the local nightclubs by the prevalence of cases, the theory being the troops would avoid those clubs. Yet the market savvy of the purveyors prevailed as they managed to find eager customers. Army leadership constantly battled the spread of the disease. Free government-issued condoms in the company orderly rooms didn't help as the troops claimed they were so thick as to be worthless. The extent of the problem explained why the battalion commander told me in my entrance briefing, "Any officer in this unit that gets VD will have an automatic Article 15." I was convinced.

Chapter 32 Resignation

Summer finally displaced the Hawk, and time had arrived for me to announce my career plans. At this point in my career, I finally agreed with my high school guidance counselor. I would resign.

As a regular Army officer, I had to request a resignation from the service at least 90 days prior to leaving. I borrowed the appropriate book of regulations and typed my own letter following the Army template. I presented it to Lieutenant Colonel Higgins, and his face sagged in surprise and perhaps dismay.

"Rob, you shouldn't resign, you should extend and take a company command in the battalion. You have tremendous career potential."

I had practiced my answers and confidently replied, "Thanks for the consideration sir, but I have carefully evaluated my path and firmly believe myself and the nation would be better served by my taking a civilian job that uses my technical education and ability."

"Well I'm disappointed. I even rated you top officer in the battalion." Higgins paused to rub his chin. "However, I can understand. Good luck to you."

"Thank you sir." I came to attention and saluted.

As I walked back to my desk in the S3 hut, I was relieved Higgins didn't grill me about staying in the Army. That however came from Colonel White, Commander of the 2nd Engineer Brigade, our higher headquarters. I received a note the next day saying I was to drive to Youngsan and meet with the Colonel. The commander had thinning grey hair and appeared much older than the other officers in the brigade. He cordially sat with me on a couch in his office and presented his reasons why I should stay in the regular Army. The conversation reminded me a bit about my first time buying a car; the Ford salesman kept throwing out reasons I should buy and while I eventually bought the car, after an hour with the commander, I still had resigned. He reluctantly signed my paperwork.

As he signed White said, "According to the regulations you have to be counseled by the first flag-ranked officer in your chain of command." I was aware of this having studied the rules. "For the Second Engineer Brigade, Lieutenant General Louis Menetrey, commander of the Combined Field Army in Uijeonbu would be the one. The adjutant will make an appointment for you. Best wishes to you Captain."

A few days later, JH drove me to me to the General's appointment in silence, and I wondered what kind of sell the General might make. I entered the CFA headquarters and announced myself. The General's administrative assistant took my paperwork and entered the commander's office. I could hear him explain the purpose of the visit, then he walked out and handed me the signed paperwork. "You're good to go."

I raised my eyebrows, reached for the completed resigna-

tion documents and said, "Thank you." Surprised, I was nonetheless glad a three-star general had a more pressing matters than an
officer's resignation.

The ride back to Camp Mercer felt totally different. I had
been on this road many times and now I knew my active duty commitment to the nation was ending. Excitement bubbled within at
the opportunity to start a new chapter even though there were a lot
of unknowns, especially since I did not have a job waiting back in
the USA and could not conduct a job search while in Korea.

The word quickly spread in the battalion, and it came as a
shock to most as no one could remember a regular Army officer
resigning while in Korea. My peers, the other officers, said they
understood my decision. The enlisted men however had a different point of view. Specialist Stengle summed it up. He entered my
work area one afternoon. and said,"Hey Sir, how could you resign?
We thought you were a lifer."

"Well Stengle, it's just I feel my career will be better as a
civilian."

"But sir, you talked lots of us into reenlisting."

"Yes I did Stengle, but the potential opportunities you have
in the Army are one thing. I feel it's different for me. My opportunity lies in using my engineering degrees in the civilian world. We
all have to evaluate what we think works best for us."

Stengle slouched and nodded in agreement. "I guess you're
right, sir, but we are sure going to miss you."

"I appreciate that." Then I rose and put my arm around his
massive shoulders, as far as it would reach at least. "And I feel
better knowing you will be doing a great job for the Army. Keep up
the good work."

In the last month of my tenure in Korea, Higgins changed
command with a new lieutenant colonel, McNally. McNally was
anxious to make his mark and decided to take the unit to the field

in his first two weeks on the job. Since this would be in late August, it was close to the end of the government's fiscal year, and due to my prior planning, we had depleted our annual budget of fuel and training ammunition and had no access to US Army training areas. The S3 deferred to me to brief the new commander about the shortage of training supplies and despite what I thought was a thorough and logical case about why it would be difficult to conduct an FTX on two-week notice, McNally overruled, and we had to prepare for the field. The decision left me totally annoyed as it meant I would be in the field a week before my departure from Korea but nonetheless I quickly got together with Major Kim and scouted out some training areas. We found, as I briefed, all of the areas normally reserved for US units were taken, so Kim and I obtained permission to use a regular ROK army area to the west.

With two weeks to go, the battalion deployed to a relatively small and narrow valley we hadn't visited before. Due to the terrain, the TOC set up in a cabbage field halfway up the mountain with our communication section taking a flat spot at the top of the mountain pass for better AM radio line of sight.

Just as we set up, the skies broke and monsoons arrived. Making matters worse, McNally decreed we would only use two-man pup tents, and not the more comfortable and much larger General Purpose Medium tents. Although every soldier in Korea was issued one half of a pup tent, we never used them as they were basic and virtually useless. To erect a pup tent each of us had to buddy up and use our tent half with another person's tent half to make a primitive shelter which in essence was nothing more than a canvas sheet hanging from a clothes line. As the torrential rain fell the field quickly turned into a quagmire and the pup tents offered little protection from the elements and certainly none from the nasty mud. Needless to say, troop morale plummeted, and it took strong leadership by the officers in the S3 to set an example to keep the troops moving.

After our first night in the field rolling in mud, myself and my office mate and now tent mate, took a ride to the battalion headquarters for our first staff meeting. When we arrived at the bivouac area I noticed the battalion commander, executive officer and sergeant major were staying in a GP Medium tent.

Still smarting from the decision to overrule the S3, I didn't find much to admire in the new commander but seeing him violate one of the most basic rules of leadership, using different rules for himself and staff than the troops irked me.

I approached McNally and, in the rain, asked, "Sir, didn't you order us to use pup tents?"

"I did."

"Then what's the story about the GP Medium?"

"We need them to run the battalion."

Perhaps emboldened by my very near departure but truly appalled by the bad leadership I said, "Is that so, meanwhile the rest of the battalion is stuck in the mud in pup tents. Unbelievable. That is the worst leadership by example I have ever seen." I saluted and left.

When I returned to the TOC, I told the troops, "Forget the pup tents, set up our regular tents. Let's get out of this rain and mud."

"What do we tell the commander?" Wheelen asked.

"Tell him we need them to run the TOC."

Stengle and Dumphries gave each other high fives, "Way to go, Captain."

The larger tents helped a bit to counter the mud, but the rain continued to pour and everything we had was wet or splattered.

The remainder of the exercise went without incident, well, maybe with one incident. A regular ROK military police unit ambushed our communications section and took our soldiers prisoner. Since we were operating in a ROK area, it turns out, unbeknownst to us, we did not have permission to use the flat spot at the top of the mountain as an AM radio relay station. The ROK army, like Sergeant Bronkly, recognized the strategic value of such a location, but were concerned about spies or infiltrators using it to radio information to the North, so they monitored it. The local commander might have been extra edgy as a US soldier had recently been reported as kidnapped by the north, and they suspected the communists of more hegemony. Their patrol used live ammo to apprehend our troops, and fortunately no one was shot.

Myself, Major Kim and the Battalion Executive Officer had to "bail out" our troops and apologize for the unauthorized intrusion. Back to our command post I reminded the Executive Officer this was a result of the hasty decision to conduct a field training exercise without time to fully coordinate, but frankly, I didn't drive home the point as I knew in three days I'd be turning in my field gear and heading to the land of the big PX.

Chapter 33 Seventy-Two Hours Over Oakland

September 15 1983 - The chartered airline touched down in San Francisco International Airport. As the wheels turned toward the taxiway, it felt good to back in the good old USA, even if it was in the home of America's looney bin. I didn't expect any parade or fanfare, and there was none, just an olive drab Army bus sitting next to the airport taxi stand. The bus filled up with soldiers sweaty and grubby after the long trans-Pacific flight. Despite never seeing California before, jet lag overtook me and I dozed as the driver worked the bus up highway 101 and across the Bay Bridge to Oakland Army Terminal. The base lay at the foot of the Bay Bridge, facing out over the harbor toward the skyline.

The sun shone brightly on a Saturday morning across the white washed warehouses of the gritty army terminal. The bus stopped at a block-long warehouse where the out processing from active duty would occur. Since I was the only officer out processing I didn't have to wait in line, the NCO incharge sent me to a desk at the end of the building. I gave my orders to an enlisted clerk who started filling out a batch of paperwork. He worked efficiently, zipping through the forms, then suddenly he swore.

"Something wrong?" I asked raising my chin to get a better look at what he was doing.

"Oh no sir, I've never out processed an officer from Korea. Not familiar with this DF."

I heard that a few times in the past few weeks.

The clerk flipped his pencil and started erasing the error. In a few minutes he said, "Sir, you are out processed. Just go to the table over there and the transportation officer will cut you a ticket to your home of record."

"Thank you." The painless process a refreshing change from Army bureaucracy.

The transportation officer turned out to be a grumpy civilian. Since it was Saturday morning the best he could do was to schedule a commercial flight on Monday.

"There are some barracks across the street here, no BOQ on the terminal. Just cross the street and make a right. You're in room 112." He handed me a key with a brass tag.

I dropped off my luggage in a sparse room in temporary barracks and found the charge of quarters, a soldier who looked way too old to be a private, in the orderly room.

"Private, how do I get to the club from here. I need to cash a check."

He glanced up from an Army-issued comic book, PS, Preventive Maintenance Monthly. "Sorry sir, but there is no club at the depot and the bank is closed for the weekend. Opens Monday at oh-nine hundred hours."

"Really, nothing open."

"Well sir this is a depot, we don't have facilities like a regular Army base."

"That's great." My sleepiness made me too tired to complain about visiting the San Francisco area with only ten dollars in US currency. Darn, I should have planned better, my chance to tear up the town down the tubes with a pocket full of effectively worthless Korean Won.

I found a pay phone in the hallway, dropped a quarter in the slot and dialed 0-516-342-1699, my parents' number.

My Mom answered the call and accepted the charges.

"Hello Mom, it's Rob, I'm calling from California."

"Oh Robert, is that you? You sound so far away." Her New York accent rekindled memories of home.

"Not as far as I was. Made it to the USA. I leave San Francisco Monday morning, flying to JFK on TWA flight 615. Arrive in the evening."

"Oh, I'm so happy."

"Me too, don't forget to pick me up."

"Monday evening, yes Robert, your father and I will ."

"Great Mom. See you in a few days. Love you." Our terse conversation was common for collect calls as they were twice as expensive as regular toll calls.

"Bye son."

"Good bye." I hung up the black plastic handset and shuffled back to my room. To stay awake I washed my face with cold water and changed into running shorts and sneakers. I took a leisurely jog across the terminal crossing railroad tracks and running among dilapidated World War War II vintage buildings. The base's glory days had passed. Seven or so years ago, the facility would have been swarming with soldiers and equipment coming and going to Vietnam. Now the empty corridors of the logistics center grew weeds and mirrored the nation's feelings towards the military and particularly the soldiers.

Despite the nation's history being replete with war, and practically every generation having at least one, the American psyche in the early 80s still had not recovered from the trauma of ten difficult years in jungles of Southeast Asia. Except for the few families with soldiers on active duty, the country would sooner forget about the military. At least the base had no San Francisco hippies ready to curse me out like they did to many returning Vietnam veterans.

As I jogged, I crossed an old cobble stone path, carefully placing my steps not to trip in the irregular voids. Just like the assembly of these odd-shaped stones made a road, my service added a brick that filled a small spot in the nation's fortress. It represented a reluctant soldier whose luck held out long enough to return home to a loving mother, and a proud but relieved father, and to rekindle a relationship with a wonderful woman.

Standing back and considering the structure my relatives helped forge, one can't help but be grateful and awed by the courage and selflessness of my extended family's ancestors. Yet, one must be taken aback by the effort and cost, both material and human, and wonder when will our genus become smart enough to realize no money, no religion, no reason, can justify war. What can I offer other than to heed the stories of soldiers, but more importantly learn from them?

Made in the USA
Columbia, SC
20 April 2019